Harcourt

Texas GoMath!

Grade K

Assessment Guide

- Prerequisite Skills Inventory
- Beginning-of-Year, Middle-of-Year, and End-of-Year Benchmark Tests
- Module Tests in TEXAS Assessment Format
- Individual Record Forms
- Correlations to Texas Essential Knowledge and Skills for Mathematics

Copyright © by Houghton Mifflin Harcourt Publishing Company

All rights reserved. No part of this work may be reproduced or transmitted in any form or by any means, electronic or mechanical, including photocopying or recording, or by any information storage and retrieval system, without the prior written permission of the copyright owner unless such copying is expressly permitted by federal copyright law. Requests for permission to make copies of any part of the work should be addressed to Houghton Mifflin Harcourt Publishing Company, Attn: Contracts, Copyrights, and Licensing, 9400 Southpark Center Loop, Orlando, Florida 32819-8647.

Printed in the U.S.A.

ISBN 978-0-544-06038-8

2 3 4 5 6 7 8 9 10 0868 22 21 20 19 18 17 16 15 14 13

4500430467 A B C D E F G

If you have received these materials as examination copies free of charge, Houghton Mifflin Harcourt Publishing Company retains title to the materials and they may not be resold. Resale of examination copies is strictly prohibited.

Possession of this publication in print format does not entitle users to convert this publication, or any portion of it, into electronic format.

Contents

© Houghton Mifflin Harcourt Publishing Company

Tests and Record Forms

© Houghton Mifflin Harcourt Publishing Company

© Houghton Mifflin Harcourt Publishing Company

Overview of *Texas GO Math!* Assessment

How Assessment Can Help Individualize Instruction

The *Assessment Guide* contains several types of assessment for use throughout the school year. The following pages will explain how these assessments can help teachers evaluate children's understanding of the Texas Essential Knowledge and Skills (TEKS). This *Assessment Guide* also contains Individual Record Forms (IRF) to help guide teachers' instructional choices to improve children's performance. The record forms may be used to monitor children's progress toward their mastery of the Texas Essential Knowledge and Skills for this grade.

Diagnostic Assessment

Prerequisite Skills Inventory in the *Assessment Guide* should be given at the beginning of the school year or when a new child arrives. The multiple-choice test assesses children's understanding of prerequisite skills. Test results provide information about the review or intervention that children may need in order to be successful in learning the mathematics related to the TEKS for the grade level. The IRF for the Prerequisite Skills Inventory provides suggestions for intervention based on the child's performance.

Beginning-of-Year Test in the *Assessment Guide*, is multiple-choice format and should be given early in the year to determine which skills for the current grade children may already understand. This benchmark test will facilitate customization of instructional content to optimize the time spent teaching specific objectives. The IRF for the Beginning-of-Year Test provides suggestions for intervention based on the child's performance.

Show What You Know in the *Student Edition* is provided for each unit. It assesses prior knowledge from previous grades as well as content taught earlier in the current grade. Teachers can customize instructional content using the suggested intervention options. The assessment should be scheduled at the beginning of each unit to determine if children have the prerequisite skills for the unit.

© Houghton Mifflin Harcourt Publishing Company

Formative Assessment

Are You Ready? items appear in the *Assessment Guide*. These are quick checks administered by the teacher to determine if children have the prerequisite skills they need for a particular lesson in the *Texas GO Math! Student Edition*. If several children have trouble with the Are You Ready? items, teachers may wish to review concepts before teaching the next lesson.

Middle-of-Year Test in the *Assessment Guide* assesses the same TEKS as the Beginning-of-Year Test, allowing children's progress to be tracked and providing opportunity for instructional adjustments, when required. The test contains multiple-choice items.

Summative Assessment

Module and Unit Assessments in the *Texas GO Math! Student Edition* indicate whether additional instruction or practice is necessary for children to master the concepts and skills taught in the module or unit. These tests include constructed-response and multiple-choice items.

Module and Unit Tests in the *Assessment Guide* evaluate children's mastery of concepts and skills taught in the module or unit. There is a test for each module. When only one module comprises a unit, the unit test assesses the content in just that module. When there are multiple modules in a unit, there are designated module tests and a comprehensive unit test. These tests contain multiple-choice items.

End-of-Year Test in the *Assessment Guide* assesses the same TEKS as the Beginning- and Middle-of-Year Tests. The test contains multiple-choice items. It is the final benchmark test for the grade level. When children's performance on the End-of-Year Test is compared to performance on Beginning- and Middle-of-Year Tests, teachers are able to document children's growth.

© Houghton Mifflin Harcourt Publishing Company

Using Correlations to TEKS

The final section of the *Assessment Guide* contains correlations to the TEKS. To identify which items in the *Assessment Guide* test a particular TEKS, locate that TEKS in the chart. The column to the right will list the test and specific items that assess the TEKS. Correlations to TEKS are also provided in the Individual Record Form for each test.

Assessment Technology

Online Assessment System offers flexibility to individualize assessment for each child. Teachers can assign entire tests from the *Assessment Guide* or build customized tests from a bank of items. For customized tests, specific TEKS can be selected to test.

Multiple-choice and fill-in-the-blank items are automatically scored by the Online Assessment System. This provides immediate feedback. Tests may also be printed and administered as paper-and-pencil tests.

The same intervention resources are available in the Online Assessment System as in the *Assessment Guide*. So, whether children take tests online or printed from the Online Assessment System, teachers have access to materials to help children succeed in *Texas GO Math!*

© Houghton Mifflin Harcourt Publishing Company

Data-Driven Decision Making

Texas GO Math! allows for quick and accurate data-driven decision making so teachers will have more instructional time to meet children's needs. There are several intervention and review resources available with *Texas GO Math!* Every lesson in the *Student Edition* has a corresponding lesson in the *Texas GO Math! Response to Intervention Tier 1 Lessons* online resource. There are also *Tier 2 Skills* and *Tier 3 Examples* available for children who need further instruction or practice. For online intervention lessons, children may complete lessons in *Soar to Success Math*. These resources provide the foundation for individual prescriptions for students who need extra support.

Using Individual Record Forms

The *Assessment Guide* includes Individual Record Forms (IRF) for all tests. On these forms, each test item is correlated to the TEKS it assesses. There are intervention resources correlated to each item as well. A common error explains why a child may have missed the item. These forms can be used to:

- Follow progress throughout the year.
- Identify strengths and weaknesses.
- Make assignments based on the intervention options provided.

© Houghton Mifflin Harcourt Publishing Company

Name ______________________

Are You Ready?
Lesson 1.1

1. Name something of which you have one.

Notes:

2. Name something of which you have two.

Notes:

Name ______________________

Are You Ready?
Lesson 1.2

1. What have you seen someone write?

Notes:

2. When would you write numbers?

Notes:

© Houghton Mifflin Harcourt Publishing Company

Name ______________________

Are You Ready?
Lesson 1.3

1. What number(s) come after 1 and 2 when you count?

Notes:

2. Show 3 fingers.

Notes:

Name ______________________

Are You Ready?
Lesson 1.4

1. Name something with three wheels.

Notes:

2. Name something with four wheels.

Notes:

© Houghton Mifflin Harcourt Publishing Company

Name ______________________

Are You Ready?
Lesson 2.1

1. Can you count to 5? Show me if you can.

Notes:

---

2. Hold up all your fingers on one hand. How many fingers do you have up?

Notes:

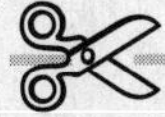

Name ______________________

Are You Ready?
Lesson 2.2

1. Where do you see the number 5 in the room?

Notes:

2. Listen. Count and tell how many claps you hear. (Clap 5 times.)

Notes:

© Houghton Mifflin Harcourt Publishing Company

Name ____________________

Are You Ready?
Lesson 2.3

1. Tell how many fingers you see. (Hold up two fingers for about 2 seconds. Repeat.) How many fingers did you see?

Notes:

2. Tell how many fingers you see this time. (Hold up five fingers for about 2 seconds. Repeat.) How many fingers did you see?

Notes:

Name ____________________

Are You Ready?
Lesson 2.4

1. Count forward to 3.

Notes:

2. When you count backward from 3, you start at 3. Count backward from 3.

Notes:

© Houghton Mifflin Harcourt Publishing Company

Name ______________________________

Are You Ready?
Lesson 2.5

1. (Put 3 counters in your hand.) How many counters do you see?

Notes:

2. (Empty your hand.) Now how many counters do you see?

Notes:

© Houghton Mifflin Harcourt Publishing Company

Name ______________________________

Are You Ready?
Lesson 3.1

1. What does it mean to put things in order?

Notes:

2. Put these cards in order. (Place three number cards down in a row in this order – 2, 3, 1.)

Notes:

Name ______________________________

Are You Ready?
Lesson 3.2

1. (Show two math books or other like items.) Can you show me two things that are the same?

Notes:

2. Hold up two fingers on each hand. How do you know you have the same number of fingers up on both hands?

Notes:

© Houghton Mifflin Harcourt Publishing Company

Name ______________________

Are You Ready?
Lesson 3.3

1. (Show two sets of 4 counters.) What number of counters is in each set?

Notes:

2. (Put two more in the bottom set.) Describe the sets now.

Notes:

Name ______________________

Are You Ready?
Lesson 3.4

1. (Show 3 of one small item and 2 of another small item.) Show how you can compare the number of items in the sets.

Notes:

2. Which set has fewer items?

Notes:

© Houghton Mifflin Harcourt Publishing Company

Name ______________________

Are You Ready?
Lesson 4.1

1. (Show 5 individual connecting cubes.) How many cubes are there?

Notes:

2. (Put the same cubes together in a cube train.) How many cubes are there now? How do you know?

Notes:

Name ______________________

Are You Ready?
Lesson 4.2

1. (Show 5 fingers.) How many fingers do you see? (Put one more finger up.) Now how many fingers are there?

Notes:

2. Start at 3 and count to 6.

Notes:

© Houghton Mifflin Harcourt Publishing Company

Name ____________________

Are You Ready?
Lesson 4.3

1. The number after 6 is 7. Start at 7 and count backwards to 1.

Notes:

2. If you have 6 kites, how many more do you need to have 7 kites?

Notes:

Name ____________________

Are You Ready?
Lesson 4.4

1. Sometimes 7 is a lot. Would you eat seven sandwiches for lunch?

Notes:

2. Name something you would eat 7 of for lunch.

Notes:

© Houghton Mifflin Harcourt Publishing Company

Name ____________________

Are You Ready?
Lesson 4.5

1. (Put out number cards 1 through 7 in random order.) Put the cards in counting order.

Notes:

---

2. (Put out 10 counters.) Show me a set of 7 counters.

Notes:

Name ____________________

Are You Ready?
Lesson 4.6

1. Start at 3 and count to 8.

Notes:

2. Put up all the fingers on one hand. How many more fingers do you put up to show 8 fingers?

Notes:

© Houghton Mifflin Harcourt Publishing Company

Name ______________________

Are You Ready?
Lesson 5.1

1. Is this sentence silly or real? Six children sit in eight chairs. Explain your answer.

Notes:

2. Name some things you count, but you cannot see.

Notes:

Name ______________________

Are You Ready?
Lesson 5.2

1. Start at 3 and count to 9

Notes:

2. Take 5 long steps. Would you go farther if you took 9 long steps? Why?

Notes:

© Houghton Mifflin Harcourt Publishing Company

Name ______________________________

Are You Ready?
Lesson 5.3

1. Each chair is full. What does that mean?

Notes:

2. Name some other things you might fill.

Notes:

Name ______________________________

Are You Ready?
Lesson 5.4

1. When you count objects, what do you know about the last number you say?

Notes:

2. (Provide 4 red cubes and 5 blue cubes.) Make a set of 7 cubes. Now make a set of 7 cubes that is different.

Notes:

© Houghton Mifflin Harcourt Publishing Company

Name ______________________

Are You Ready?
Lesson 6.1

1. Why is it important to count correctly?

Notes:

2. Hold up all your fingers on both hands. Without counting, tell me how many fingers you have up

Notes:

Name ______________________

Are You Ready?
Lesson 6.2

1. When you count to 10, what numbers do you say after 5?

Notes:

2. (Provide a set of 8 counters and a set of 5 counters.) Which set would you rather have? Why?

Notes:

© Houghton Mifflin Harcourt Publishing Company

Name ______________________________________

Are You Ready?
Lesson 6.3

1. (Show 8 red counters and 7 yellow counters.) Which set has the greater number? How do you know?

Notes:

---

2. Which would you rather have, 6 pieces or 4 pieces of your favorite fruit? Why?

Notes:

Name ______________________________________

Are You Ready?
Lesson 6.4

1. When you count what number do you say just after 8?

Notes:

2. When you count backward from 8, what number do you say next?

Notes:

© Houghton Mifflin Harcourt Publishing Company

Name ____________________

Are You Ready?
Lesson 6.5

1. (Show a set of 8 counters. Provide a set of 10 additional counters.) Make a set with fewer counters.

Notes:

2. (Show a set of 5 counters. Provide a set of 10 additional counters.) Make a set with more counters.

Notes:

Name ____________________

Are You Ready?
Lesson 6.6

1. When you count what number is two numbers after 7?

Notes:

2. When you count what number is two numbers before 7?

Notes:

© Houghton Mifflin Harcourt Publishing Company

Name ______________________________

Are You Ready?
Lesson 7.1

1. If a ten frame is full, how many counters does it have in it?

Notes:

2. (Draw or show a ten frame with 8 counters in it and a ten frame with 6 counters in it below the other ten frame.) Without counting tell which ten frame has more counters in it? How can you tell?

Notes:

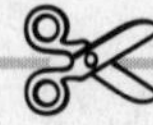

Name ______________________________

Are You Ready?
Lesson 7.2

1. Start at 4 and count to 12.

Notes:

2. If you have 11 eggs and get one more, how many eggs do you have?

Notes:

© Houghton Mifflin Harcourt Publishing Company

Name ______________________________

Are You Ready?
Lesson 7.3

1. Can you put 11 counters in a ten frame? Why?

Notes:

2. (Show 10 counters in a ten frame.) How many more counters do you need to show 12?

Notes:

Name ______________________________

Are You Ready?
Lesson 7.4

1. Start at 10 and count to 14.

Notes:

2. When you count to 13, how many numbers do you say after 10?

Notes:

© Houghton Mifflin Harcourt Publishing Company

Name ______________________________

Are You Ready?
Lesson 7.5

1. (Provide 14 counters with 10 in a ten frame and 4 below and a set of 14 counters.) Which set is easier to see how many are in it? Why?

Notes:

---

2. (Provide 15 counters and a ten frame.) Show the number 14.

Notes:

Name ______________________________

Are You Ready?
Lesson 7.6

1. Count forward from 10 to 15.

Notes:

2. Count backward from 13 to 10.

Notes:

© Houghton Mifflin Harcourt Publishing Company

Name ______________________

Are You Ready?
Lesson 8.1

1. What number is one more than 13?

Notes:

2. What number is one less than 13?

Notes:

Name ______________________

Are You Ready?
Lesson 8.2

1. Start at 10 and count to 16.

Notes:

2. (Show two ten frames with 10 counters in one of the ten frames.) How many more counters do you need to show 17?

Notes:

© Houghton Mifflin Harcourt Publishing Company

Name ____________________

Are You Ready?
Lesson 8.3

1. (Put out number cards 8 through 17 in random order.) Put the cards in counting order.

Notes:

2. Where might you see the number 18?

Notes:

Name ____________________

Are You Ready?
Lesson 8.4

1. (Write the numbers 11 through 19 in a vertical list.) Describe what is alike and what is different about these numbers.

Notes:

2. (Hold up all 10 fingers.) Hold up more fingers to show 15.

Notes:

© Houghton Mifflin Harcourt Publishing Company

Name ____________________

Are You Ready?
Lesson 8.5

1. What number comes after 18?

Notes:

2. How many counters is 10 and 9 more?

Notes:

Name ____________________

Are You Ready?
Lesson 8.6

1. (Show 18 with counters in two ten frames.) How many more counters are needed to have 20?

Notes:

2. If one team has 19 points and another team has 20, which team has more points?

Notes:

© Houghton Mifflin Harcourt Publishing Company

Name ______________________________

Are You Ready?
Lesson 8.7

1. If you have 10 counters and 5 counters, how many counters do you have?

Notes:

2. What number comes before 17?

Notes:

Name ______________________________

Are You Ready?
Lesson 8.8

1. What number is one more than 16?

Notes:

2. What number is one less than 20?

Notes:

© Houghton Mifflin Harcourt Publishing Company

Name ________________________________

Are You Ready?
Lesson 9.1

1. (Show a set with 1 yellow counter and 2 red counters and another set with 1 red counter and 2 yellow counters.) How many counters are in each set? How are the sets alike?

Notes:

2. How are the sets different?

Notes:

Name ________________________________

Are You Ready?
Lesson 9.2

1. (Provide 6 two-color counters.) Show 3 in two different ways.

Notes:

2. If you show 3 with three counters that are yellow, how many are red?

Notes:

© Houghton Mifflin Harcourt Publishing Company

Name ____________________

Are You Ready?
Lesson 9.3

1. (Provide 10 two-color counters.) Show 4 in two different ways.

Notes:

2. (Provide 10 two-color counters.) Show 5 in two different ways.

Notes:

Name ____________________

Are You Ready?
Lesson 9.4

1. (Put out 5 yellow counters.) Turn over 1 or more of the counters and tell the numbers that make 5.

Notes:

2. (Put out 4 yellow counters.) Turn over 1 or more of the counters and tell the numbers that make 4.

Notes:

© Houghton Mifflin Harcourt Publishing Company

Name ____________________

Are You Ready?
Lesson 10.1

1. If you show 5 with five counters that are red, how many are yellow?

Notes:

2. (Provide 10 two-color counters.) Show 5 two different ways.

Notes:

Name ____________________

Are You Ready?
Lesson 10.2

1. (Provide 14 two-color counters.) Show 6 two different ways.

Notes:

2. (Provide 14 two-color counters.) Show 7 two different ways.

Notes:

© Houghton Mifflin Harcourt Publishing Company

Name ______________________

Are You Ready?
Lesson 10.3

1. (Provide 16 two-color counters.) Show 8 two different ways.

Notes:

2. If you show 8 with eight counters that are red, how many are yellow?

Notes:

Name ______________________

Are You Ready?
Lesson 10.4

1. (Provide 18 two-color counters.) Show 9 two different ways.

Notes:

2. If there are no red counters, how many yellow counters do you need to show 9?

Notes:

© Houghton Mifflin Harcourt Publishing Company

Name ______________________

Are You Ready?
Lesson 10.5

1. (Provide 10 two-color counters.) Show 5 two different ways.

Notes:

2. (Provide 5 two-sided counters, red side up.) Turn over 1 or more of the counters and tell the numbers that make 5.

Notes:

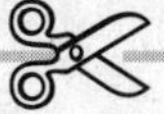

Name ______________________

Are You Ready?
Lesson 10.6

1. (Provide 6 two-sided counters, red side up.) Turn over 1 or more of the counters and tell the numbers that make 6.

Notes:

2. (Provide 7 two-sided counters, yellow side up.) Turn over 1 or more of the counters and tell the numbers that make 7.

Notes:

© Houghton Mifflin Harcourt Publishing Company

Name ____________________

Are You Ready?
Lesson 10.7

1. (Put out 8 two-sided counters, yellow side up.) Turn over 1 or more of the counters and tell the numbers that make 8.

Notes:

2. (Put out 9 two-sided counters, red side up.) Turn over 1 or more of the counters and tell the numbers that make 9.

Notes:

Name ____________________

Are You Ready?
Lesson 10.8

1. If there are 0 yellow counters, how many red counters do you need to show 10?

Notes:

2. (Put out 10 two-sided counters, red side up.) Turn over 1 or more of the counters and tell the numbers that make 10.

Notes:

© Houghton Mifflin Harcourt Publishing Company

Name ___________________________________

Are You Ready?
Lesson 11.1

1. What does the plus symbol between two numbers mean?

   Notes:

2. If you have 7 cubes and then you find one more, how many cubes do you have?

   Notes:

Name ___________________________________

Are You Ready?
Lesson 11.2

1. (Put out 2 blue cubes and 1 yellow cube.) Tell me something about the cubes.

   Notes:

2. (Provide 2 blue cubes.) Here are 2 yellow cubes. (Give child 2 yellow cubes.) Say an addition sentence that tells about the cubes.

   Notes:

© Houghton Mifflin Harcourt Publishing Company

Name ____________________

Are You Ready?
Lesson 11.3

1. (Provide 5 blue counters.) Use the cubes to act out this story and tell me the answer. Isabel has 3 blue counters. Shane gives her 1 more.

Notes:

2. Use the counters to show an addition story. Say a number sentence about the story.

Notes:

Name ____________________

Are You Ready?
Lesson 11.4

1. (Provide 5 cubes.) Use the cubes to act out the story and say an addition sentence that tells about the story. There are 2 plates on the table. Gina puts one more plate on the table. How many plates are there now?

Notes:

2. Tell an addition story about 2 plus 2 equals 4.

Notes:

© Houghton Mifflin Harcourt Publishing Company

Name ____________________

Are You Ready?
Lesson 12.1

1. What does the minus sign between two numbers mean?

Notes:

2. If you have 5 cubes and you give one away, how many do you have?

Notes:

Name ____________________

Are You Ready?
Lesson 12.2

1. (Provide a 5-cube train.) Take 2 off the cube train. Say a subtraction sentence that tells about the cubes.

Notes:

2. (Provide a 5-cube train.) Take 4 off the cube train. Say a subtraction sentence that tells about the cubes.

Notes:

© Houghton Mifflin Harcourt Publishing Company

Name ______________________________

Are You Ready?
Lesson 12.3

1. (Provide 5 blue cubes.) Use the cubes to act out this story and tell me the answer. Lucy has 3 blue cubes. She gives Rob one of the cubes.

Notes:

2. Use the cubes to show a subtraction story. Say a number sentence about the story.

Notes:

Name ______________________________

Are You Ready?
Lesson 12.4

1. (Provide 5 cubes.) Use the cubes to act out the story and say a subtraction sentence that tells about the story. There are 5 carrots on the table. Gina eats one. How many carrots are there now?

Notes:

2. Tell a subtraction story about 5 minus 2 equals 3.

Notes:

© Houghton Mifflin Harcourt Publishing Company

Name ______________________

Are You Ready?
Lesson 13.1

1. When you count forward, what number comes before 9?

Notes:

2. When you count forward, what number comes after 9?

Notes:

Name ______________________

Are You Ready?
Lesson 13.2

1. (Provide 8 cubes.) Use the cubes to show 7 and 1 more. Say an addition sentence about having 1 more than 7.

Notes:

2. Use the cubes to show 7 and 1 less. Say a subtraction sentence about having 1 less than 7.

Notes:

© Houghton Mifflin Harcourt Publishing Company

Name ____________________

Are You Ready?
Lesson 13.3

1. (Provide 7 green cubes and 7 yellow cubes.) Choose 6 cubes and tell an addition story about them.

Notes:

2. (Provide 7 green and 7 yellow cubes.) Choose 7 cubes and tell an addition story about them.

Notes:

Name ____________________

Are You Ready?
Lesson 13.4

1. (Provide 9 green cubes and 9 yellow cubes.) Choose 8 cubes and tell an addition story about them.

Notes:

2. (Provide 9 green and 9 yellow cubes.) Choose 9 cubes and tell an addition story about them.

Notes:

© Houghton Mifflin Harcourt Publishing Company

Name ______________________

Are You Ready?
Lesson 13.5

1. (Provide 10 red cubes and 10 yellow cubes.) Choose 10 cubes and tell an addition story about them.

Notes:

2. Rory said addition is putting groups together. Is he correct? Explain.

Notes:

Name ______________________

Are You Ready?
Lesson 13.6

1. What are some things that come in groups of the same number?

Notes:

2. 3 plus 3 equals 6 is a doubles addition sentence. Tell another doubles addition sentence.

Notes:

© Houghton Mifflin Harcourt Publishing Company

Name ____________________

Are You Ready?
Lesson 14.1

1. (Provide 6 two-sided counters, red side up.) Turn over 1 or more of the counters and tell the numbers that make 6.

Notes:

2. (Provide 7 two-sided counters, yellow side up.) Turn over 1 or more of the counters and tell the numbers that make 7.

Notes:

Name ____________________

Are You Ready?
Lesson 14.2

1. What does subtraction mean?

Notes:

2. How can you find 7 minus 1 without subtracting?

Notes:

© Houghton Mifflin Harcourt Publishing Company

Name ______________________

Are You Ready?
Lesson 14.3

1. (Write $8 - 3 = 5$.) Tell a subtraction story about the subtraction sentence.

Notes:

2. Say the subtraction sentence that tells about the story. There are 9 balloons. 3 float away. There are 6 left.

Notes:

Name ______________________

Are You Ready?
Lesson 14.4

1. (Write $10 - 2 = 8$.) Tell a subtraction story about the subtraction sentence.

Notes:

2. (Write $10 - 5 = ?$) Tell a subtraction story about the subtraction sentence and find the answer.

Notes:

© Houghton Mifflin Harcourt Publishing Company

Name ____________________

Are You Ready?
Lesson 15.1

1. What do people do with coins?

Notes:

2. (Put out 7 pennies.) How many coins are there?

Notes:

Name ____________________

Are You Ready?
Lesson 15.2

1. (Put out several pennies, some heads up, others tails up.) What is the name of this kind of coin?

Notes:

2. (Put out several pennies and some nickels.) Which coins are pennies? Take them out of the group of coins.

Notes:

© Houghton Mifflin Harcourt Publishing Company

Name ____________________

Are You Ready?
Lesson 15.3

1. (Put out several nickels, some heads up, others tails up, different nickel design, if possible.) What is the name of this kind of coin?

Notes:

2. (Put out several pennies and some nickels.) Which coins are nickels? Take them out of the group of coins.

Notes:

Name ____________________

Are You Ready?
Lesson 15.4

1. (Put out several dimes, some heads up, others tails up.) What is the name of this kind of coin?

Notes:

2. (Put out pennies, nickels, and dimes.) Which coins are dimes? Take them out of the group of coins.

Notes:

© Houghton Mifflin Harcourt Publishing Company

Name 

Are You Ready?
Lesson 15.5

1. (Put out several quarters, some heads up, others tails up, and with different designs, if possible.) What is the name of this kind of coin?

Notes:

2. (Put out pennies, nickels, dimes, and quarters.) Which coins are quarters? Take them out of the group of coins.

Notes:

© Houghton Mifflin Harcourt Publishing Company

Name ____________________

Are You Ready?
Lesson 16.1

1. Start at 11 and count to 20.

Notes:

---

2. Tell the number that comes before 14.

Notes:

Name ____________________

Are You Ready?
Lesson 16.2

1. Count from 34 to 40.

Notes:

2. What numbers come before and after 30?

Notes:

© Houghton Mifflin Harcourt Publishing Company

Name ______________________________________

Are You Ready?
Lesson 16.3

1. Count from 75 to 85.

Notes:

2. When you count from 1 to 100, which number to you say first – 56 or 65?

Notes:

Name ______________________________________

Are You Ready?
Lesson 16.4

1. Start at 30 and count by tens to 100.

Notes:

2. When you count by tens, what number do you say first, 30 or 50?

Notes:

© Houghton Mifflin Harcourt Publishing Company

Name ________________________________

Are You Ready?
Lesson 17.1

1. (Put out 3 large circles and 1 small circle.) Which are the same size?

Notes:

2. (Put out a large circle, a small circle, and a small triangle.) Which two are the same shape?

Notes:

Name ________________________________

Are You Ready?
Lesson 17.2

1. (Put out a circle, a square, and a triangle.) Which is a circle?

Notes:

2. (Put out a large circle, 2 small circles, 1 large triangle, and 1 small triangle.) How many circles are there?

Notes:

© Houghton Mifflin Harcourt Publishing Company

Name ______________________________

Are You Ready?
Lesson 17.3

1. (Put out a circle, and square, and a triangle.) Which is a triangle?

Notes:

---

2. (Put out 2 large triangles, 2 small triangles, 1 large circle, and 1 small circle.) How many triangles are there?

Notes:

Name ______________________________

Are You Ready?
Lesson 17.4

1. (Put out a circle, a rectangle, and a triangle.) Which is a rectangle?

Notes:

2. (Put out a large rectangle, a small rectangle, a large circle, and a small circle.) How many circles are there?

Notes:

© Houghton Mifflin Harcourt Publishing Company

Name ______________________________

1. (Put out a circle, a square, and a triangle.) Which is a square?

Notes:

---

2. (Put out a large square, a small square, a large circle, and a small circle.) How many squares are there?

Notes:

© Houghton Mifflin Harcourt Publishing Company

Name ____________________

Are You Ready?
Lesson 18.1

1. (Put out a cube and a square.) Which figure is a square?

Notes:

2. (Put out a cylinder and a circle.) Which figure is a circle?

Notes:

Name ____________________

Are You Ready?
Lesson 18.2

1. (Put out a cylinder, a cube, and a cone.) Which is a cylinder?

Notes:

2. (Put out a cylinder.) Tell me two things you know about a cylinder.

Notes:

© Houghton Mifflin Harcourt Publishing Company

Name ___

Are You Ready?
Lesson 18.3

1. (Put out a cylinder, a cube, and a cone.) Which is a cone?

Notes:

2. (Put out a cone.) Tell me two things you know about a cone.

Notes:

Name ___

Are You Ready?
Lesson 18.4

1. (Put out a cylinder, a cube, and a sphere.) Which is a sphere?

Notes:

2. (Put out a sphere.) Tell me something you know about a sphere.

Notes:

© Houghton Mifflin Harcourt Publishing Company

Name ___________________________________

Are You Ready?
Lesson 18.5

1. (Put out a cylinder, a cube, and a sphere.) Which is a cube?

Notes:

---

2. (Put out a cube.) Tell me something you know about a cube.

Notes:

© Houghton Mifflin Harcourt Publishing Company

Name ____________________

Are You Ready?
Lesson 19.1

1. Your uncle grows a big pumpkin in his garden. What might you want to know about the pumpkin?

Notes:

2. Juan has a new thermos. What is one thing he may want to know about it?

Notes:

Name ____________________

Are You Ready?
Lesson 19.2

1. There are some sharpened pencils in a pencil jar. You can choose one. Why might you want to compare the pencils?

Notes:

2. If you have two cube trains that are different lengths, why would you compare them?

Notes:

© Houghton Mifflin Harcourt Publishing Company

Name ______________________

Are You Ready?
Lesson 19.3

1. How are length and height different?

Notes:

2. How are height and length the same?

Notes:

Name ______________________

Are You Ready?
Lesson 19.4

1. If a green cube train is longer than a blue cube train, does it have more cubes or fewer cubes?

Notes:

2. If a green cube tower is shorter than a yellow cube tower, does it have more cubes or fewer cubes?

Notes:

© Houghton Mifflin Harcourt Publishing Company

Name ______________________________

Are You Ready?
Lesson 20.1

1. (Provide connecting cubes - 2 blue, 2 orange, and 2 red. Hold up 1 red cube.) What color is this cube? Show another cube of the same color.

Notes:

2. (Provide the same cubes as above.) Show a cube of a different color.

Notes:

Name ______________________________

Are You Ready?
Lesson 20.2

1. (Provide a blue triangle and a red triangle.) How are these alike?

Notes:

2. (Provide the same shapes as Lesson 20.2 exercise 1.) How are these different?

Notes:

© Houghton Mifflin Harcourt Publishing Company

Name ________________________________

1. (Provide a red triangle, a red circle, a blue triangle, and a blue circle.) Sort these into two groups.

Notes:

---

2. (Provide a red triangle, a red circle, a blue triangle, and a blue circle.) Sort these into two groups a different way.

Notes:

© Houghton Mifflin Harcourt Publishing Company

Name ______________________________

1. (Provide a set of attribute blocks.) What are the ways you could sort and classify these blocks?

Notes:

2. (Provide 2 small circles and 1 large circle, 1 large triangle and 2 small triangles.) Sort these pieces into two groups.

Notes:

© Houghton Mifflin Harcourt Publishing Company

Name ______________________________

Are You Ready?
Lesson 21.1

1. Name some coins you know.

Notes:

2. (Provide 3 pennies and 4 dimes.) How many pennies are there?

Notes:

Name ______________________________

Are You Ready?
Lesson 21.2

1. What does it mean to "earn" money?

Notes:

2. What other way could you get money?

Notes:

© Houghton Mifflin Harcourt Publishing Company

Name ____________________

Are You Ready?
Lesson 21.3

1. What are some ways people earn money?

Notes:

2. What are some other ways people receive money?

Notes:

Name ____________________

Are You Ready?
Lesson 21.4

1. Name something that you would spend money on because you need it.

Notes:

2. Name something that you would spend money on because you want it.

Notes:

© Houghton Mifflin Harcourt Publishing Company

Name ____________________

○ 4

○ 3

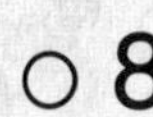
○ 8

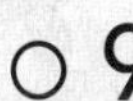
○ 9

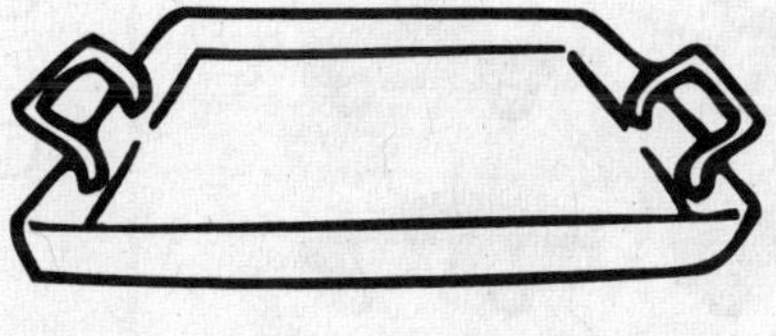

○

○

DIRECTIONS Fill in the bubble for the correct answer. **1.** Count the crayons. How many are there? **2.** Count the turtles. How many are there? **3.** Which tray has 0 cartons of milk on it?

GO ON

© Houghton Mifflin Harcourt Publishing Company

4

0 ○   3 ○

5

○ 20
○ 19

6

○ 15
○ 16

7

7

○ 1
○ 7

DIRECTIONS **4.** Emma has zero strawberries. Which number shows how many strawberries she has? **5.** Count the dolls. How many are there? **6.** Count the trucks. How many are there? **7.** Look at the first number. Which number is the same?

GO ON

© Houghton Mifflin Harcourt Publishing Company

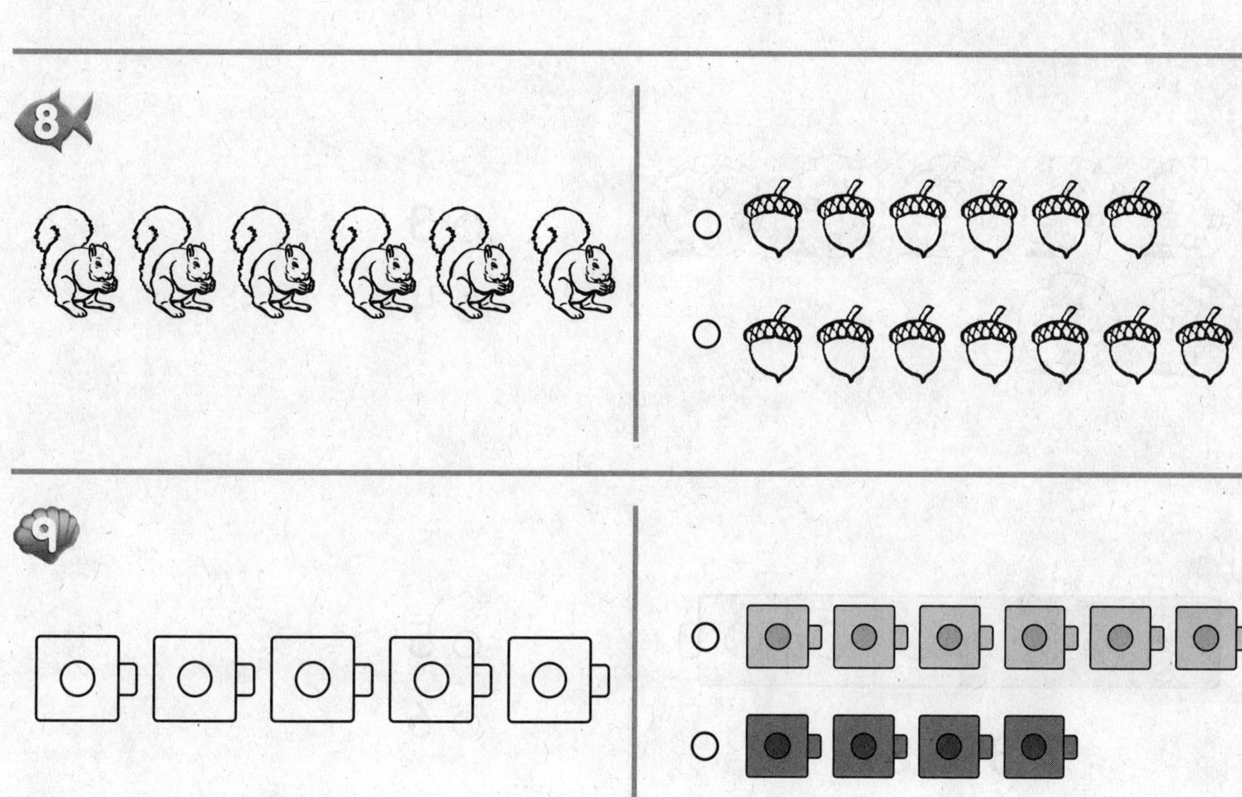

10

3 and 3
2 and 4
1 and 5

6 and 1
6 and 2
6 and 3

DIRECTIONS **8.** Count the squirrels. Which set of acorns has more than the number of squirrels? **9.** Count the white cubes. Which set has fewer cubes? **10.** Which shows ways to make 6?

GO ON

© Houghton Mifflin Harcourt Publishing Company

11

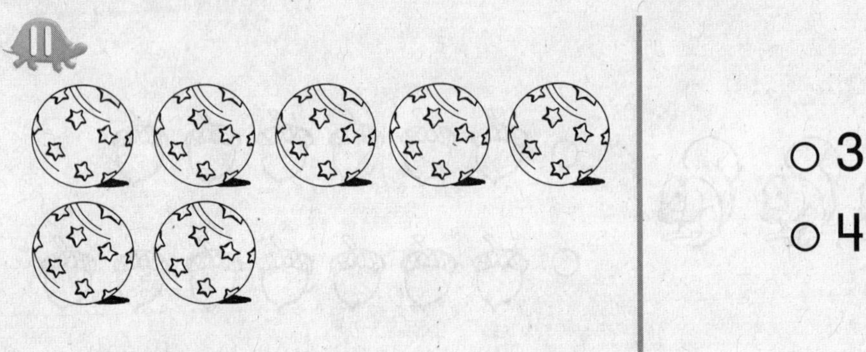

○ 3
○ 4

12

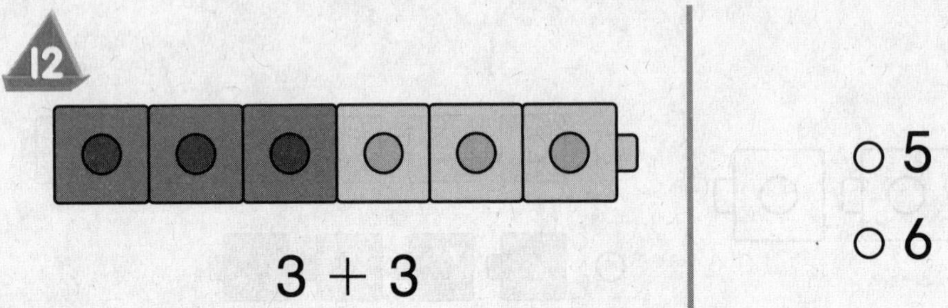

○ 5
○ 6

13

○ ○

DIRECTIONS 11. There are 7 balls. How many more balls do you need to make a group of 10? **12.** Derrick joins 3 dark gray cubes and 3 light gray cubes. How many cubes does he have altogether? **13.** Which model shows 5 hens with 2 leaving?

GO ON

© Houghton Mifflin Harcourt Publishing Company

12, 13, 14, 15, 16, ▬

○ 18

○ 17

○ 

○ 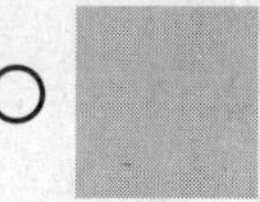

○ alike

○ different

○ alike

○ different

DIRECTIONS **14.** Count by ones. What number comes next? **15.** Look at the shapes. Which shape belongs in this set? **16.** Are these shapes alike or different? **17.** Are these coins alike or different?

© Houghton Mifflin Harcourt Publishing Company

Name ____________________

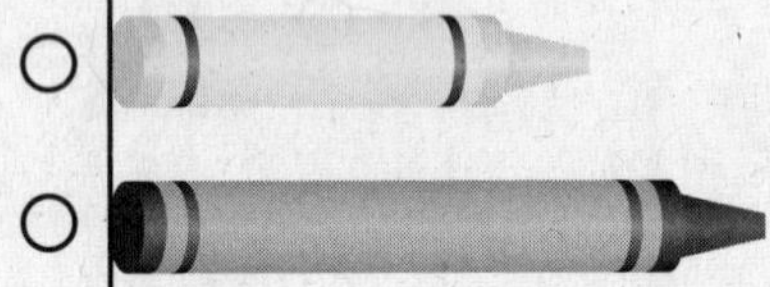

DIRECTIONS **18.** Which shape is large? **19.** Which crayon is shorter? **20.** Which fruit is heavier?

STOP

© Houghton Mifflin Harcourt Publishing Company

Name ______________________________

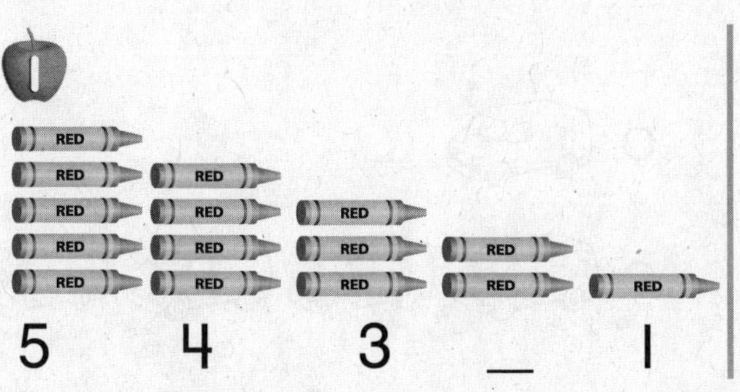

5 4 3 _ 1

○ 4
○ 2

○ 5, 4, 3, 2, 1
○ 1, 2, 3, 4, 5

2
two

○ 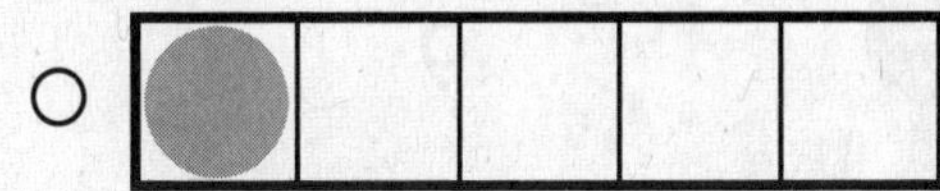
○ 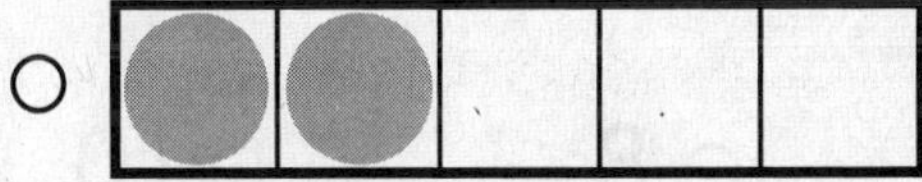

○ 
○ 

DIRECTIONS Fill in the bubble for the correct answer. **1.** What is the missing number in order by counting backward? **2.** Count the dots. What order do they show? **3.** Look at the number. Which five frame shows that number? **4.** Count the trucks. Which set shows a greater number of cars than the number of trucks?

© Houghton Mifflin Harcourt Publishing Company

5

○

○

6

○

○

7 9

○ 8 ○ 10

8 7

○ 8 ○ 6

9

○ ○

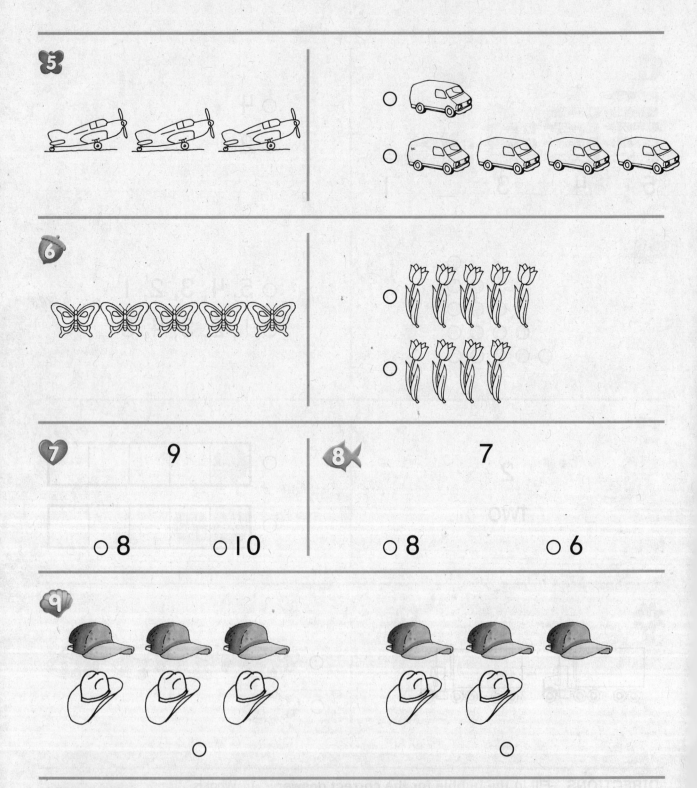

DIRECTIONS **5.** Count the planes. Which set shows a number of vans that is less than the number of planes? **6.** Which set has the same number as the butterfly set? **7.** Look at the number. Which number is one more? **8.** Look at the number. Which number is one less? **9.** Which sets show the same number of hats?

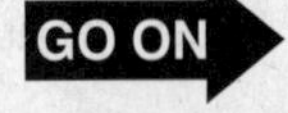

© Houghton Mifflin Harcourt Publishing Company

Name ______________________________

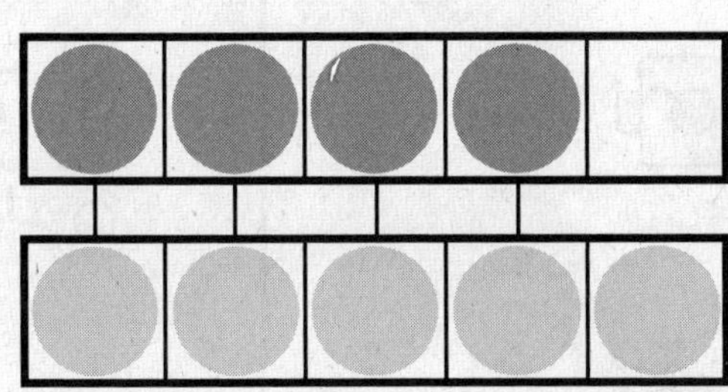

○ 

○ 

○ 9 is less than 10

○ 9 is greater than 10

○ 15 is less than 14

○ 15 is greater than 14

○ 

○ 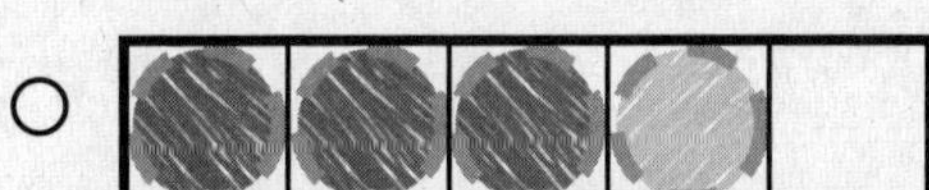

DIRECTIONS **10.** Count how many in each set. Which set has 1 more? **11.** There are 9 balls. What is true about 9? **12.** There are 15 stars. What is true about 15? **13.** Which model shows 3 as 1 and 2?

© Houghton Mifflin Harcourt Publishing Company

Name ______________________________

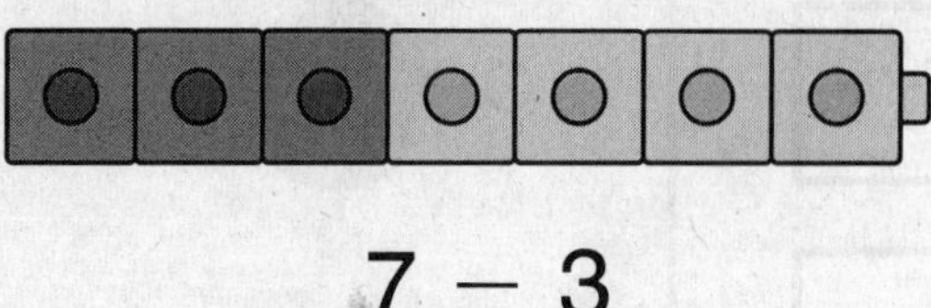

7 − 3

○ 7
○ 4

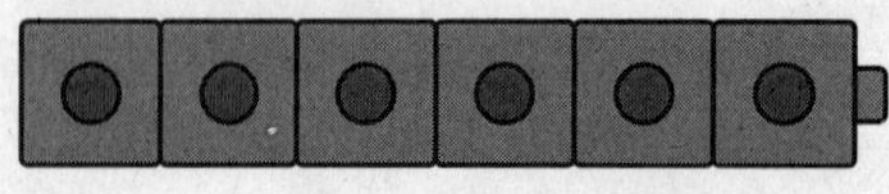

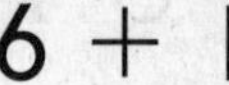

6 + 1

○ 7
○ 5

2 + 3

○ 3
○ 5

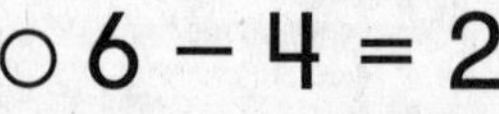

○ 6 − 4 = 2

○ 4 − 2 = 2

DIRECTIONS **14.** Look at the seven-cube train. Three cubes are dark gray the rest are light gray. How many are light gray? **15.** Rebecca has 6 cubes. What number is one more? **16.** There are 2 fish. Three more fish join them. How many fish are there now? **17.** There are 6 frogs. Four hop away. What does this picture show?

GO ON

© Houghton Mifflin Harcourt Publishing Company

18

○  

○  

19

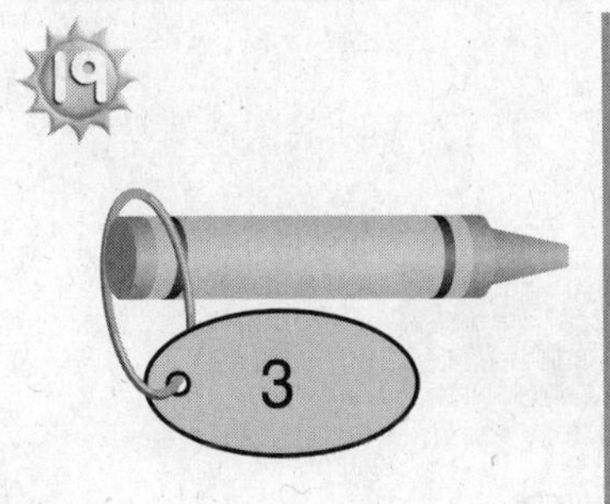

○   

○  

31	32	33	34	35	36	37	38	39	40
41	42	43	44	45	46	47		49	50

○ 58

○ 48

61	62	63	64	65	66	67	68	69	70
71	72	73	74	75	76	77	78	79	80

○ 66, 67, 68 ○ 70, 71, 72

DIRECTIONS **18.** David uses 2 nickels to buy a pencil. Which set shows the coins he used? **19.** Which set of pennies shows the number you need to buy the crayon? **20.** Point to each number as you count. What is the missing number? **21.** Point to each number as you count. Which numbers come after 69?

GO ON

© Houghton Mifflin Harcourt Publishing Company

Name ______________________

22

○

○

23

○

○

24

○

○

25

○

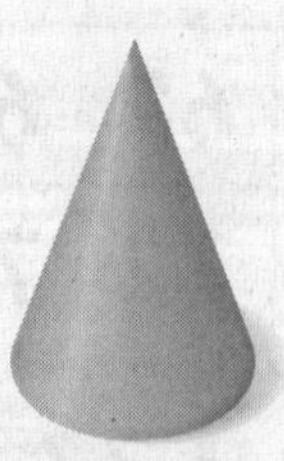

○

DIRECTIONS **22.** Which shape is a circle? **23.** Which shape is a triangle? **24.** Which object is shaped like a cylinder? **25.** Which shape is a cone?

GO ON

© Houghton Mifflin Harcourt Publishing Company

26

○ ○

27

○ 3 sides
○ curved

28

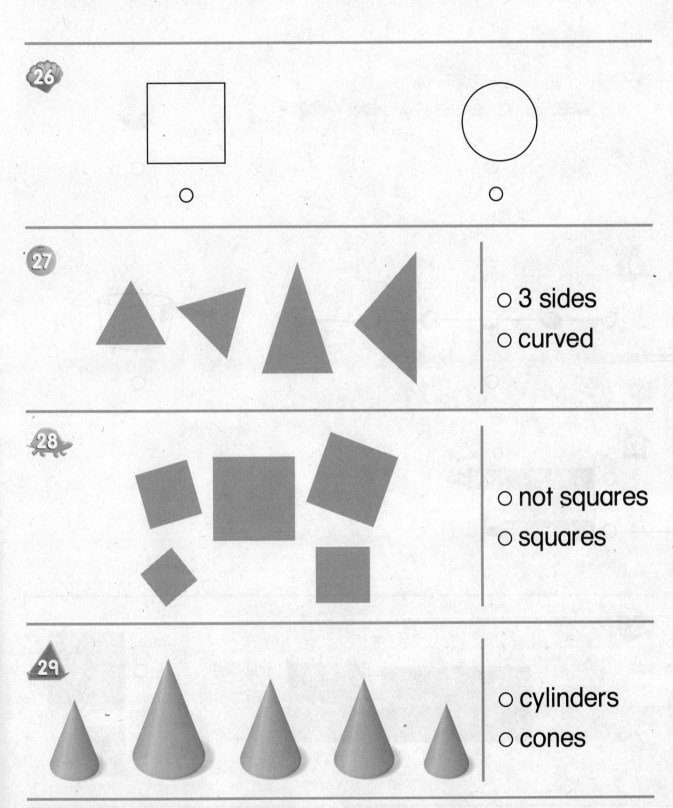

○ not squares
○ squares

29

○ cylinders
○ cones

DIRECTIONS **26.** Which shape is a flat surface on a cube? **27.** Look at the shapes. Which describes all the shapes? **28.** Eddie sorted his shapes. What is a name for this group of shapes? **29.** Helen sorted her shapes. What is a name for this group of shapes?

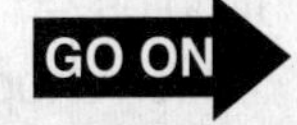

© Houghton Mifflin Harcourt Publishing Company

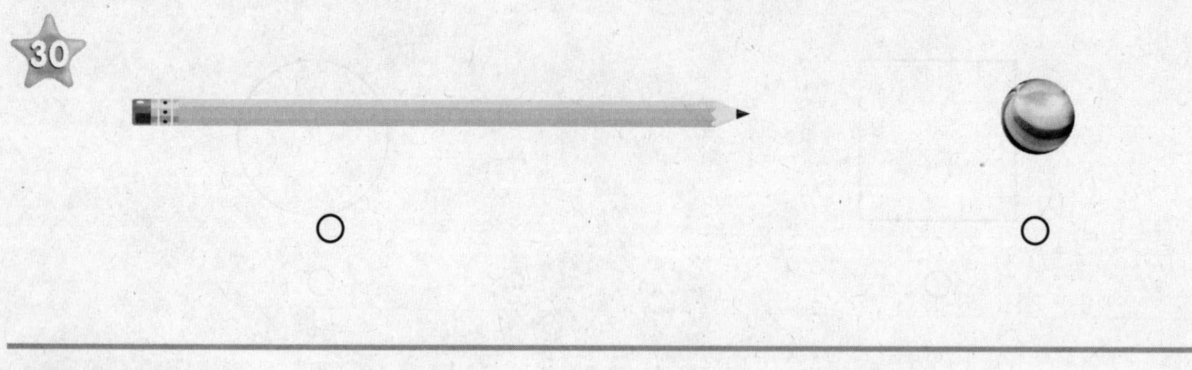

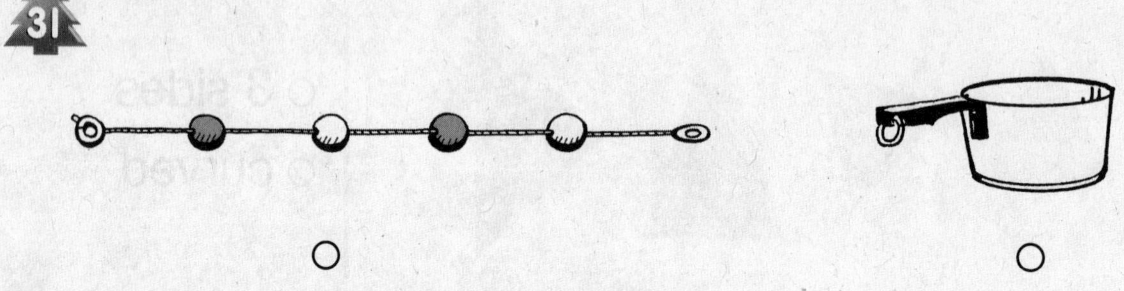

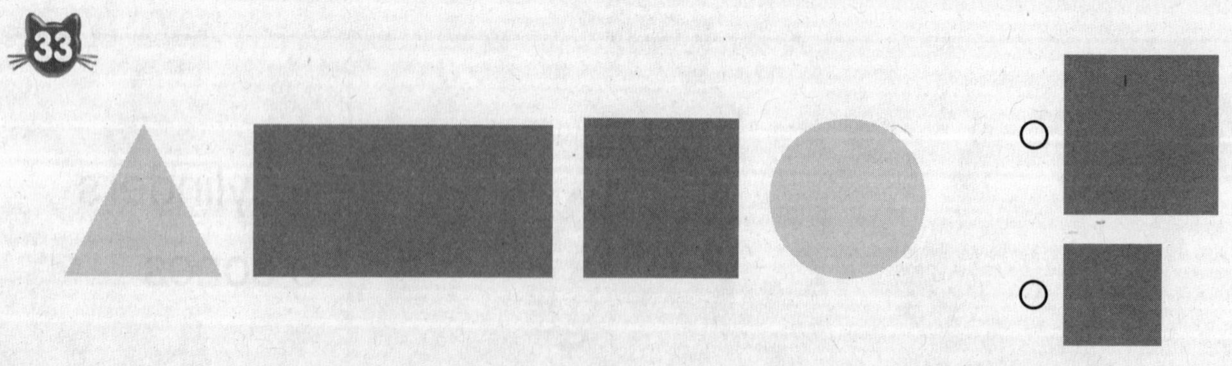

DIRECTIONS **30.** Which object would you most likely measure to find how long it is? **31.** Which object would you most likely measure to find how much it holds? **32.** Which crayon is longer? **33.** Kevin sorted these shapes. Which shape belongs in this set?

GO ON

© Houghton Mifflin Harcourt Publishing Company

34

○ ○

35

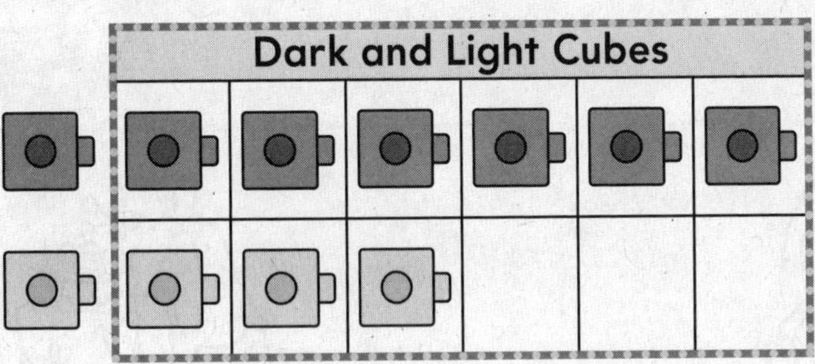

○ 7

○ 6

Favorite Color						
Brown	○	○	○			
Yellow	○	○	○	○	○	

○ brown
○ yellow

DIRECTIONS **34.** Look at how the shapes are sorted. Which shape belongs in the last category? **35.** Read the graph. How many dark gray cubes are there? **36.** Read the graph. Which color do most people like?

© Houghton Mifflin Harcourt Publishing Company

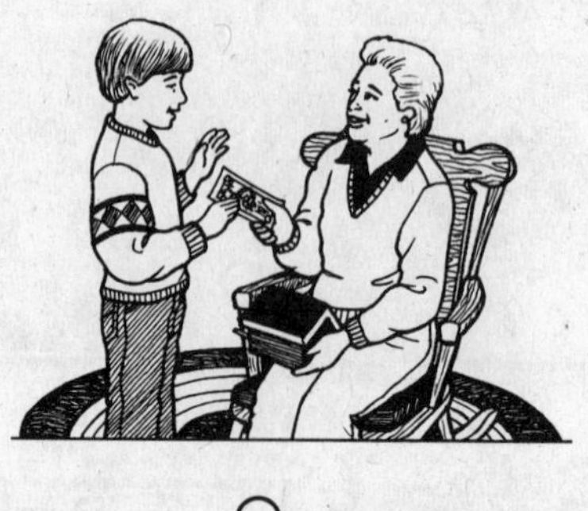

DIRECTIONS **37.** Which shows a picture of someone working to earn income? **38.** Which shows a child receiving money as a gift? **39.** Which person needs to know about car parts? **40.** Which picture shows a need?

© Houghton Mifflin Harcourt Publishing Company

Name ________________________________

○ 5, 4, 3, 2, 1 ○ 1, 2, 3, 4, 5

○ 5, 4, 3, 2, 1 ○ 1, 2, 3, 4, 5

7, ____, 9,

○ 10

○ 8

4

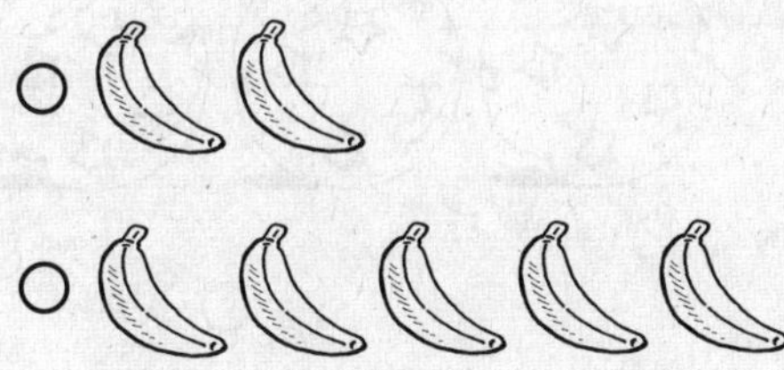

DIRECTIONS Fill in the bubble for the correct answer. **1.** Which numbers are in forward counting order? **2.** Which numbers are in backward counting order? **3.** Look at the number. Which is the missing number? **4.** Count the orange slices. Which set shows a number of bananas that is less than the number of orange slices?

GO ON

© Houghton Mifflin Harcourt Publishing Company

5

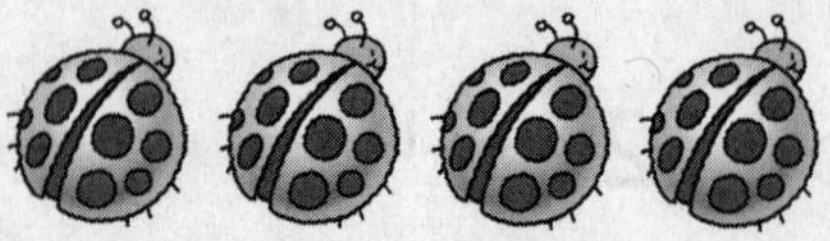

○

○

6

○

○

7 6

○ 5 ○ 7

8 8

○ 9 ○ 7

9

○ ○

DIRECTIONS **5.** Which set has the same number as the ladybug set? **6.** Count the fish. Which set shows a number of frogs that is greater than the number of fish? **7.** Look at the number. Which number is one more? **8.** Look at the number. Which number is one less? **9.** Which sets has a greater number of balls?

© Houghton Mifflin Harcourt Publishing Company

10

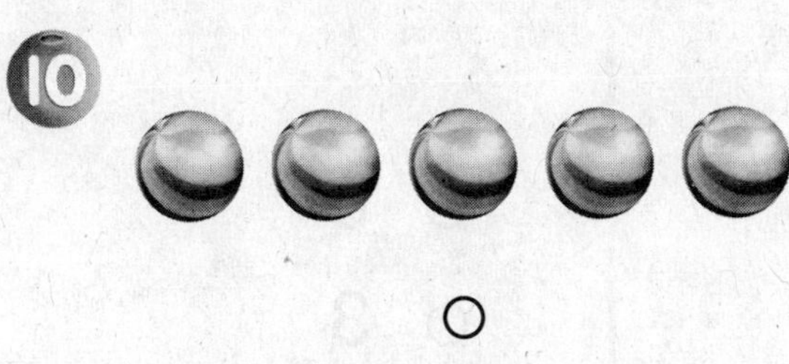

○

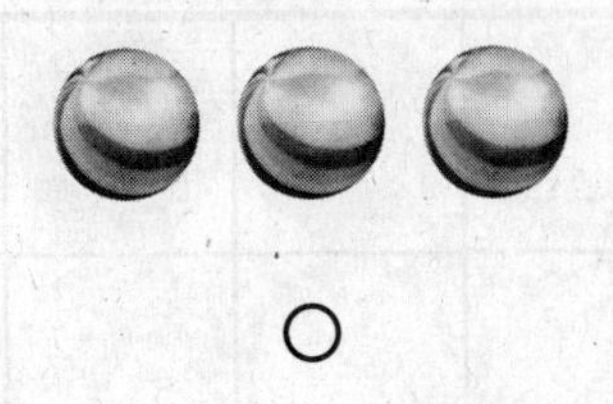

○

11

○ 9 is less than 8

○ 9 is greater than 8

12

○ 17 is less than 18

○ 17 is greater than 18

13

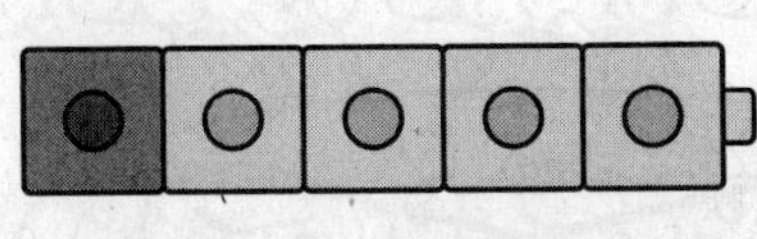

5 − 1

○ 6

○ 4

DIRECTIONS **10.** Which sets has a number of marbles that is less? **11.** There are 9 crayons. What is true about 9? **12.** There are 17 hot air balloons. What is true about 17? **13.** Look at the five-cube train. One cube is dark gray the rest are light gray. How many are light gray?

GO ON

© Houghton Mifflin Harcourt Publishing Company

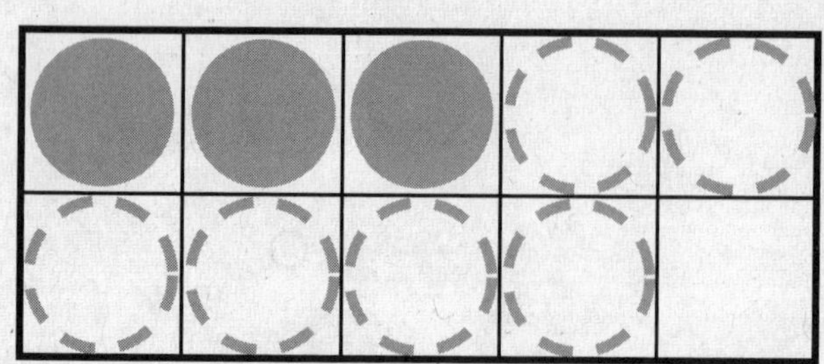

○ 6

○ 3

15

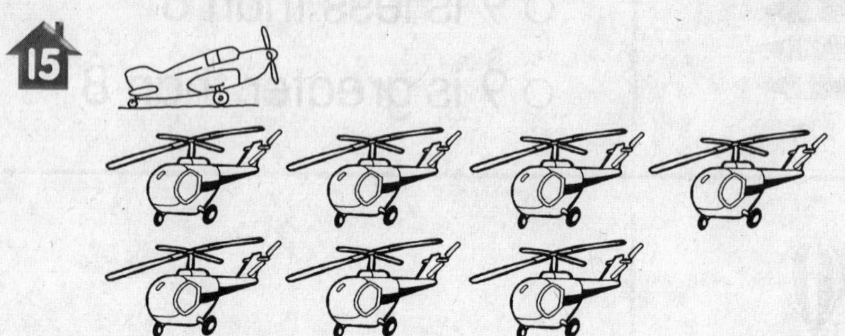

○ $2 + 6 = 8$

○ $1 + 7 = 8$

16

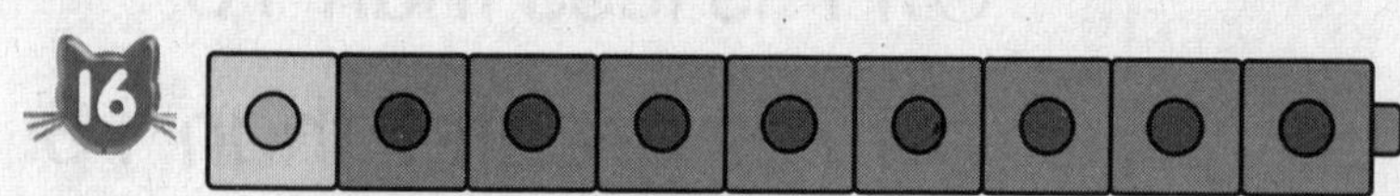

$9 - 1 =$

○ 8

○ 7

17

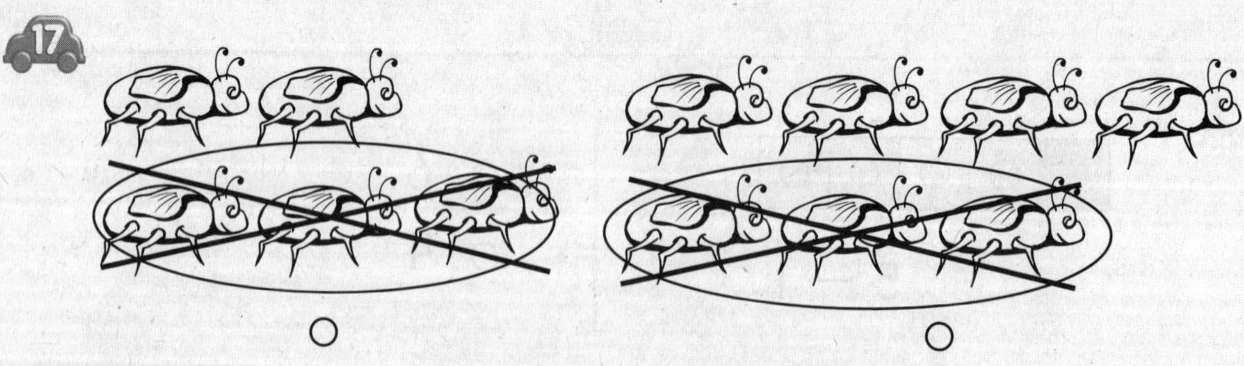

○ ○

DIRECTIONS **14.** Ryan needs to place 9 counters on the ten frame. He puts 3 dark gray counters on the ten fame. How many more counters does he need to make 9? **15.** There is 1 plane and 7 helicopters at the airport. What does this picture show? **16.** Rong has a 9-cube train. She takes away 1 cube. How many cubes are left on her train? **17.** Seven bugs are in the yard. Three bugs leave. Which picture shows how to find how many bugs are left?

© Houghton Mifflin Harcourt Publishing Company

18

○  

○  

19

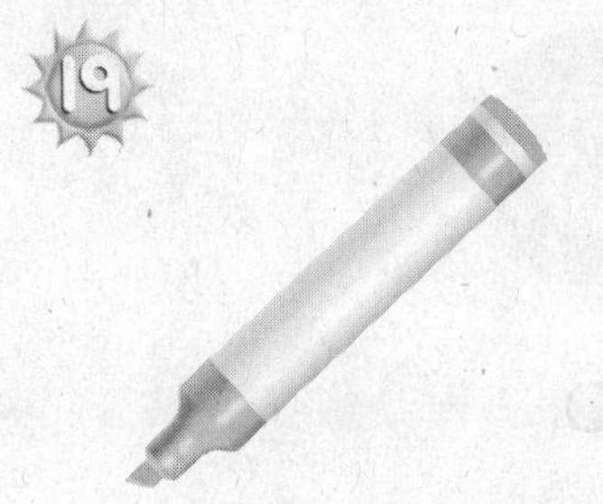

○  

○ 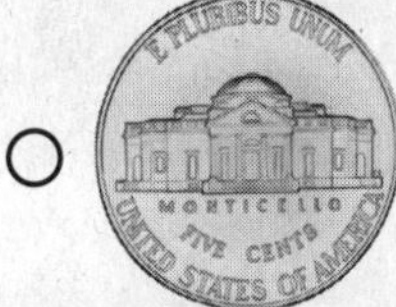 

51	52	53	54	55	56	57	58	59	60
61	62	63		65	66	67	68	69	70

○ 74

○ 64

30	40	50		70	80	90

○ 60 ○ 51

DIRECTIONS **18.** David uses 2 nickels to buy a pen. Which set shows the coins he uses? **19.** Rianna uses 2 dimes to buy a marker. Which set shows the coins she uses? **20.** Point to each number as you count. What is the missing number? **21.** Count by tens. What is the missing number?

© Houghton Mifflin Harcourt Publishing Company

22

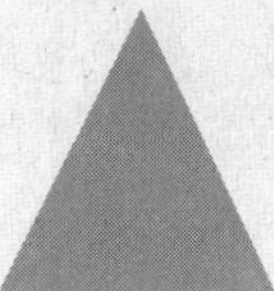

DIRECTIONS **22.** Which shape is a triangle? **23.** Which shape is a rectangle? **24.** Which object is shaped like a cone? **25.** Which shape is a sphere?

GO ON

© Houghton Mifflin Harcourt Publishing Company

Name ________________________________

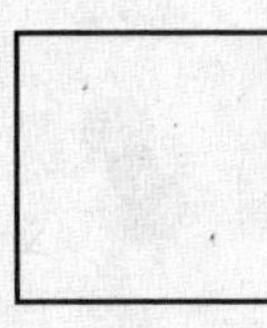

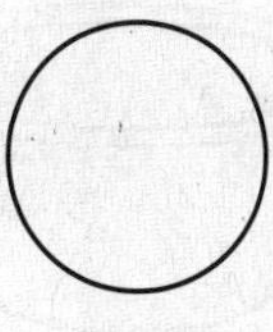

○ not rectangles

○ rectangles

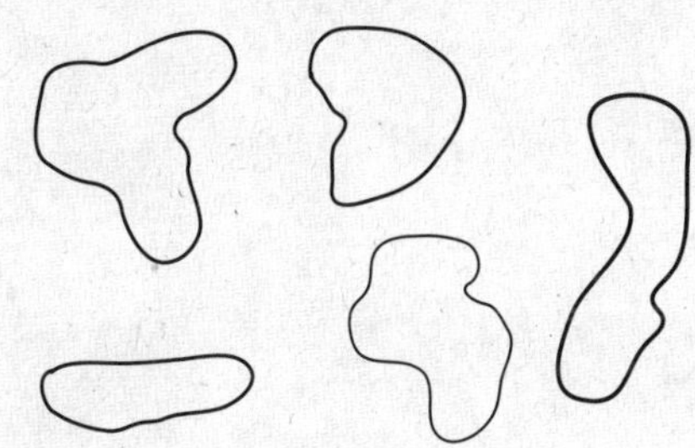

○ not triangles

○ triangles

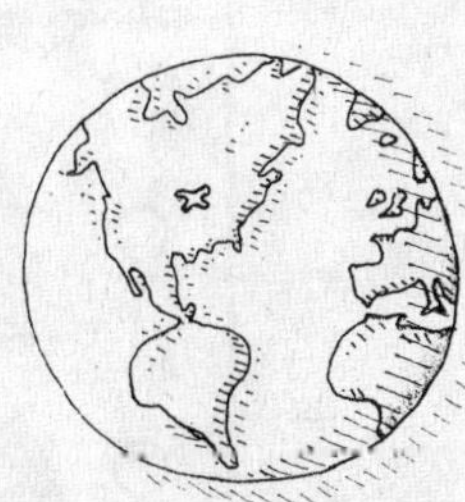

○ cylinders

○ spheres

DIRECTIONS **26.** Which shape is the flat surface of a cylinder? **27.** Amelia sorted her shapes. What is a name for this group of shapes? **28.** Look at the shapes. Which describes all the shapes? **29.** Kobe sorted his shapes. What is a name for this group of shapes?

© Houghton Mifflin Harcourt Publishing Company

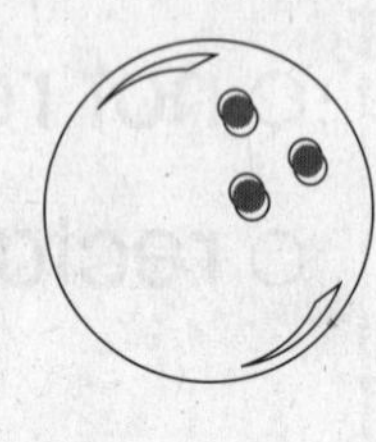

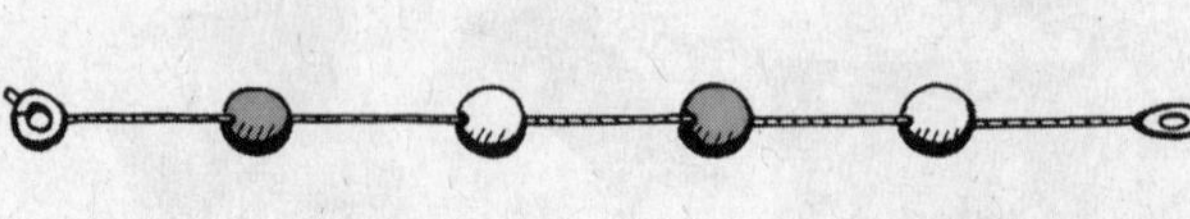

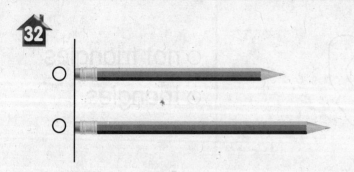

32

33

DIRECTIONS **30.** Which object would you most likely measure to find how much it holds? **31.** Which object would you most likely measure to find how heavy it is? **32.** Which pencil is shorter? **33.** Angela is sorting shapes. She wants to put another shape in her set. Which shape should she chose?

GO ON

© Houghton Mifflin Harcourt Publishing Company

Name ______________________________

34

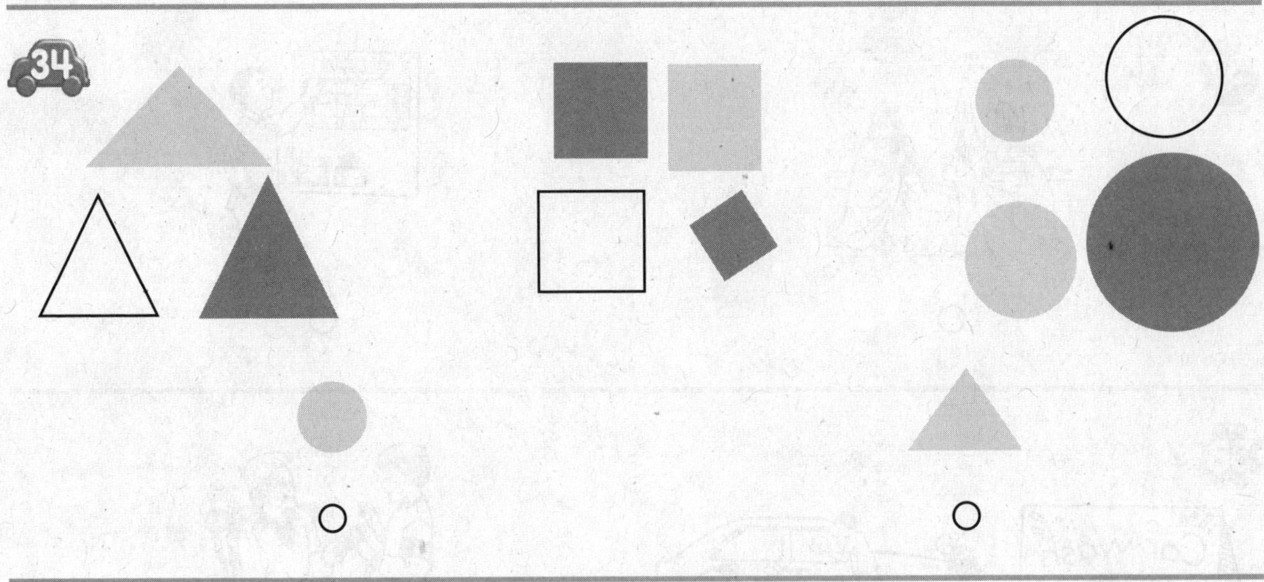

35

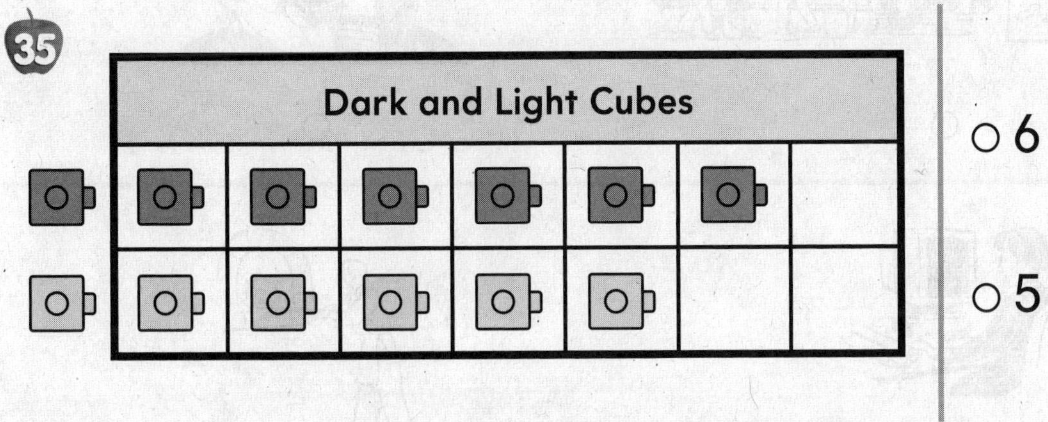

○ 6

○ 5

36

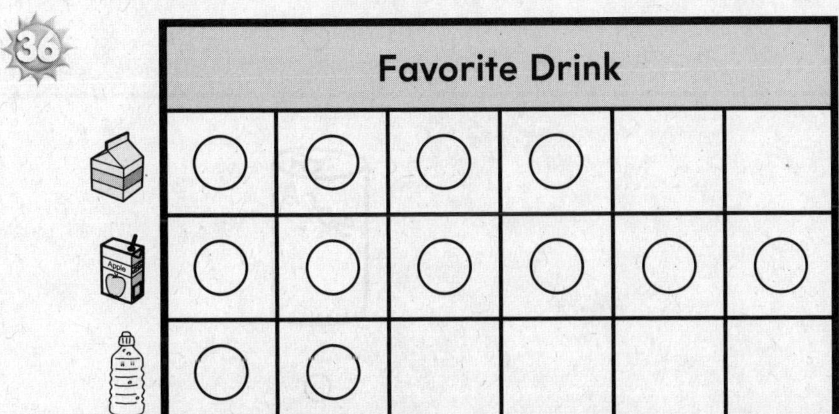

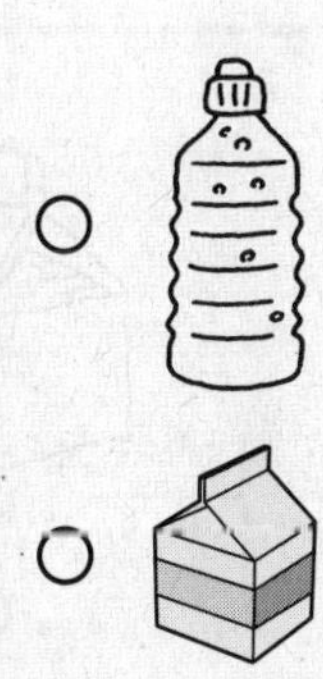

DIRECTIONS **34.** Look at how the shapes are sorted. Which shape belongs in the first category? **35.** Read the graph. How many light gray cubes are there? **36.** Read the graph. Which drink did the fewest children like?

© Houghton Mifflin Harcourt Publishing Company

Name ______________________________

DIRECTIONS **37.** Which shows a picture of someone working to earn income? **38.** Which shows a child earning money? **39.** Which person needs to know how to use a computer? **40.** Andrea drinks what she wants instead of what she needs. What did she drink?

© Houghton Mifflin Harcourt Publishing Company

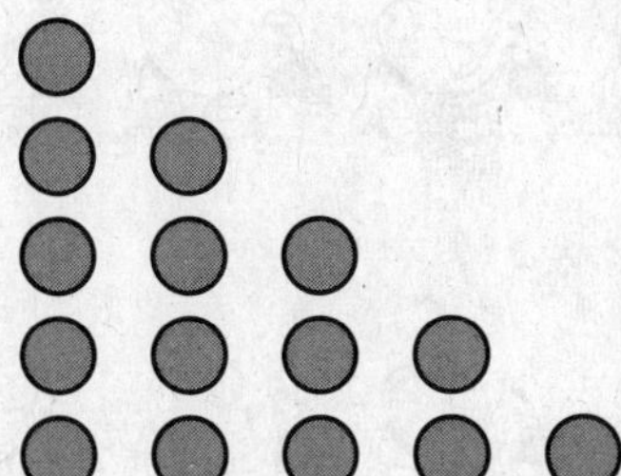

○ 5, 4, 3, 2, 1

○ 1, 2, 3, 4, 5

○ 1, 2, 3, 4, 5

○ 5, 4, 3, 2, 1

5, ____, 7

○ 4

○ 6

○ 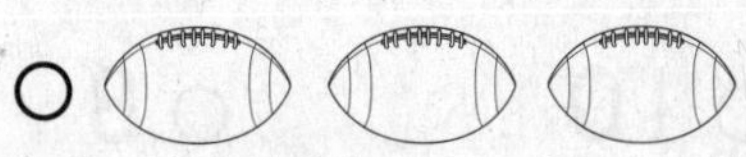

○ 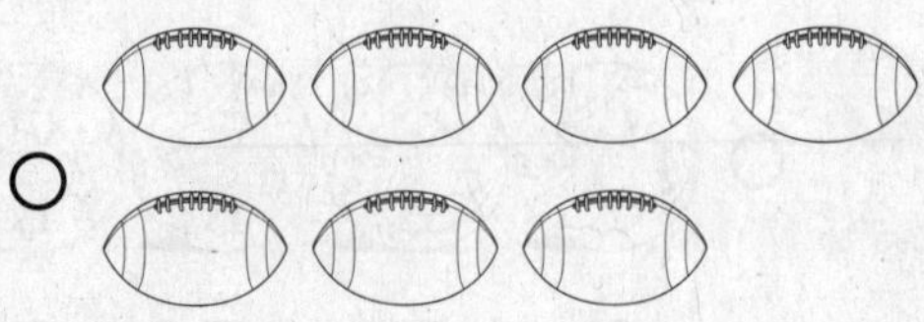

DIRECTIONS Fill in the bubble for the correct answer. 1. Count the dot towers. What order do they show? **2.** Which numbers are in backward counting order? **3.** Look at the number. Which is the missing number? **4.** Count the baseballs. Which set shows a number of footballs that is more than the number of baseballs?

GO ON

© Houghton Mifflin Harcourt Publishing Company

Name ________________________________

5

○

○

6

○

○

7 9

○ 10 ○ 8

8 5

○ 4 ○ 6

9

○

○

DIRECTIONS **5.** Count the horses. Which set shows a number of saddles that is less than the number of horses? **6.** Which set has the same number as the shovel set? **7.** Look at the number. Which number is one more? **8.** Look at the number. Which number is one less? **9.** Which sets has a greater number of balls?

© Houghton Mifflin Harcourt Publishing Company

Name ______________________

10

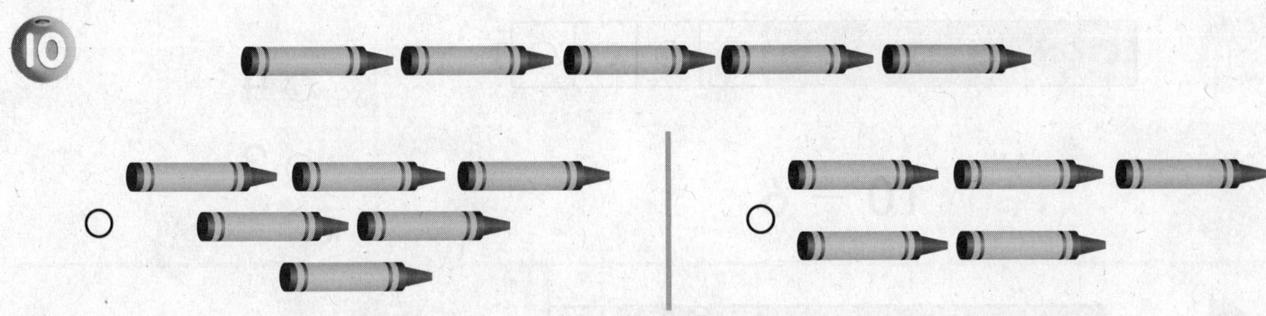

○ 

○

11

○ 7 is less than 8

○ 7 is greater than 8

12

○ 13 is less than 12

○ 13 is greater than 12

13

○ 2 and 3

○ 2 and 2

DIRECTIONS **10.** Richard has 5 crayons. Which set has the same number of crayon? **11.** There are 7 marbles. What is true about 7? **12.** There are 13 sailboats. What is true about 13? **13.** How many fish in all?

© Houghton Mifflin Harcourt Publishing Company

10 − 6

○ 4
○ 3

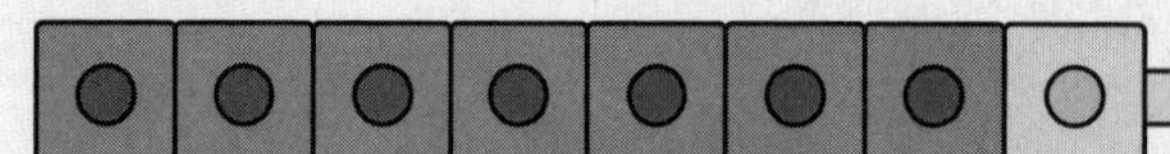

8 − 1 =

○ 9
○ 7

○ 4 − 3 = 1
○ 7 − 3 = 4

○ 3 − 2 = 1
○ 5 − 3 = 2

DIRECTIONS **14.** Amanda has a ten-cube train. She takes it apart to make 2 trains. One train has 6 cubes. How many cubes are in the other train? **15.** Mark has an 8-cube train. He takes away 1 cube. How many cubes are left on his train? **16.** There are 7 helicopters. Three leave. Which number sentence matches the story? **17.** Five cars are in a parking lot. Three drive away. Which number sentence matches the story?

© Houghton Mifflin Harcourt Publishing Company

○ 

○ 

○  

○  

61	62	63	64	65	66	67	68	69	70
71	72	73	74	75	76	77	78		80

○ 89

○ 79

21

20	30	40	50	60		80

○ 61 ○ 70

DIRECTIONS **18.** Kyle uses a dime to buy a pencil. Which shows the coin he uses? **19.** Amita uses 2 quarters to buy a stuffed penguin. Which set shows the coins she uses? **20.** Point to each number as you count. What is the missing number? **21.** Count by tens. What is the missing number?

© Houghton Mifflin Harcourt Publishing Company

Name ____

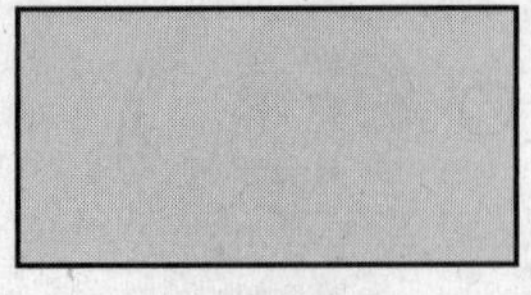
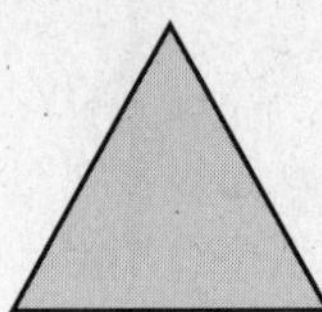

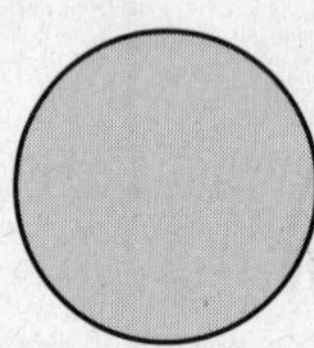

DIRECTIONS **22.** Which shape is a rectangle? **23.** Which shape is a square? **24.** Which object is shaped like a sphere? **25.** Which object is shaped like a cube?

GO ON

© Houghton Mifflin Harcourt Publishing Company

26

○ ○

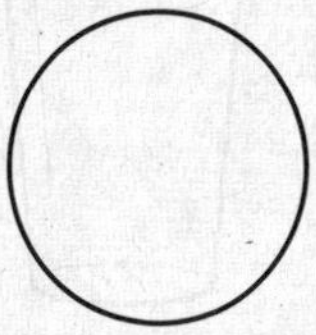

27

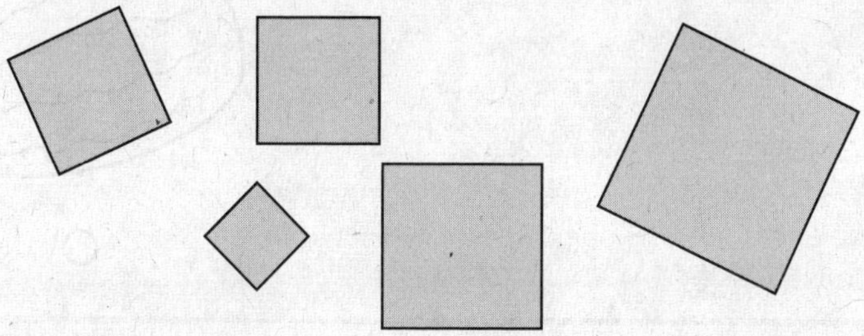

○ not squares
○ squares

28

○ spheres
○ cones

29

○ ○

DIRECTIONS **26.** Which shape is a flat surface of a cube? **27.** Peter sorted his shapes. What is a name for this group of shapes? **28.** Laney sorted her shapes. What is a name for this group of shapes? **29.** Tami is sorting her shapes. Which group does the first shape belong in?

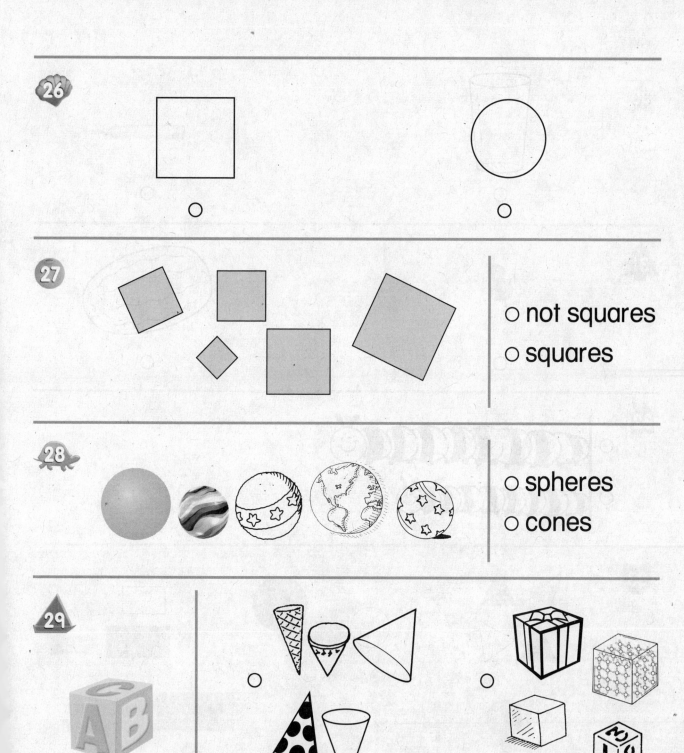

© Houghton Mifflin Harcourt Publishing Company

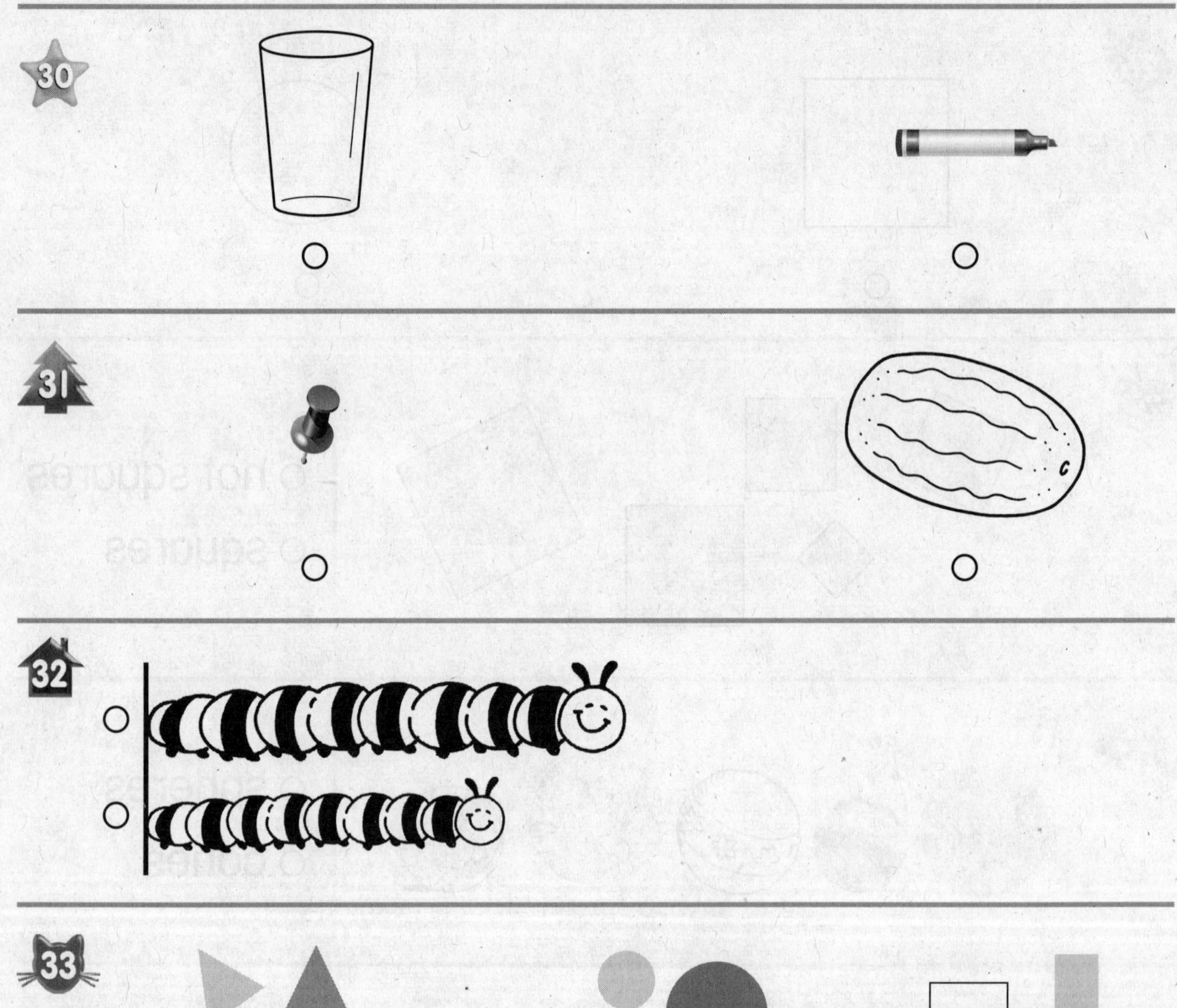

DIRECTIONS **30.** Which object would you most likely measure to find how much it holds? **31.** Which object would you most likely measure to show how heavy it is? **32.** Which caterpillar is shorter? **33.** Mindy is sorting shapes. She wants to put another shape in her second set. Which shape should she chose?

GO ON

© Houghton Mifflin Harcourt Publishing Company

34

35

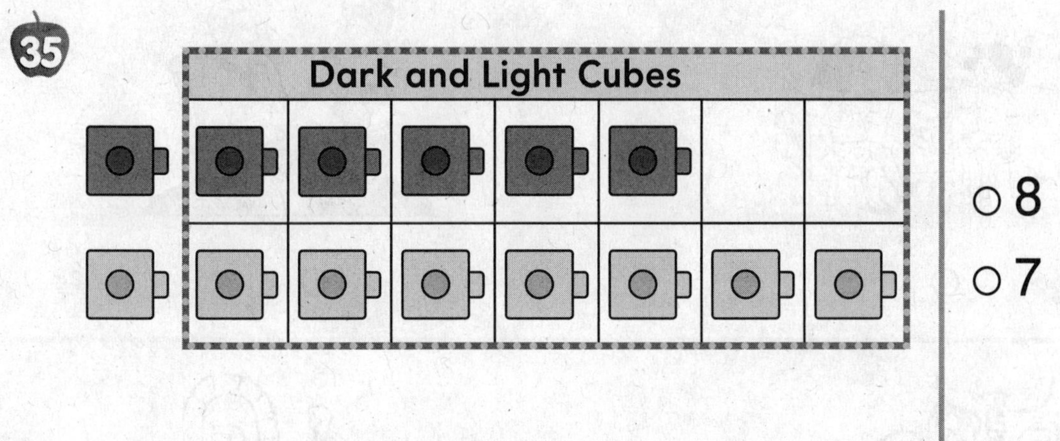

○ 8

○ 7

36

Favorite Animal						
dog	○	○	○	○	○	○
tiger	○	○	○	○		
penguin	○	○	○	○	○	

○ 

○ 

DIRECTIONS **34.** Look at how the shapes are sorted. Which shape belongs in the second category? **35.** Read the graph. How many light gray cubes are there? **36.** Read the graph. Which animal did most people like?

© Houghton Mifflin Harcourt Publishing Company

DIRECTIONS **37.** Which shows a picture of someone working to earn income? **38.** Which shows a child receiving money as a gift? **39.** Which person needs to know how to read a recipe? **40.** Danny is packing things he needs. What does he pack?

© Houghton Mifflin Harcourt Publishing Company

1

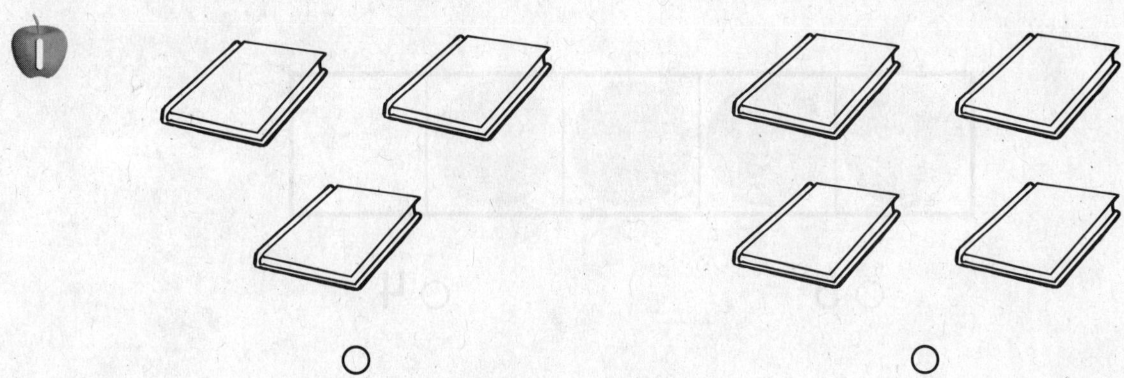

2

3

DIRECTIONS Fill in the bubble for the correct answer. **1.** Count the books in each set. Which set has four books? **2.** There are 3 puppies. One more puppy joins them. How many puppies are there now? **3.** Count the bears in each set. Which set has two bears?

© Houghton Mifflin Harcourt Publishing Company

Name ____________________

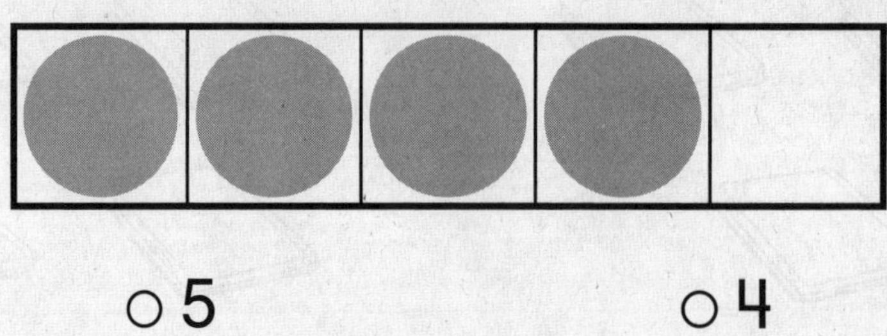

○ 5 ○ 4

5

○ 3 ○ 4

6

○ 3 ○ 4

DIRECTIONS **4.** What number does the model show? **5.** How many trees are there? **6.** Maria counted the kittens. She wrote how many kittens there are. What number did she write?

© Houghton Mifflin Harcourt Publishing Company

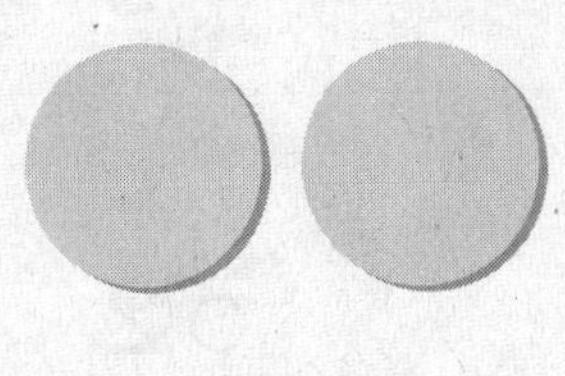

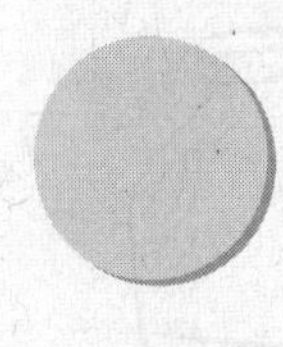

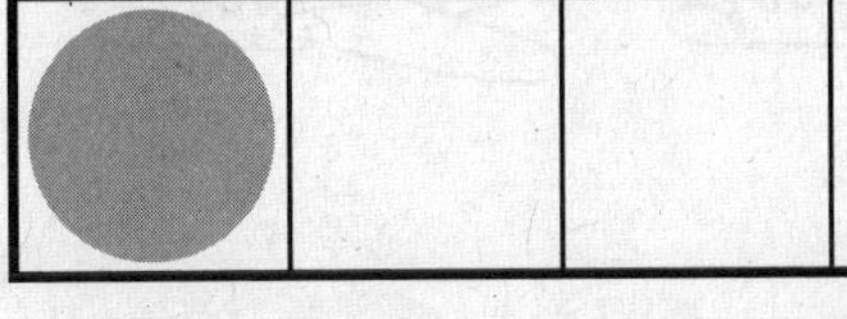

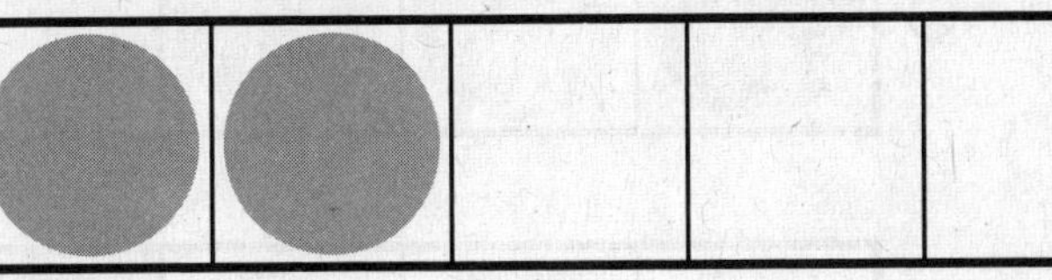

one

○ one ○ two

DIRECTIONS **7.** Two children each have an apple. Which shows a model of this problem? **8.** Look at the number. Which five frame shows that number? **9.** Count. How many fish are there?

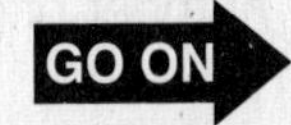

© Houghton Mifflin Harcourt Publishing Company

○ 1 ○ 2

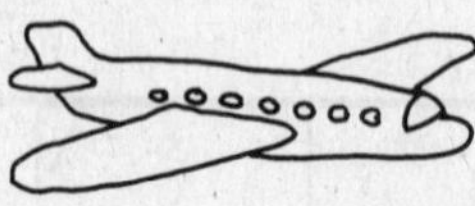  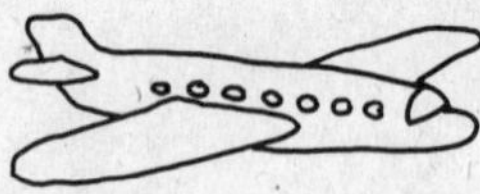 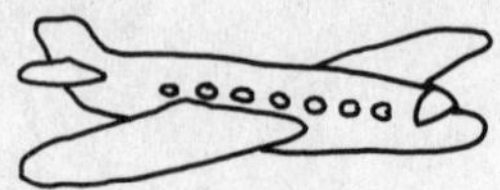

○ 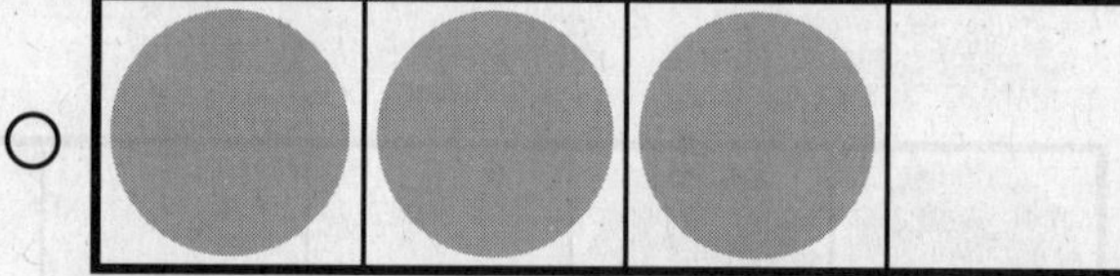

○ 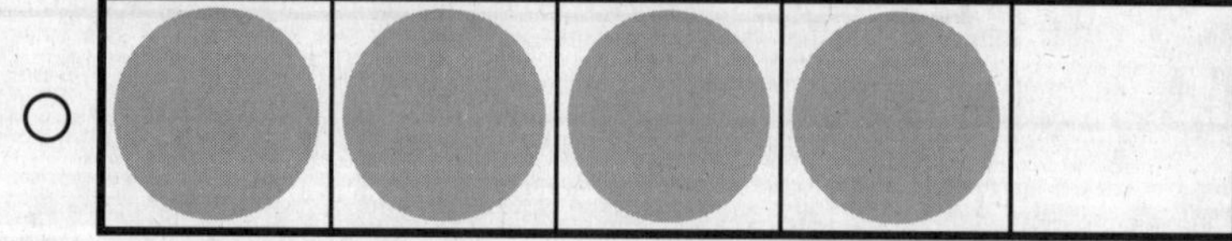

○

○

DIRECTIONS **10.** Count. What number tells how many? **11.** Count the planes. Which five frame shows the same number as the number of planes? **12.** Which set has two objects?

© Houghton Mifflin Harcourt Publishing Company

Name ______________________________

○ 4 ○ 3

○ zero ○ one

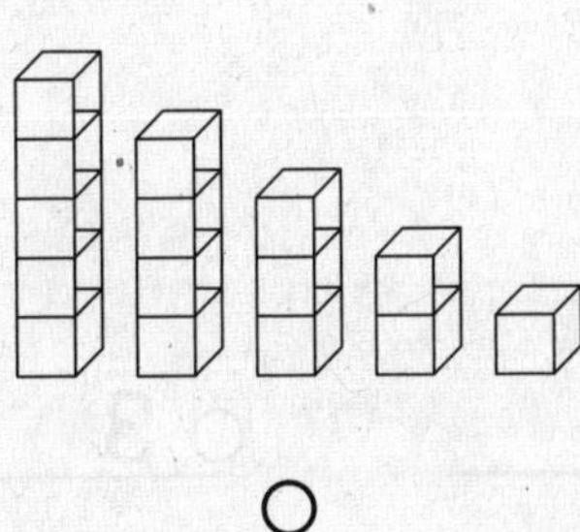

○

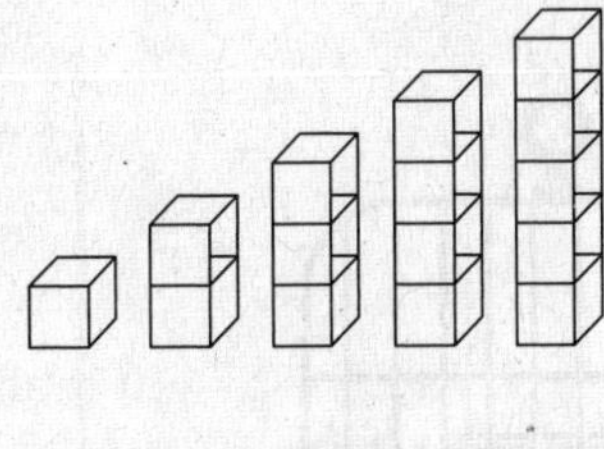

○

DIRECTIONS Fill in the bubble for the correct answer. **1.** How many frogs? **2.** How many kittens are in the box? **3.** Which picture shows counting backward?

© Houghton Mifflin Harcourt Publishing Company

○ 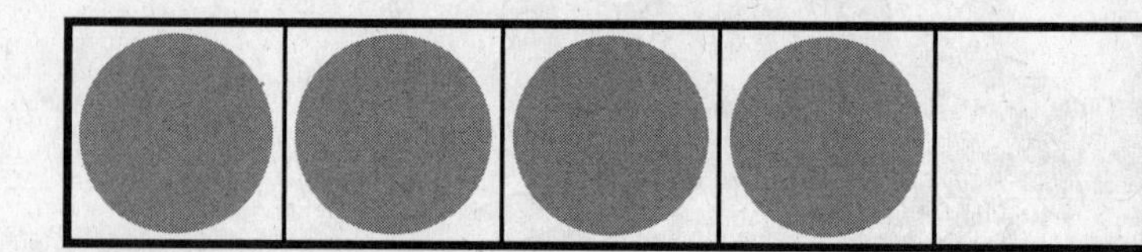

○ 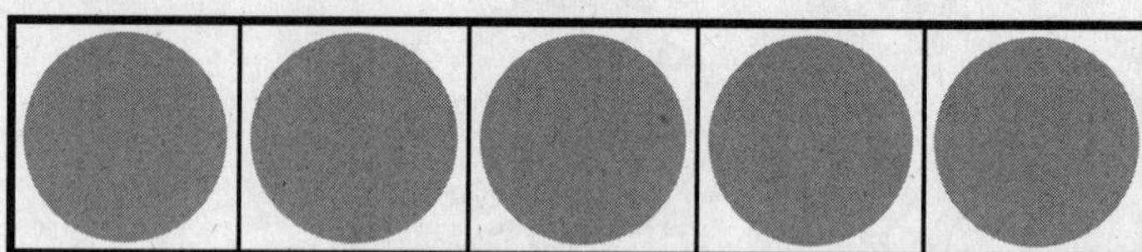

5

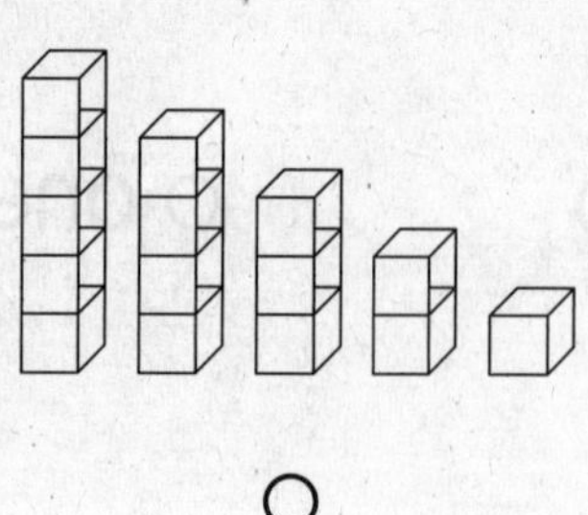

○

○

6

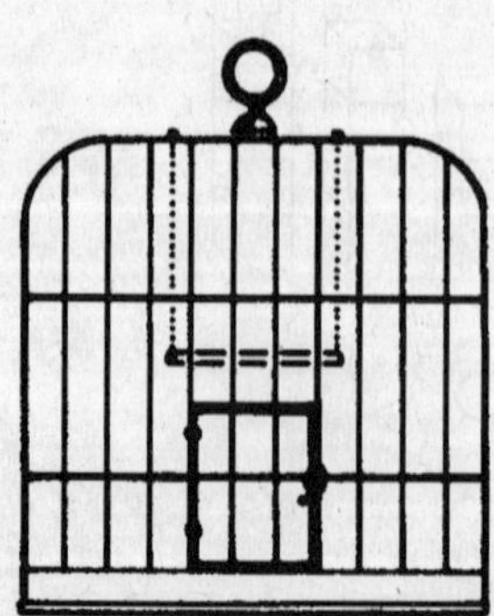

○ 0 ○ 3

DIRECTIONS **4.** Count the hot air balloons. Which shows the balloons with counters? **5.** Which picture shows counting forward? **6.** There are no birds in the cage. How many birds are in the cage?

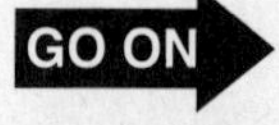

© Houghton Mifflin Harcourt Publishing Company

Name ____________________

○ ○

8

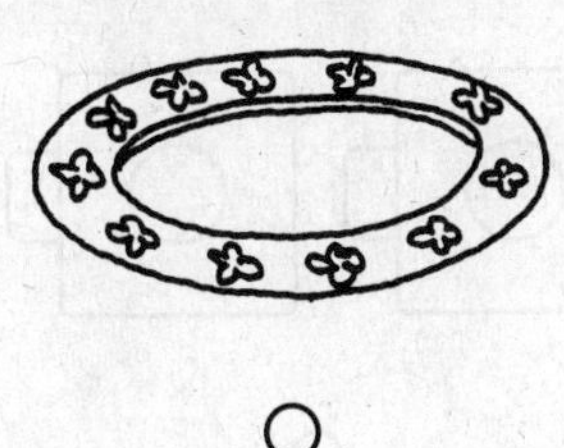

○ ○

9

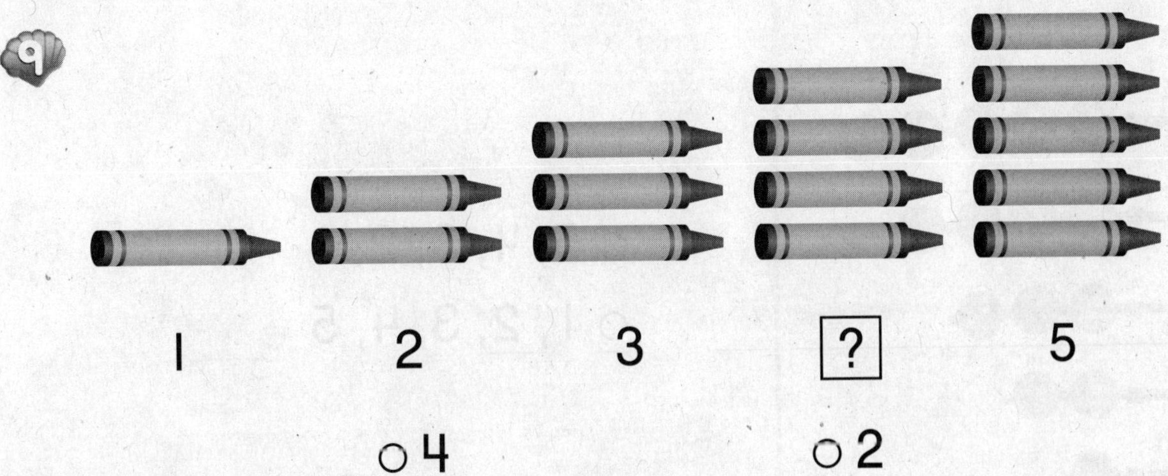

○ 4 ○ 2

DIRECTIONS **7.** Which shows four strawberries? **8.** Which plate shows 0 muffins? **9.** Look at the crayons. What is the missing number in order by counting forward?

GO ON

© Houghton Mifflin Harcourt Publishing Company

Name ___________________________

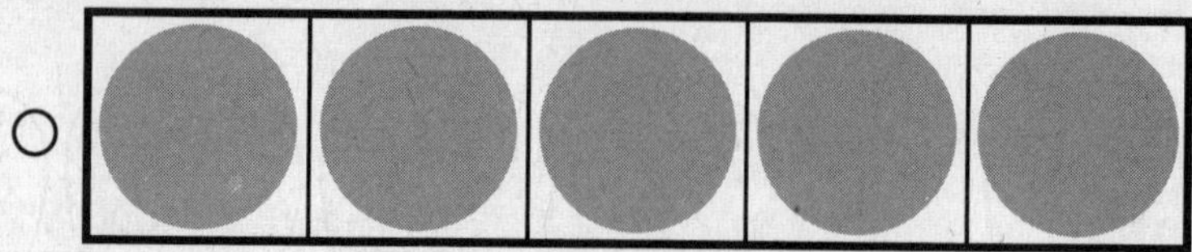

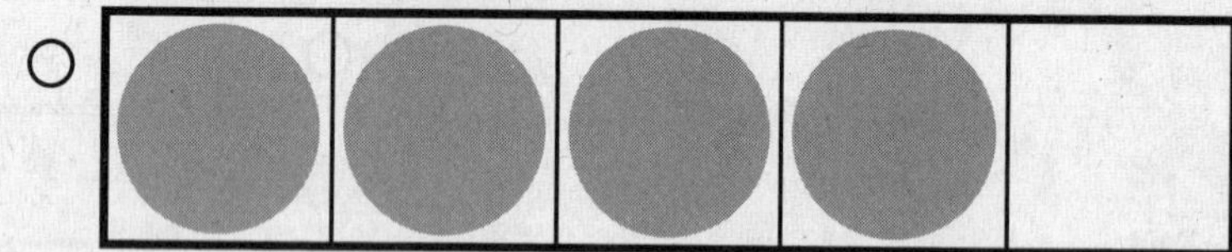

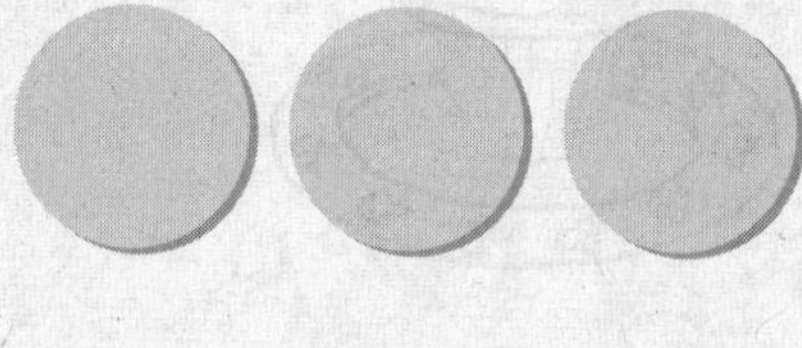

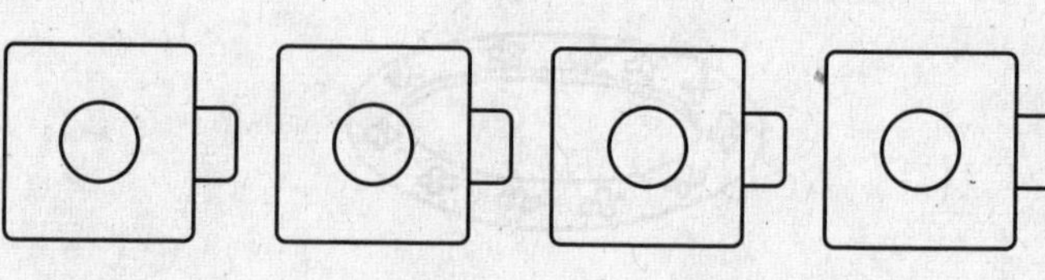

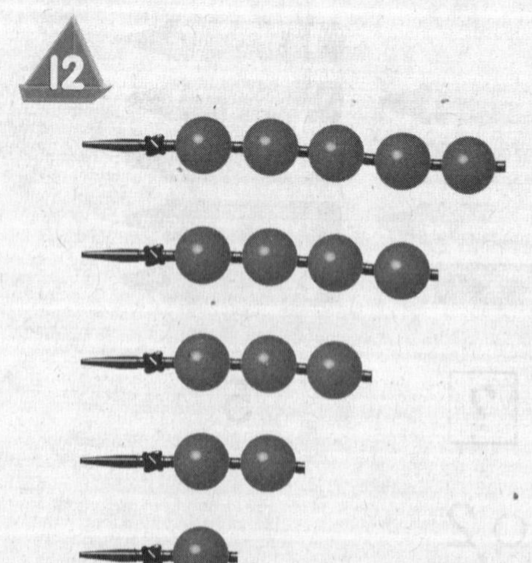

○ 5, 4, 3, 2, 1

○ 1, 2, 3, 4, 5

DIRECTIONS **10.** Which counters show 5? **11.** Which could you use to show 4? **12.** Look at the beads on each string. What order do they show?

© Houghton Mifflin Harcourt Publishing Company

Name ____________________

○ 2 ○ 4

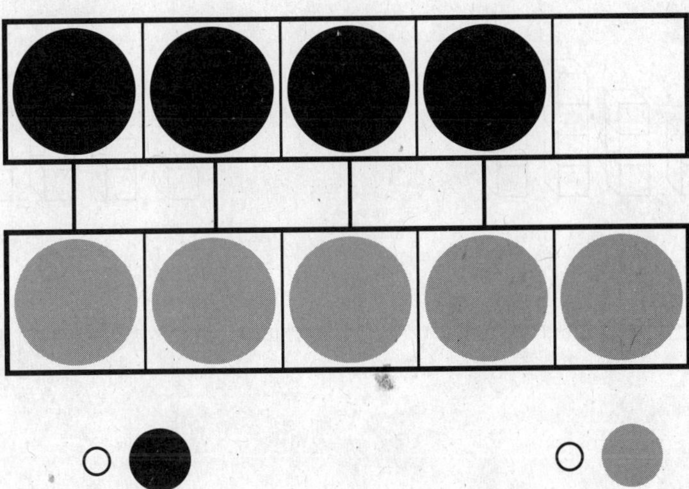

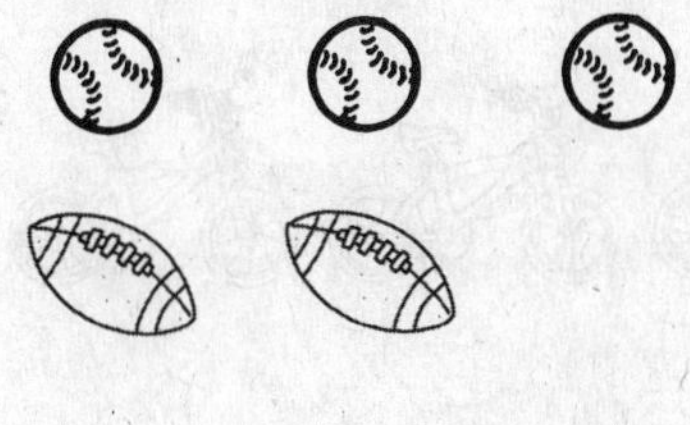

DIRECTIONS Fill in the bubble for the correct answer. **1.** Which number is greater than the number of chicks? **2.** Count how many in each set. Which set has 1 less? **3.** Which sets show the same number of balls?

GO ON

© Houghton Mifflin Harcourt Publishing Company

Name ______________________________

4

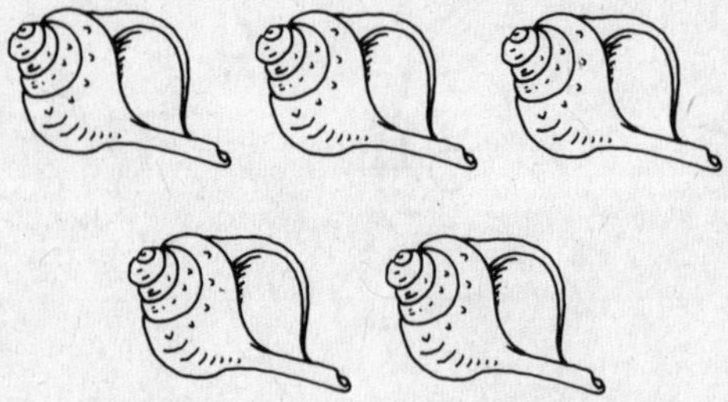

○ 3 ○ 5

5

○ ○

6

○ 

○ 

DIRECTIONS 4. Count the shells. How many are there? 5. Which block towers are in counting order? 6. Count the skateboards. Count the objects in each set. Which set has the same number of objects as the number of skateboards?

© Houghton Mifflin Harcourt Publishing Company

7

8

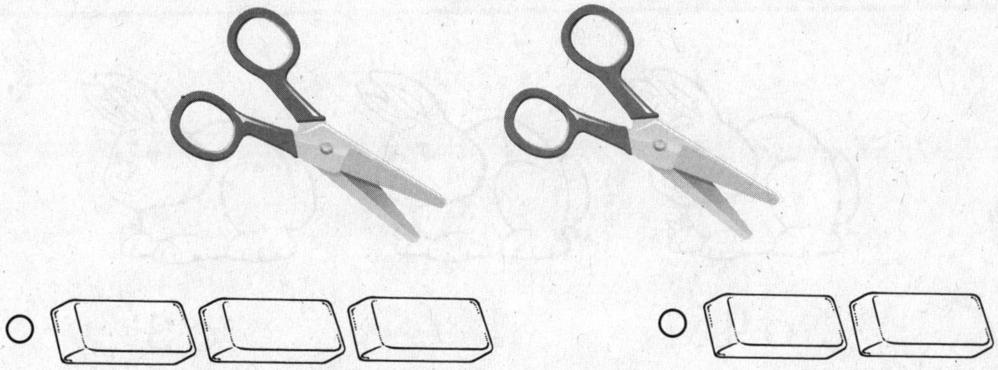

9

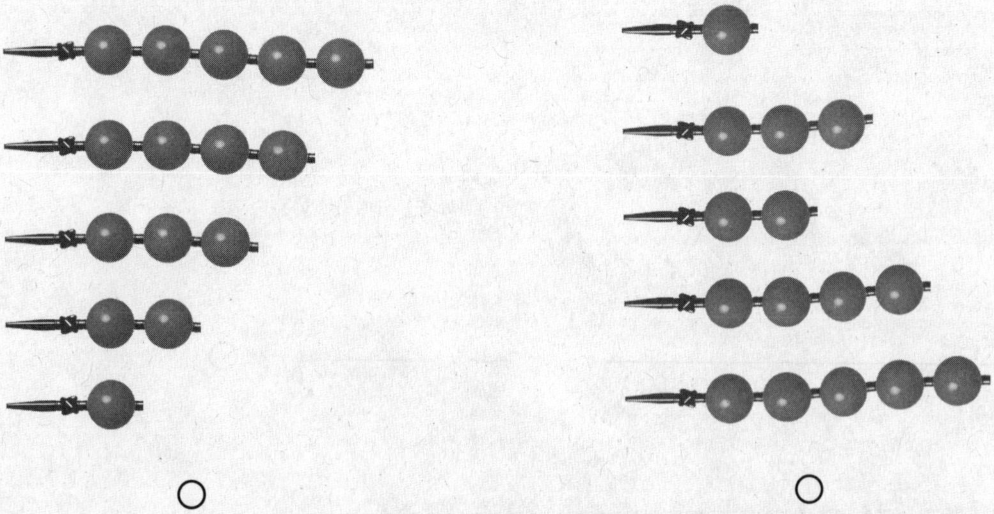

DIRECTIONS **7.** Which set has a a greater number of animals? **8.** Ryan has 2 pairs of scissors. Maria has the same number of erasers. Which shows Maria's erasers? **9.** Which bead strings are in counting order?

© Houghton Mifflin Harcourt Publishing Company

○ ○

○ 4 ○ 3

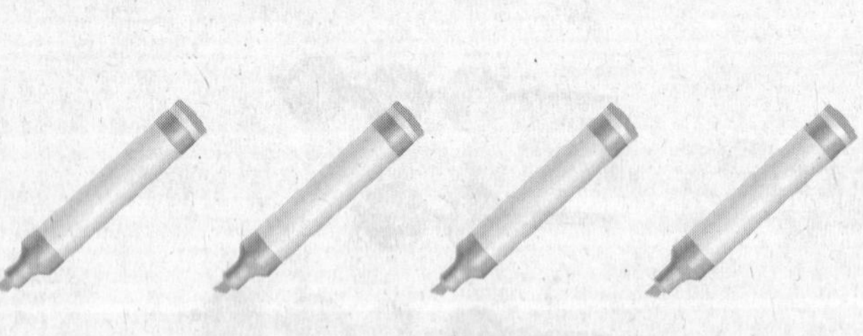

○

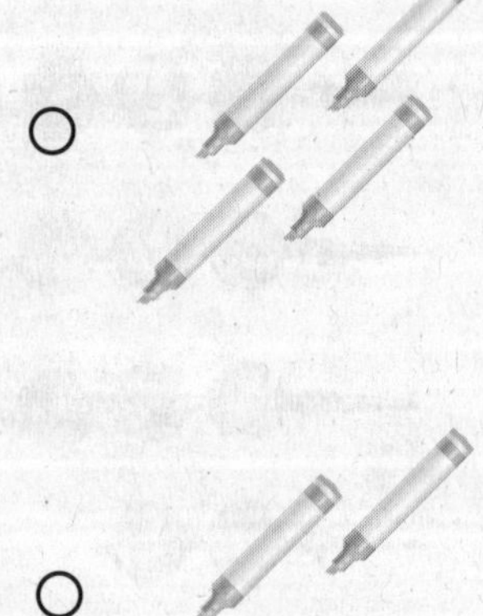

○

DIRECTIONS **10.** Count the buses. Which set shows a greater number of train engines than the number of buses? **11.** Count the bunnies. How many are there? **12.** Tyrone has 4 markers. Which set has a number of markers that is less?

© Houghton Mifflin Harcourt Publishing Company

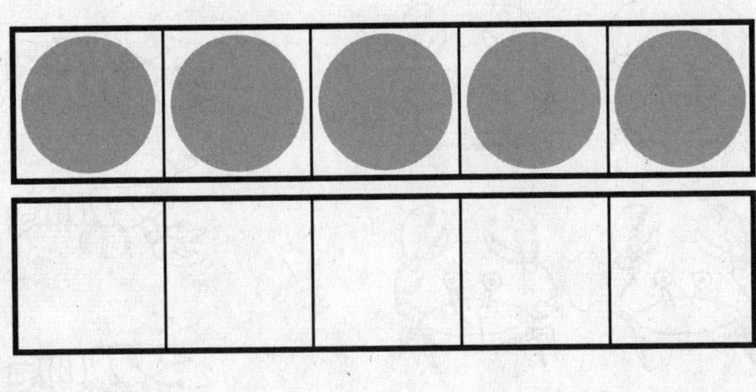

○ 5 ○ 7

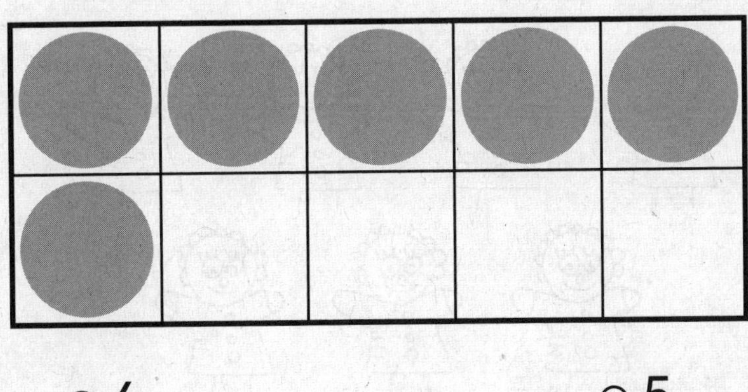

○ 6 ○ 5

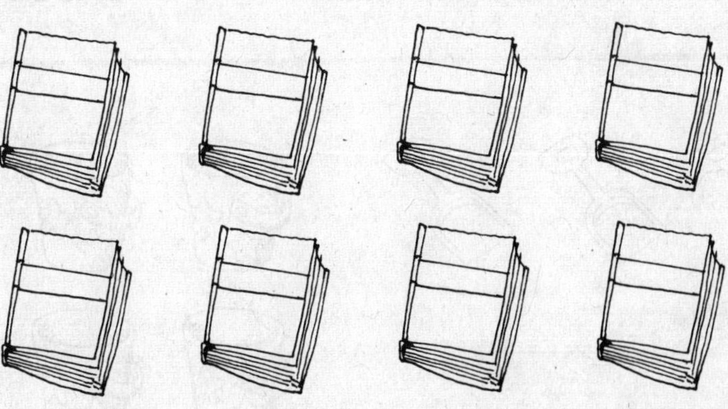

○ eight ○ seven

DIRECTIONS Fill in the bubble for the correct answer. **1.** Sofia is modeling a number. First she puts 5 counters in the ten frame. Then she puts 2 more counters. What number will she model? **2.** What number does the model show? **3.** How many books are in the set?

© Houghton Mifflin Harcourt Publishing Company

4

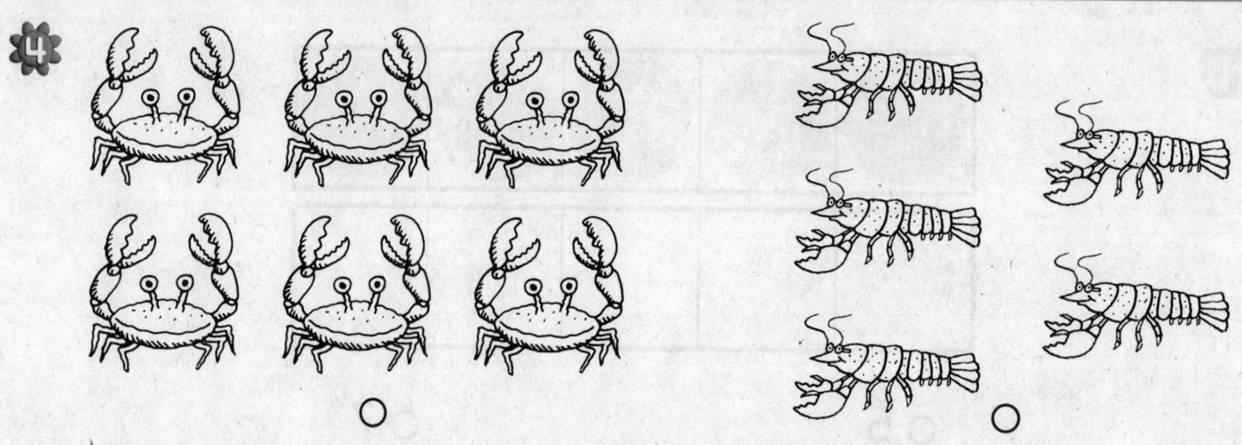

5

○ six ○ seven

6

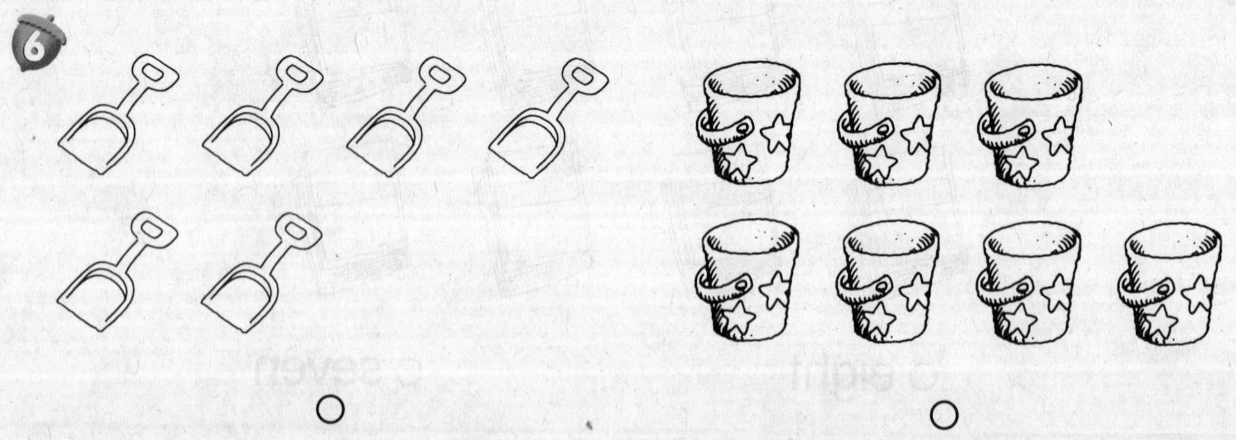

DIRECTIONS **4.** Which set shows 6 animals? **5.** How many hand puppets are in the set? **6.** Which set shows 1 more than 6?

GO ON

© Houghton Mifflin Harcourt Publishing Company

Name ______________________________

○ six ○ four

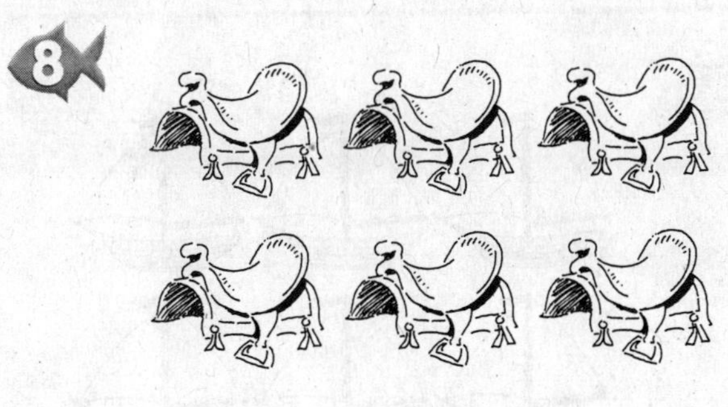

○ 

8
eight

○ 3 ○ 5 

DIRECTIONS 7. How many mice are there? 8. Which set shows seven objects? 9. Michael is modeling the number 8. He puts 5 counters in the ten frame. Which shows how many more counters he needs to model 8?

© Houghton Mifflin Harcourt Publishing Company

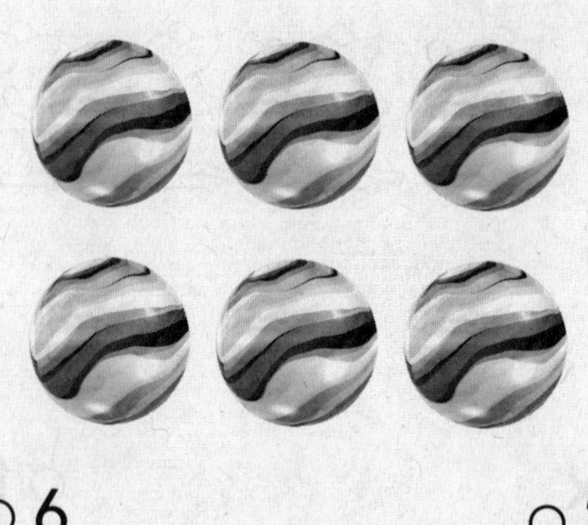

○ 6 ○ 3

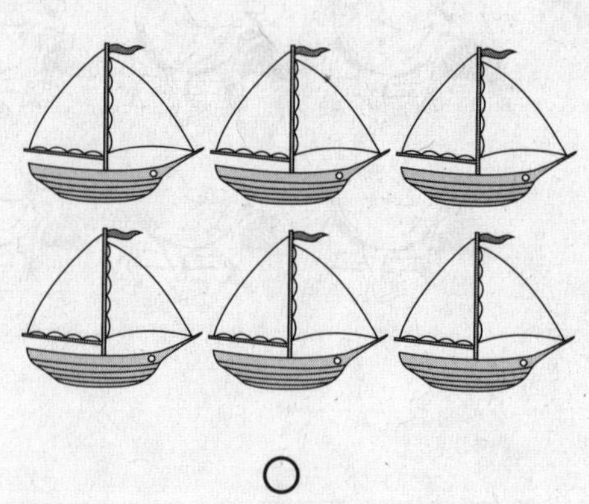

○ ○

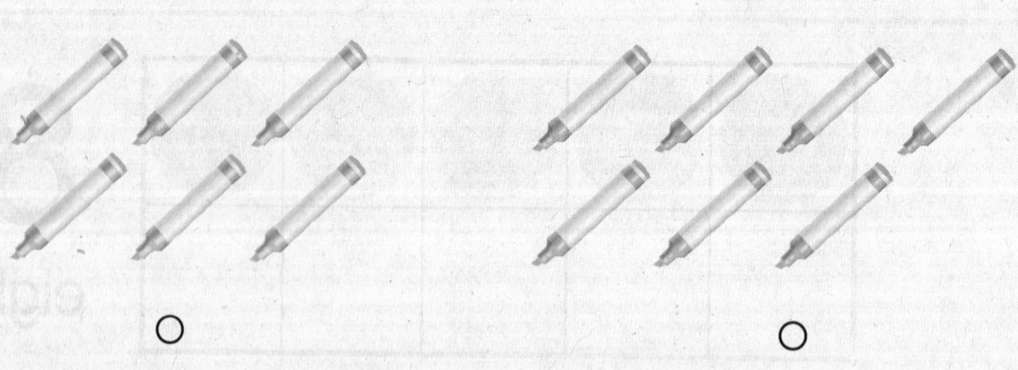

○ ○

DIRECTIONS **10.** Jose counted the marbles and wrote how many there were. What number did he write? **11.** Sam has 8 sailboats. Anna has a number of sailboats that is 2 less than 8. Which shows how many sailboats Anna has? **12.** Count the objects in each set. Which set has a number of objects that is 2 greater than 5?

© Houghton Mifflin Harcourt Publishing Company

Name ________________________________

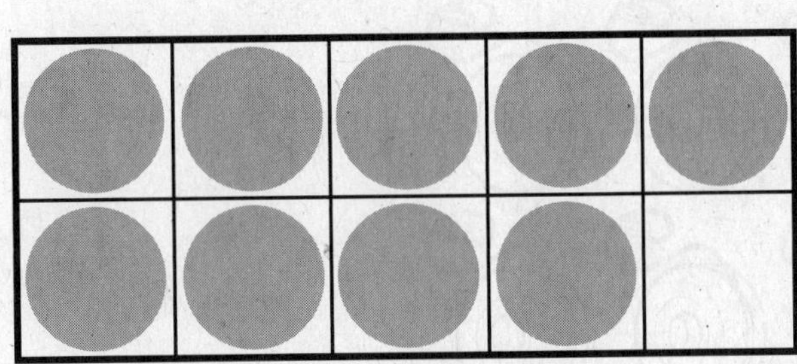

○ 9 ○ 5

○ 6 ○ 4

○ 7

○ 10

DIRECTIONS Fill in the bubble for the correct answer. **1.** Which number does this model show? **2.** How many more cubes need to be shaded to make 10? **3.** Rena counted the flowers and wrote how many. What number did she write?

GO ON

© Houghton Mifflin Harcourt Publishing Company

4

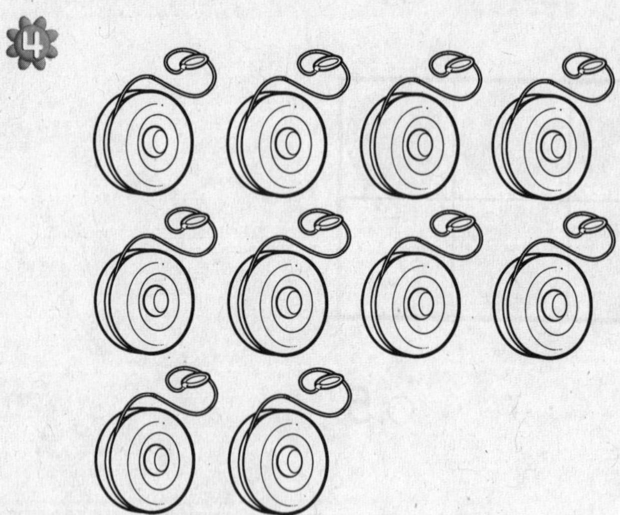

○ two

○ ten

5

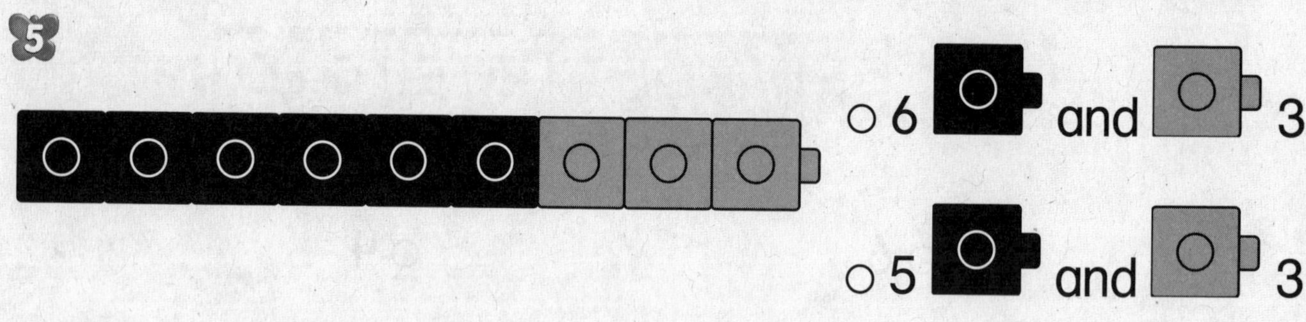

○ 6 and 3

○ 5 and 3

6

○ 9

○ 10

DIRECTIONS **4.** Count the yoyos. How many are there? **5.** Count each color of cubes on the cube train. Which pair of numbers makes nine? **6.** Julie counted the balls and wrote how many. What number did she write?

© Houghton Mifflin Harcourt Publishing Company

Name ______________________________

○ five

○ nine

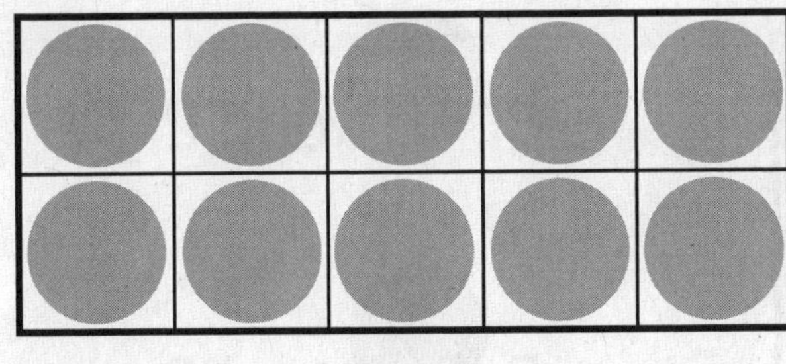

○

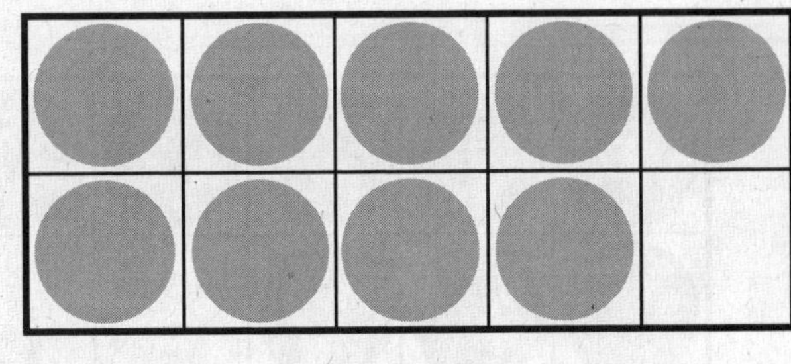

○

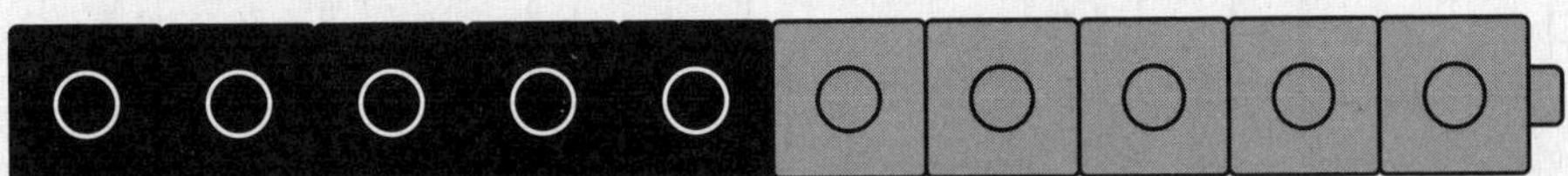

○ 5  and 5

○ 6  and 4

DIRECTIONS **7.** Count the hats. How many are there? **8.** David used counters to model 10. Which shows 10 counters? **9.** How is ten shown in the cube train?

© Houghton Mifflin Harcourt Publishing Company

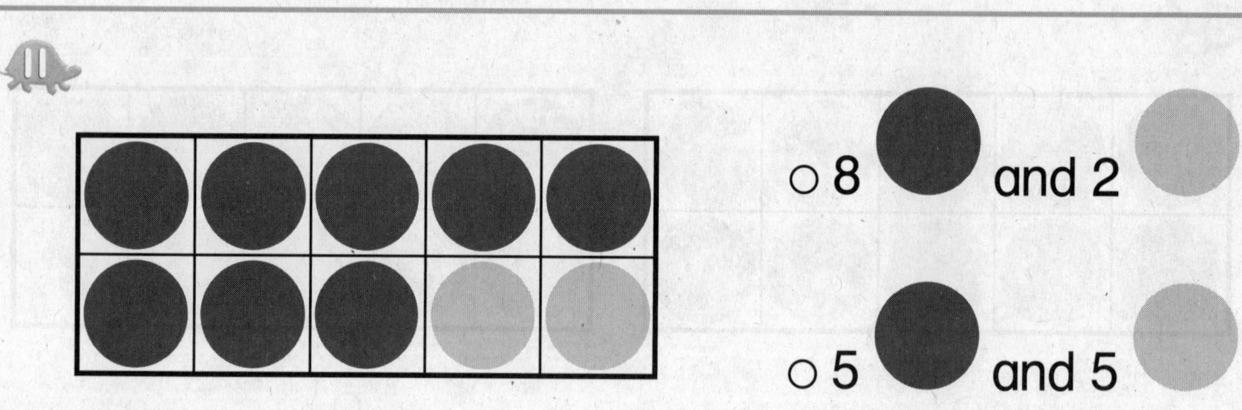

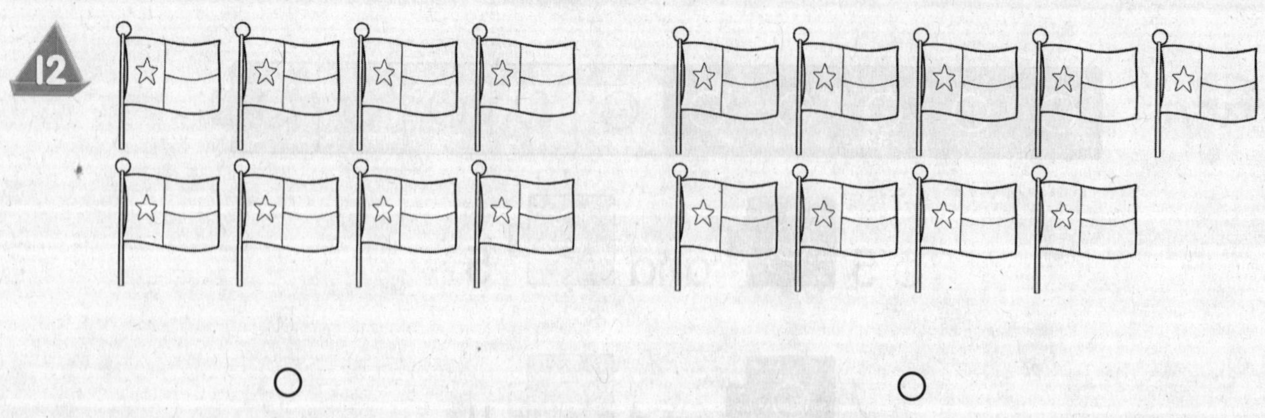

DIRECTIONS **10.** Which set shows 9 hearts? **11.** Count each color of dots on the ten frame. Which shows how many dark gray and light gray dots? **12.** Which set shows 9 flags?

© Houghton Mifflin Harcourt Publishing Company

○ 5 is less than 6 ○ 5 is greater than 6

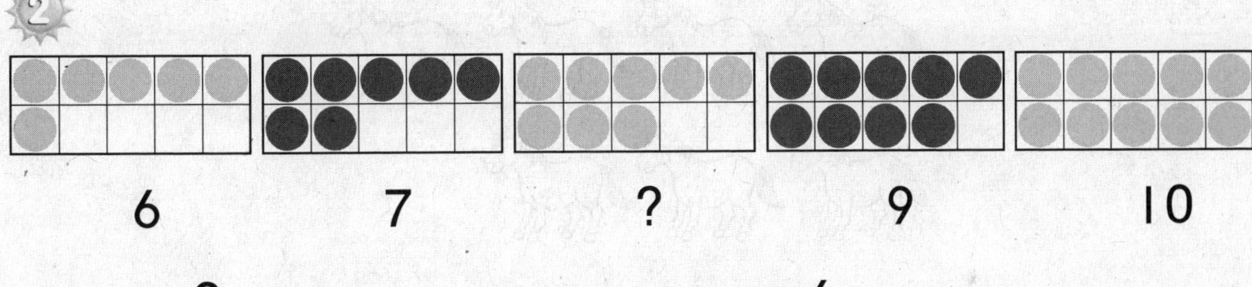

6 7 ? 9 10

○ 8 ○ 6

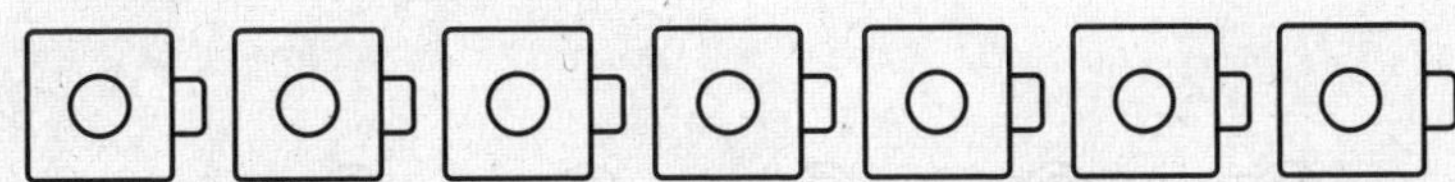

DIRECTIONS Fill in the bubble for the correct answer. **1.** There are 5 giraffes. Which is true about 5? **2.** Count the dots in each ten frame. What number is missing? **3.** Adam has 7 cubes. Which shows a set that has two less than 7?

© Houghton Mifflin Harcourt Publishing Company

○ ○

○ 8 7 9 ○ 6 7 8

○
○

DIRECTIONS **4.** Sofia has 6 muffins. Which set has a number of muffins that is one less than 6? **5.** There are 7 horses in the set. Which shows the numbers that are one less and one more than 7? **6.** Which set of stickers has less?

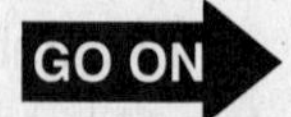

© Houghton Mifflin Harcourt Publishing Company

Name ______________________________

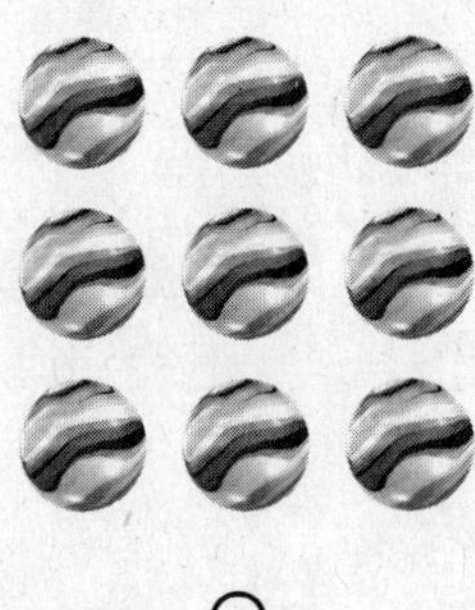

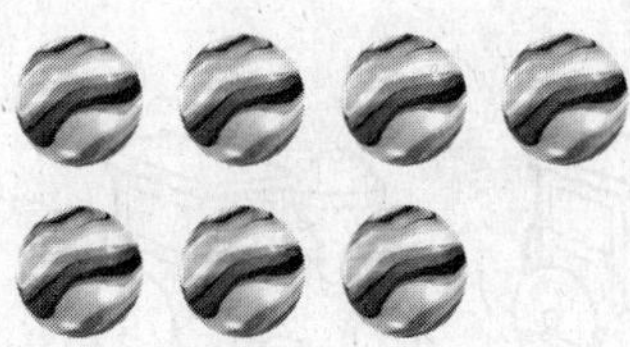

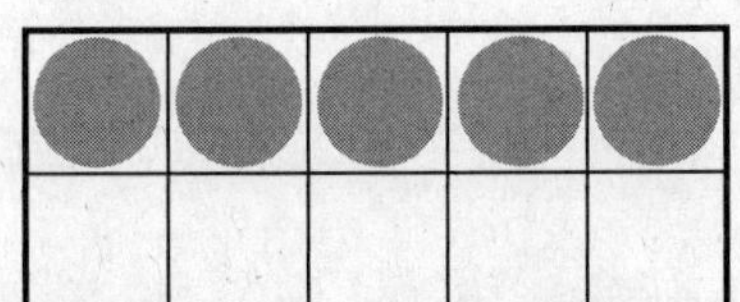

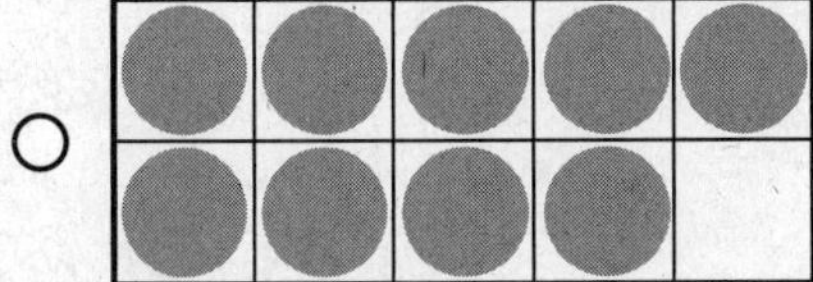

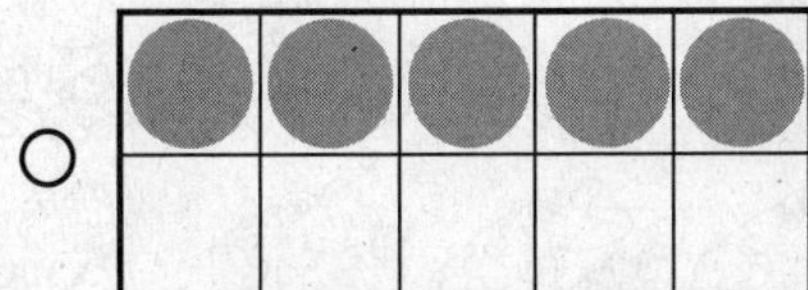

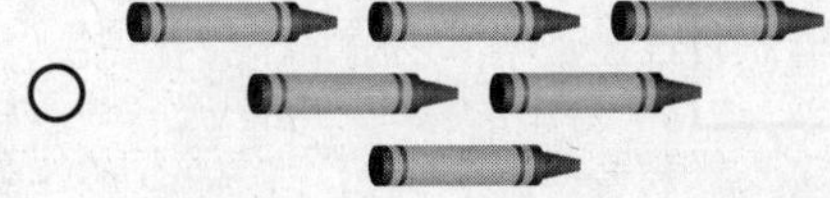

DIRECTIONS **7.** Richard has 8 marbles. Which set has one more than 8? **8.** Jose placed 5 counters on the ten frame. Which ten frame shows the same number of counters as Jose's frame? **9.** Jill has 6 crayons. Which set has two more crayons?

GO ON

© Houghton Mifflin Harcourt Publishing Company

○ 4

○ 5

○ 10

○ 6

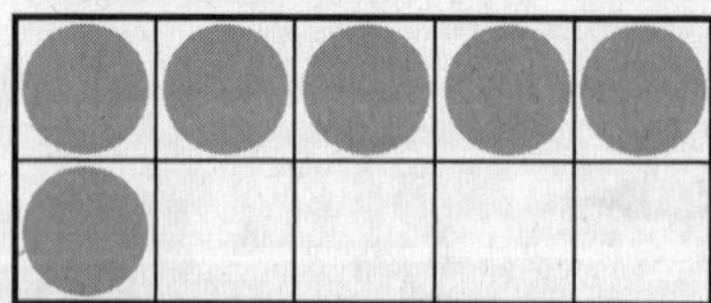

○ 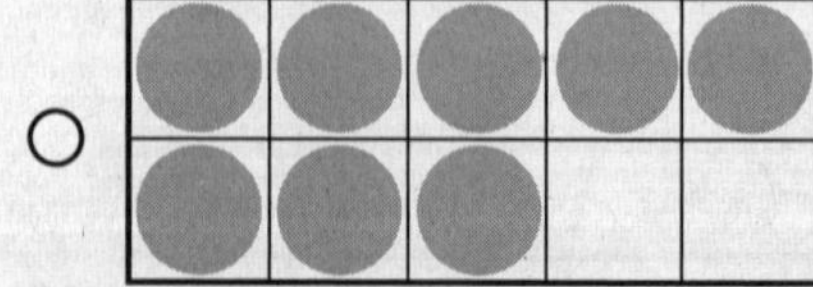

○ 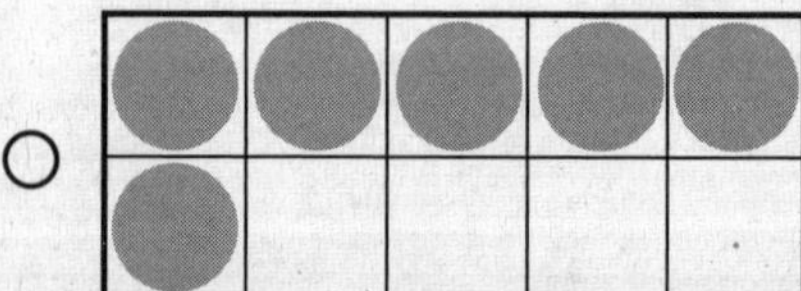

DIRECTIONS **10.** Brian has 4 toy train engines. Which number shows how many toy train engines he has? **11.** Ana has 8 frogs. Which set has a number of frogs that is less than 8? **12.** Rena placed 6 counters on the ten frame. Which ten frame shows a number of counters that is more than 6?

© Houghton Mifflin Harcourt Publishing Company

Name ____________________

1

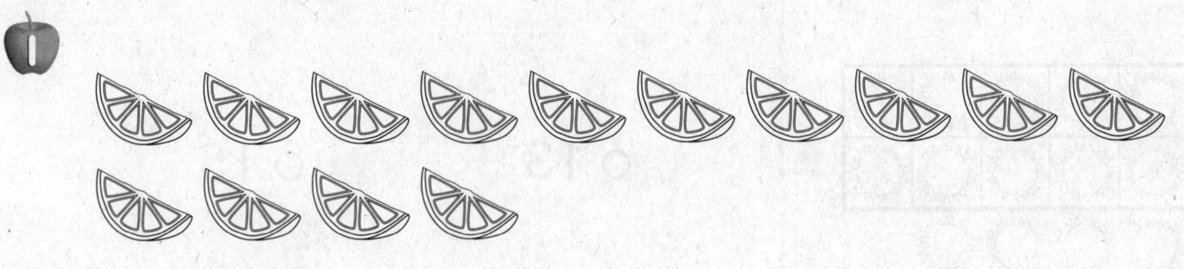

○ 15 ○ 14

2

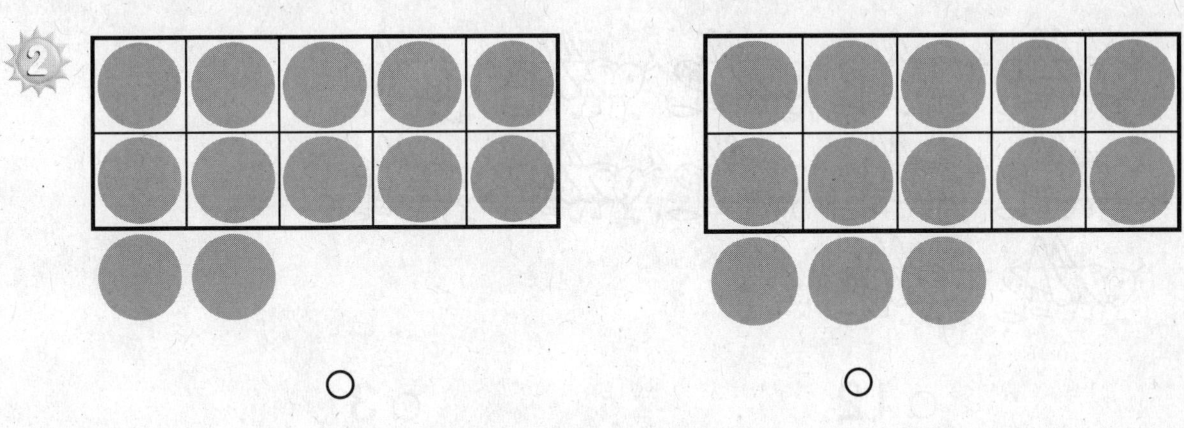

○ ○

3

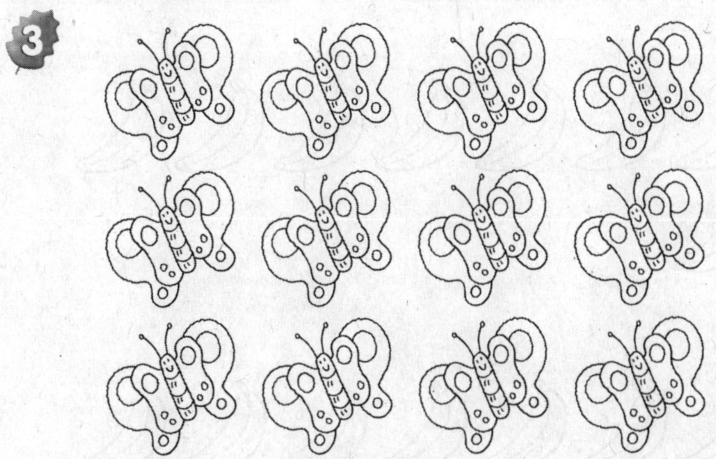

○ 12 ○ 13

DIRECTIONS Fill in the bubble for the correct answer. **1.** Ana correctly counts the orange slices and writes how many. What number does she write? **2.** Which model shows 13 counters? **3.** Count the butterflies. How many are there?

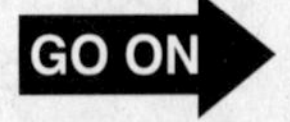

© Houghton Mifflin Harcourt Publishing Company

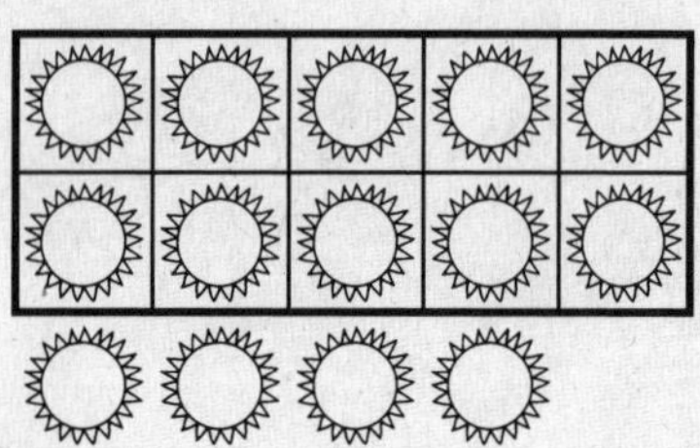

○ 13 ○ 15

○ 12 ○ 3

○

○

DIRECTIONS **4.** There are 14 suns. What number is one more? **5.** Count the grasshoppers. How many are there? **6.** Ryan sees 13 bananas. Which set has a number that is one less than 13?

GO ON

© Houghton Mifflin Harcourt Publishing Company

7

○ 11 ○ 12

8

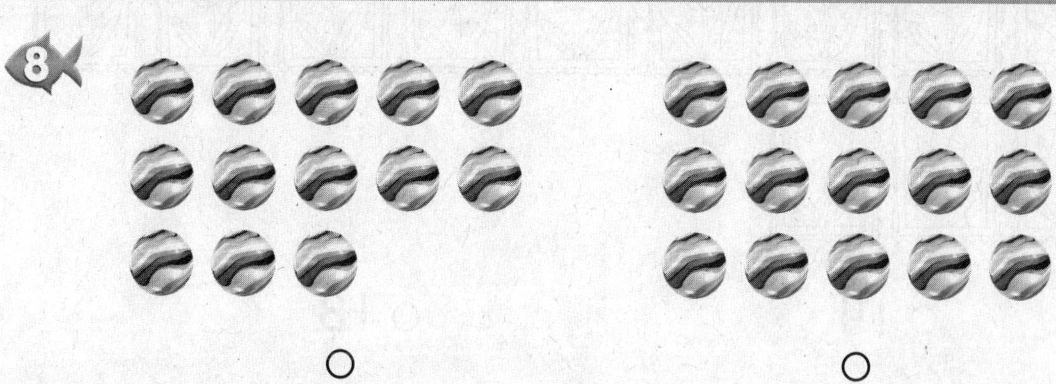

○ ○

9

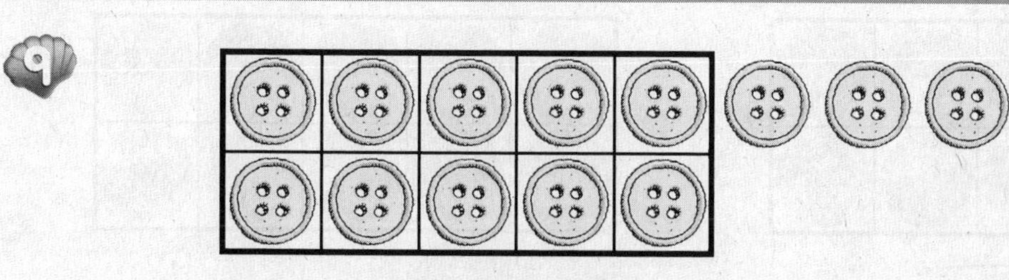

○ 13 ○ 14

DIRECTIONS **7.** Count the fish. How would you write the number of fish? **8.** Layla has 14 marbles. Which set has a number that is one more than 14? **9.** Count the buttons. How many are there?

© Houghton Mifflin Harcourt Publishing Company

Name ____________________

○ ○

○ 14 ○ 13

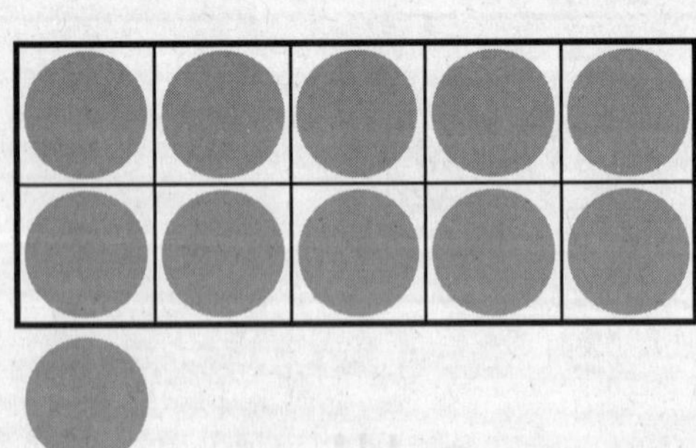

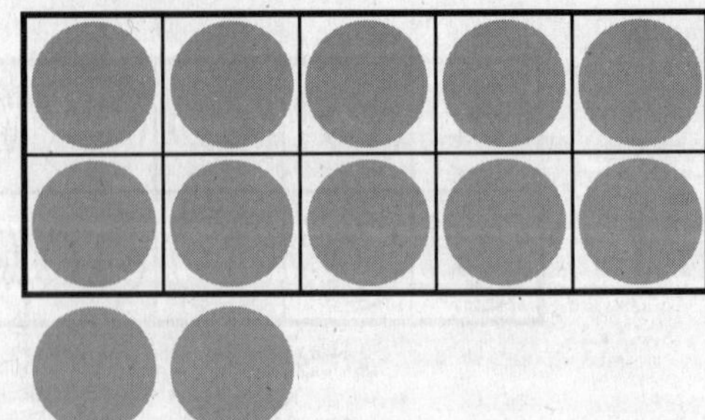

○ ○

DIRECTIONS **10.** Which set shows 15 ladybugs? **11.** Count the stamps. How many are there? **12.** Which model shows 11 counters?

© Houghton Mifflin Harcourt Publishing Company

19

○ 18 ○ 20

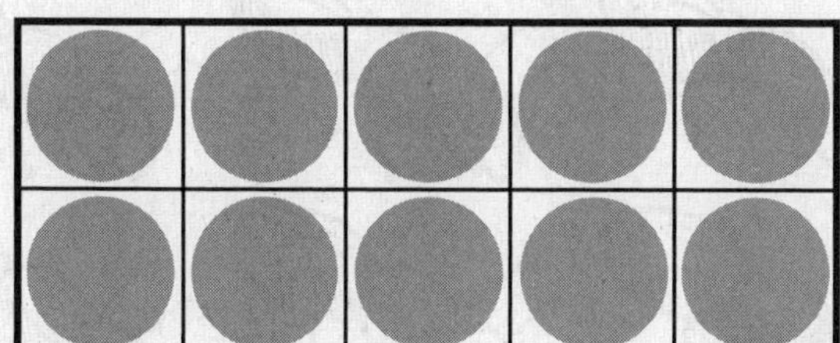

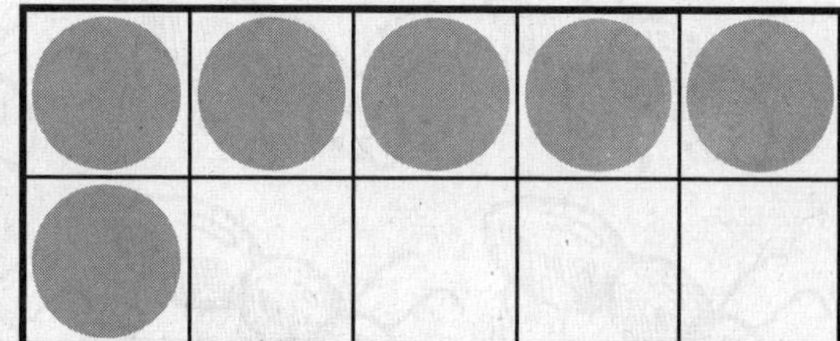

○ 17 ○ 16

○ 16 is less than 17 ○ 16 is greater than 17

DIRECTIONS Fill in the bubble for the correct answer. **1.** Look at the number. What number is one more? **2.** What number does the model show? **3.** There are 16 kittens. Which is true about 16?

© Houghton Mifflin Harcourt Publishing Company

Name ____________________

4

18

○ 17 ○ 19

5

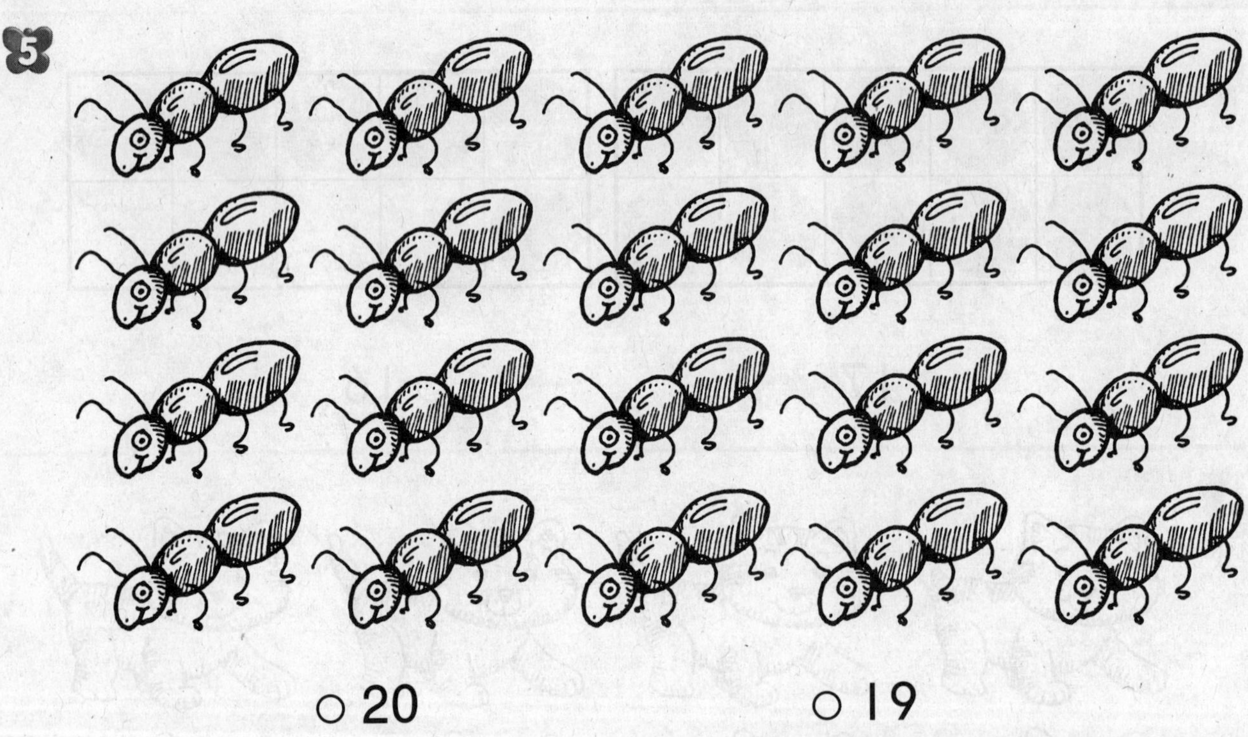

○ 20 ○ 19

6

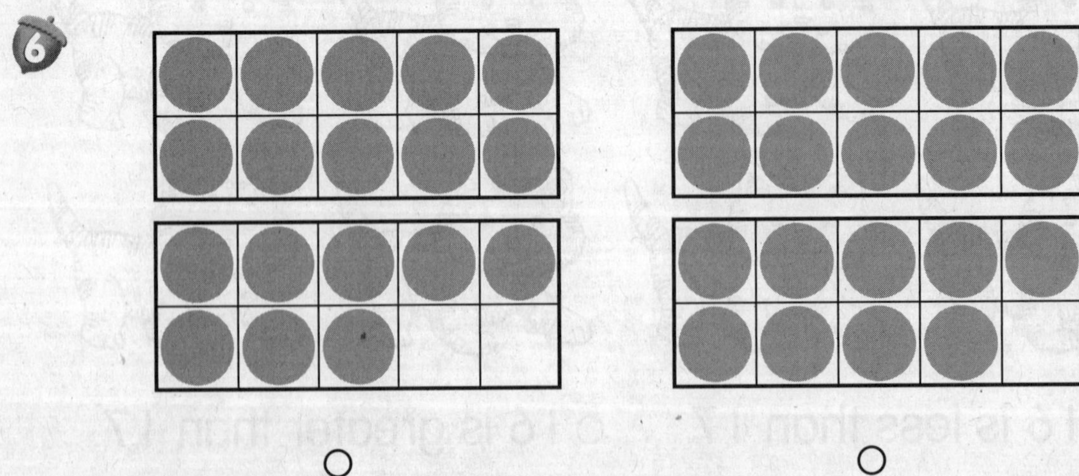

○ ○

DIRECTIONS 4. Look at the number. What number is one more? 5. Count the ants. How many are there? 6. Which model shows 18?

© Houghton Mifflin Harcourt Publishing Company

Name ______________________________

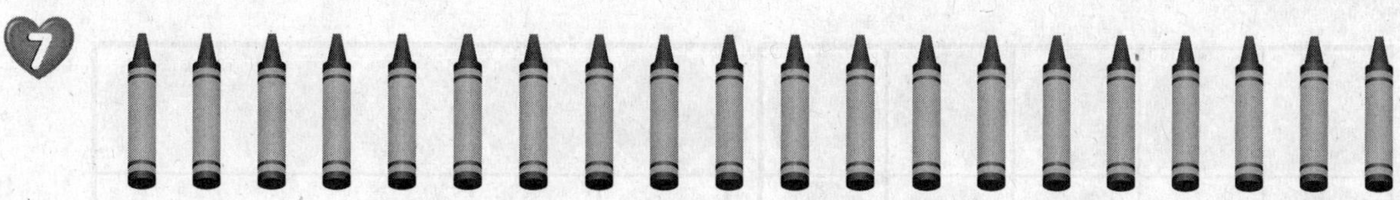

○ 19 ○ 20

○ eighteen ○ eleven

9

○ 17 ○ 18

DIRECTIONS **7.** Count the crayons. How many are there? **8.** Count the turtles. What number word tells how many? **9.** Count the stars. What number tells how many?

© Houghton Mifflin Harcourt Publishing Company

Name ________________________________

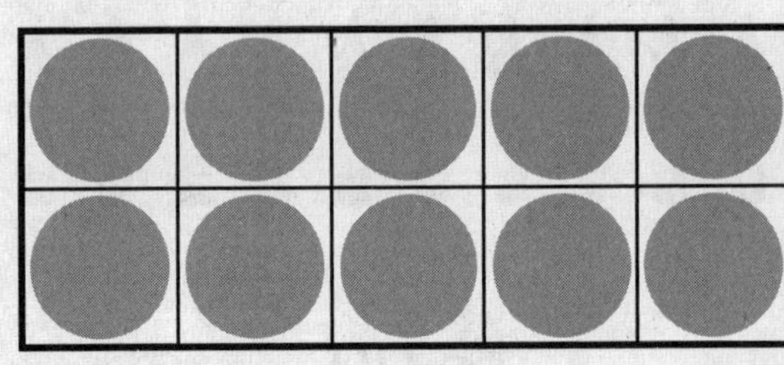

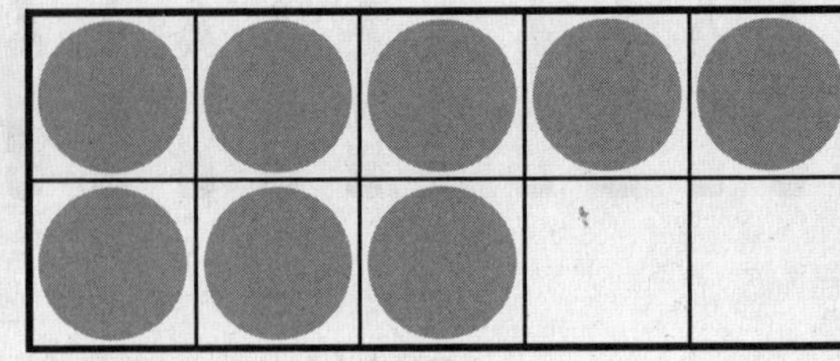

○ 18   ○ 19

10 and ______ 16

○ 6   ○ 16

○ ○

DIRECTIONS **10.** Count. What number tells how many? **11.** What number goes in the blank? **12.** Which shows 16 beads on the string?

© Houghton Mifflin Harcourt Publishing Company

Name ______________________

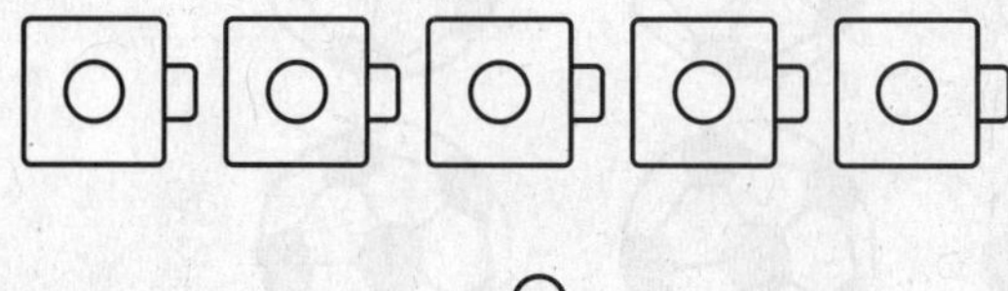

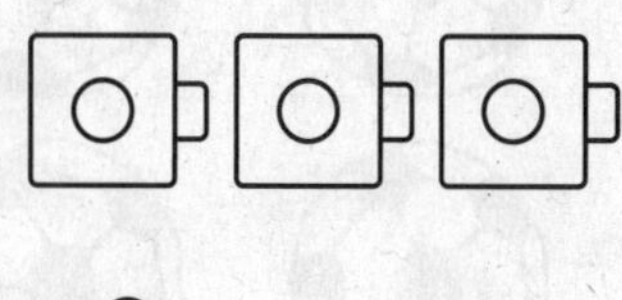

○ ○

○ 10 ○ 9

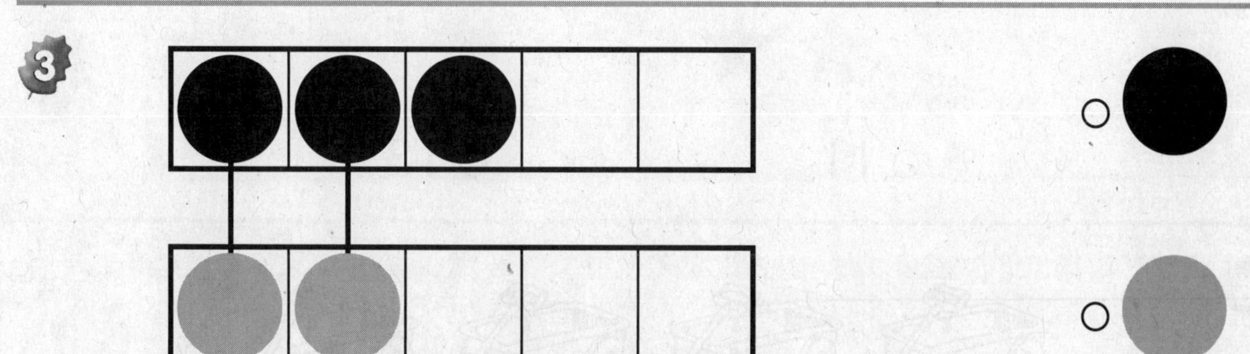

DIRECTIONS Fill in the bubble for the correct answer. **1.** Juan has 4 paintbrushes. Which shows a set that has less than 4? **2.** Count the ducks. How many are there? **3.** Count how many in each set. Which set has one less?

© Houghton Mifflin Harcourt Publishing Company

Name ____________________

○ 19 is less than 20 ○ 19 is greater than 20

○ 11 ○ 13

○ four ○ five

DIRECTIONS **4.** There are 19 soccer balls. Which is true about 19? **5.** There are 12 stars. Which number is one more? **6.** Count the wagons. How many are there?

© Houghton Mifflin Harcourt Publishing Company

○ ○

○ 20 ○ 19

2
two

○ 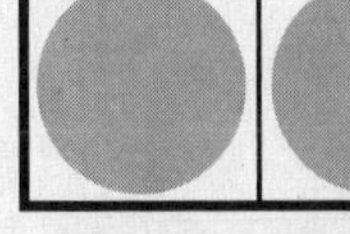

 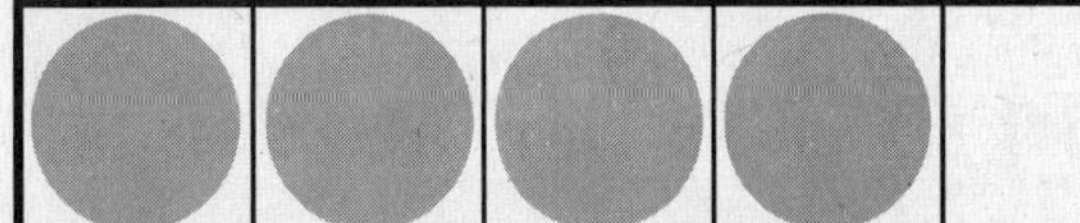

DIRECTIONS 7. Which set shows 2? 8. Count the dolls. How many are there? 9. Look at the number. Which five frame shows a set that has 2 more than that number?

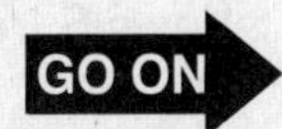

© Houghton Mifflin Harcourt Publishing Company

Name ___________________

10

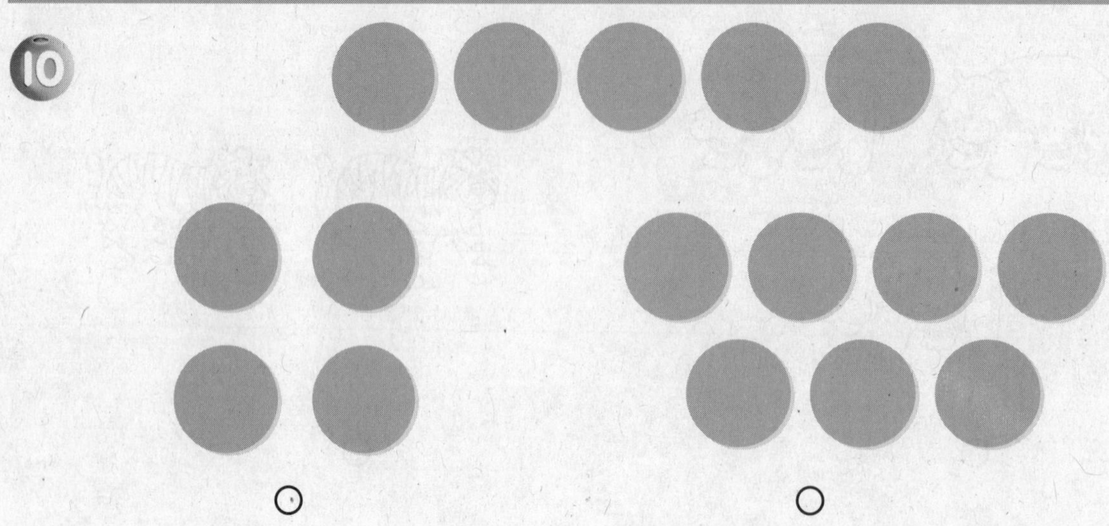

○ ○

11

1, 2, 3, 4, 5, ____, 7, 8, 9, 10

○ 4 ○ 6

12

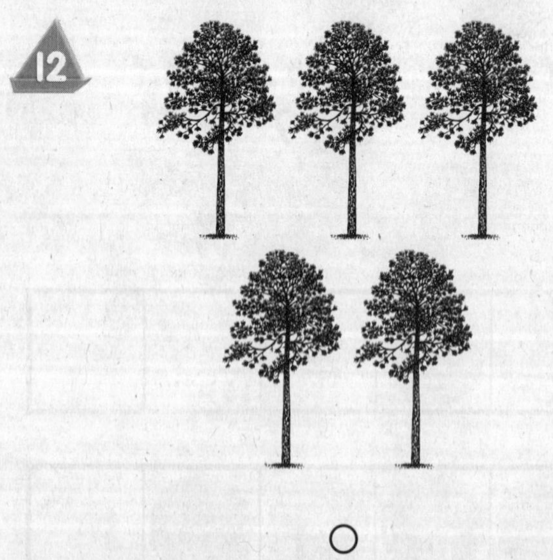

○ ○

DIRECTIONS **10.** Adam has 5 counters. Which shows a set that has more? **11.** Count forward. What is the missing number? **12.** Which set shows 5 trees?

GO ON

© Houghton Mifflin Harcourt Publishing Company

Name ______________________________

○ ○

5, 4, 3, ____, 1

○ 2 ○ 4

○ 10 ○ 9

DIRECTIONS **13.** Julie has 5 blocks. Brian has the same number of blocks. Which shows Brian's blocks? **14.** What is the missing number when you count backward? **15.** How many crayons are there?

© Houghton Mifflin Harcourt Publishing Company

16

○ ○

○ ○

18

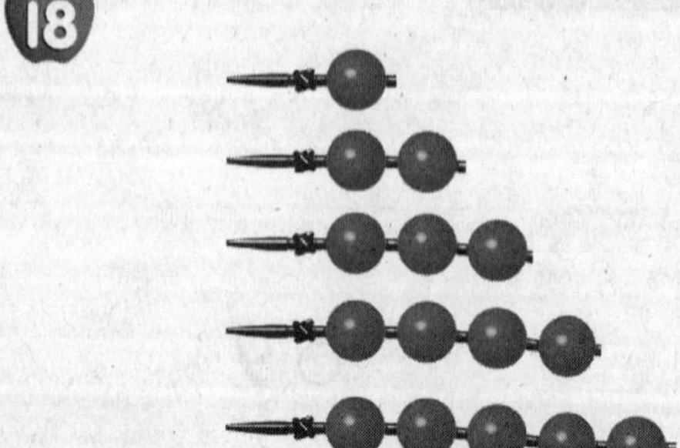

○ 5 4 3 2 1

○ 1 2 3 4 5

DIRECTIONS **16.** Bill has 6 teddy bears. Which shows a set that has one less than 6? **17.** Trish saw 6 bees. Which shows a set that has less than 6? **18.** Look at the beads on each string. What order do they show?

© Houghton Mifflin Harcourt Publishing Company

Name ____________________

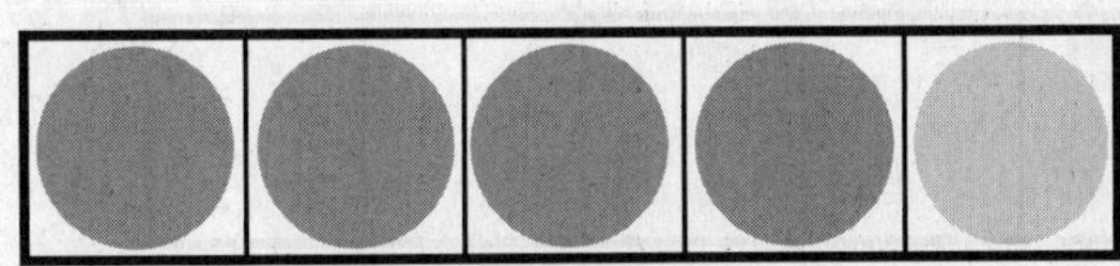

○ 5 and 1 ○ 4 and 1

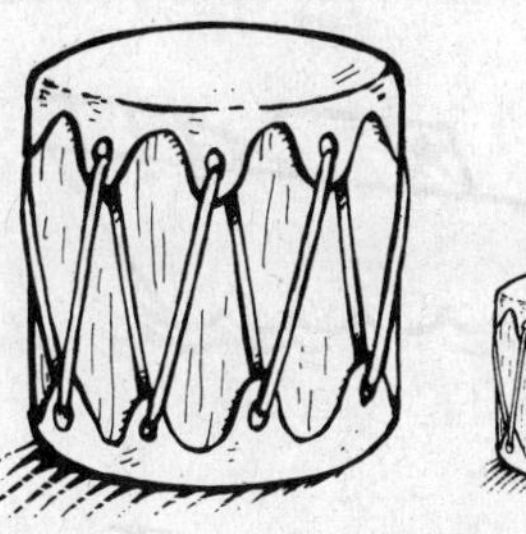

○ 2 ○ 1

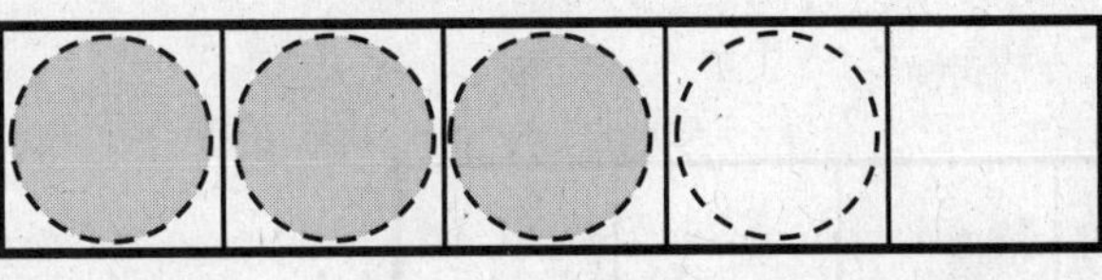

4 – 3

○ 3 ○ 1

DIRECTIONS Fill in the bubble for the correct answer. **1.** Which shows the number of counters? **2.** How many drums in all? **3.** There are 4 counters in the five frame. Three are light gray. The rest are dark gray. How many are dark gray?

© Houghton Mifflin Harcourt Publishing Company

Name ______________________________

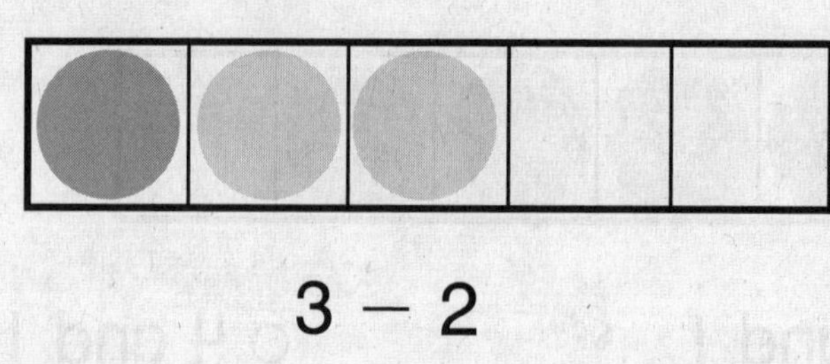

3 − 2

○ 2 ○ 1

○ 2 and 1 ○ 3 and 2

○ ○

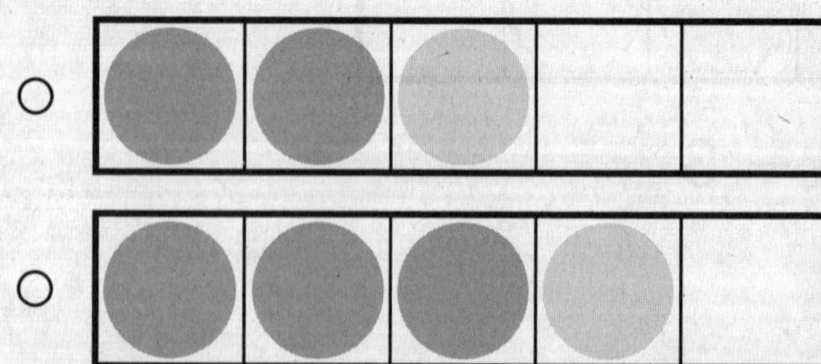

DIRECTIONS **4.** There are 3 counters in the five frame. Two are light gray. How many are dark gray? **5.** How many boats in all? **6.** Which model shows 3 as 2 and 1?

© Houghton Mifflin Harcourt Publishing Company

Name ____________________

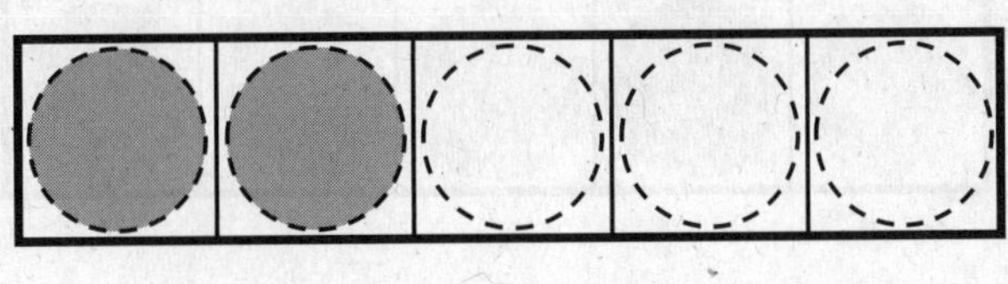

5 − 3

○ 2 ○ 3

○ 4 ○ 3

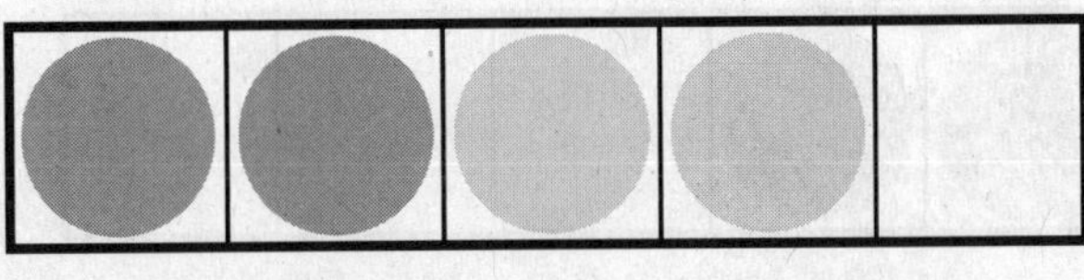

2 + 2

○ 4 ○ 5

DIRECTIONS **7.** There are 5 counters in the five frame. Three are light gray. The rest are dark gray. How many are dark gray? **8.** How many crayons? **9.** What number shows how many counters in all?

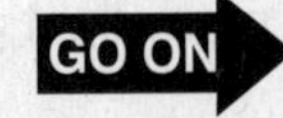

© Houghton Mifflin Harcourt Publishing Company

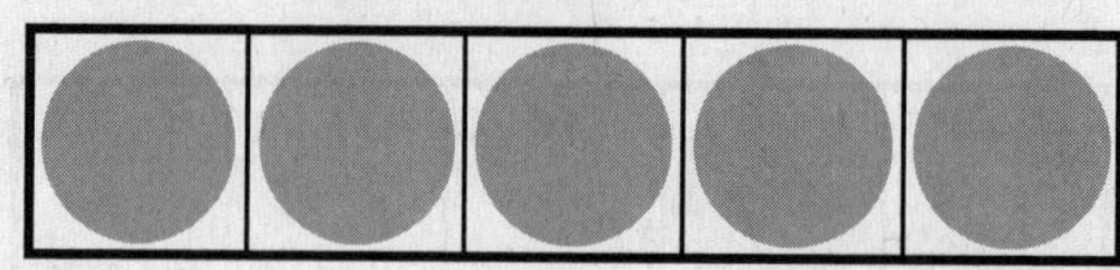

5 and 0

○ 0 ○ 5

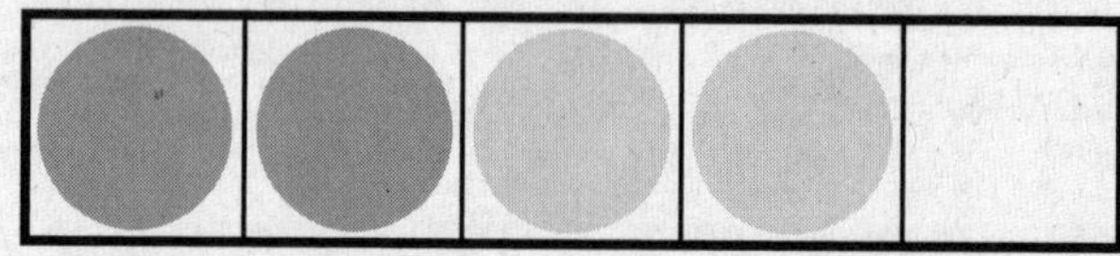

○ 2 and 2 ○ 2 and 3

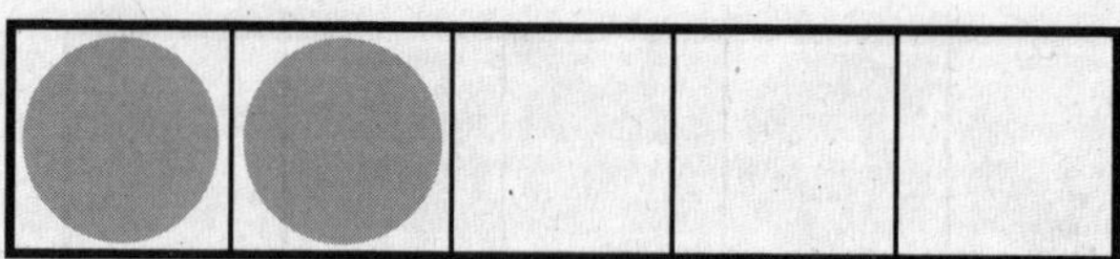

___ and ___

○ 2 and 1 ○ 2 and 0

DIRECTIONS **10.** There are 5 dark gray counters and 0 light gray counters. What number tells how many counters there are in all? **11.** Which shows the number of counters? **12.** There are 2 dark gray counters. How many light gray counters will make 2 in all?

© Houghton Mifflin Harcourt Publishing Company

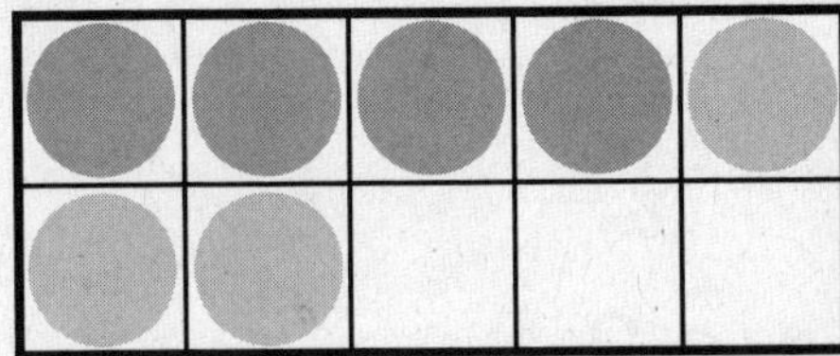

○ 5 and 1
○ 4 and 3

2

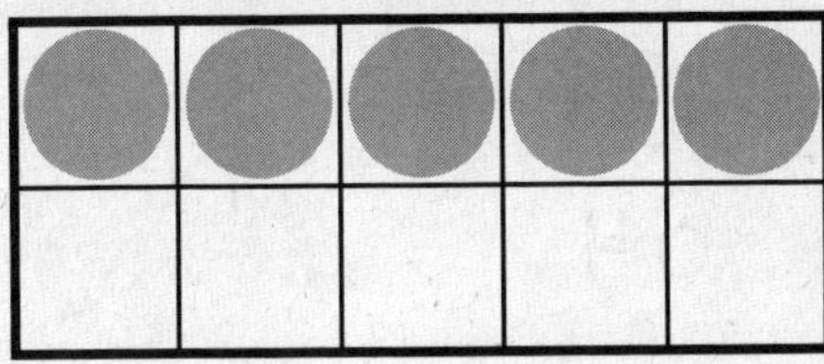

○ 3 ○ 2

3

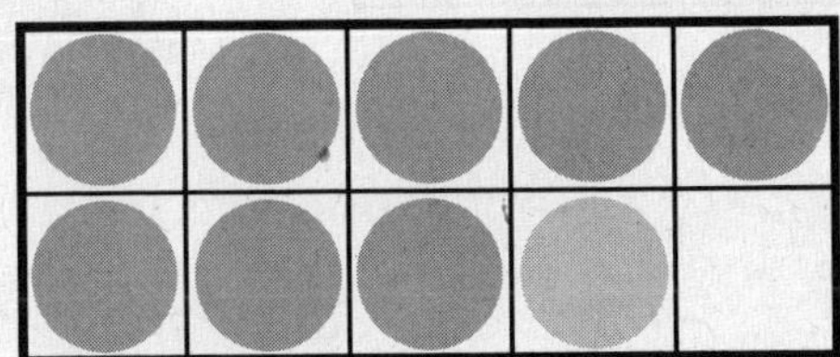

○ 7 and 3
○ 8 and 1

DIRECTIONS Fill in the bubble for the correct answer. **1.** Count the counters. How many counters are in the sets being put together? **2.** Antonio has 8 counters. Five of his counters are dark gray. The rest are light gray. How many are light gray? **3.** Which 2 numbers make 9?

GO ON

© Houghton Mifflin Harcourt Publishing Company

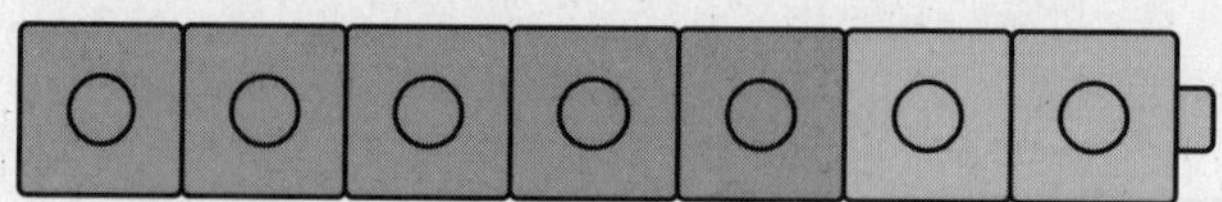

7 − 5

○ 7 ○ 2

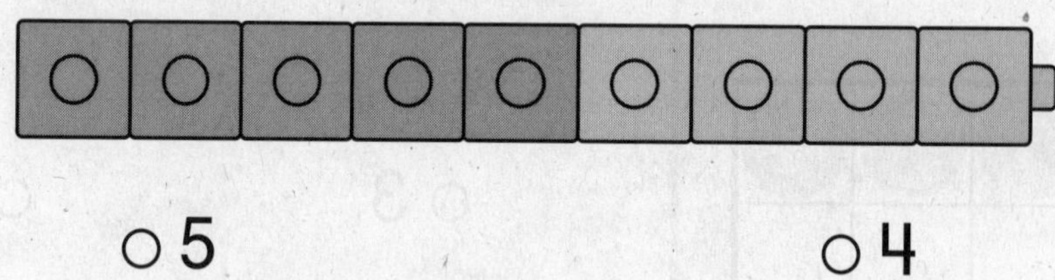

○ 5 ○ 4

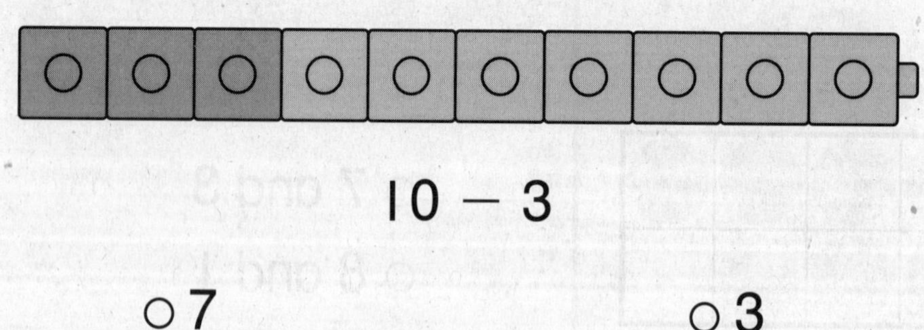

10 − 3

○ 7 ○ 3

DIRECTIONS **4.** Look at the seven-cube train. Five cubes are dark gray. The rest are light gray. How many are light gray? **5.** Take apart the nine-cube train. How many are light gray? **6.** Take apart the ten-cube train. How many are light gray?

© Houghton Mifflin Harcourt Publishing Company

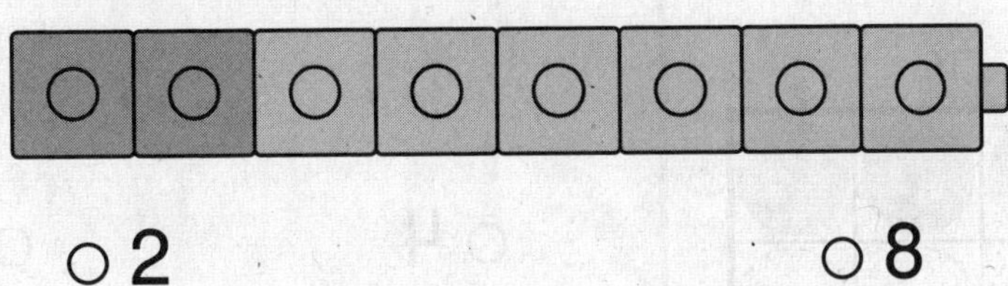

○ 2 ○ 8

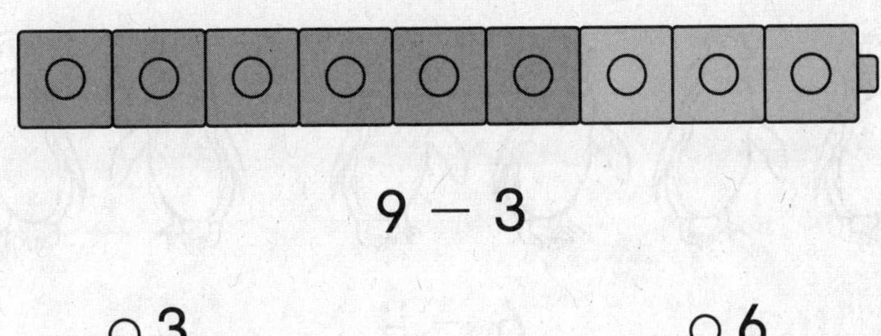

9 − 3

○ 3 ○ 6

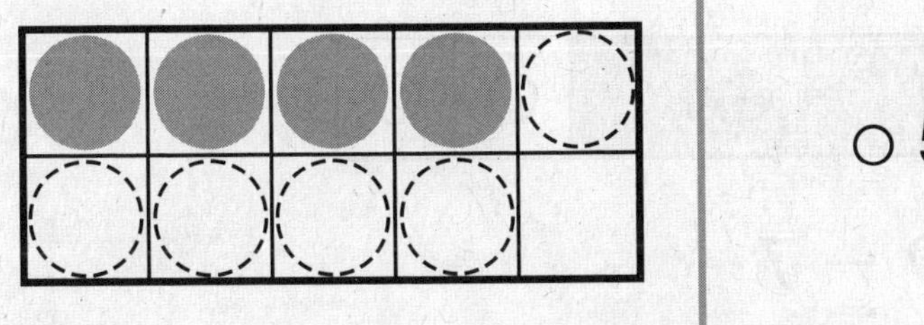

○ 5 ○ 4

DIRECTIONS **7.** There are 8 cubes. How many cubes will be left is you take away 6? **8.** There are 9 cubes on the cube train. How many cubes will be left if you take away 3? **9.** Michael needs to place 9 counters on the ten fame. He puts 4 dark gray counters on the ten fame. How many more counters does he need to make 9?

© Houghton Mifflin Harcourt Publishing Company

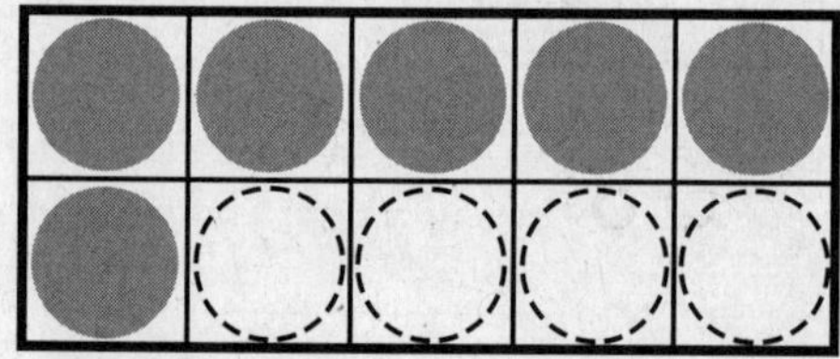

○ 4 ○ 5

6 − 4

○ 3 ○ 2

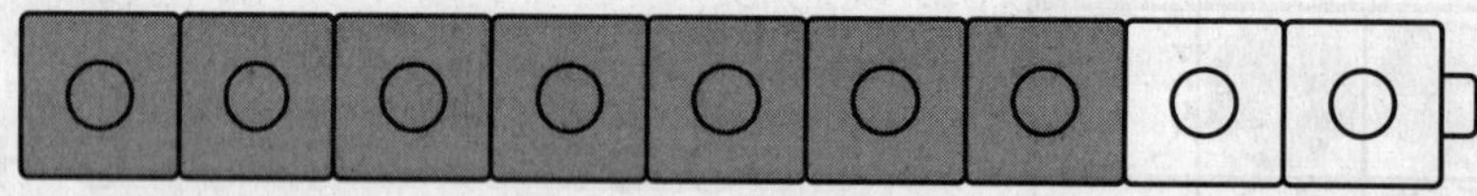

9 − 7

○ 2 ○ 3

DIRECTIONS **10.** Claudia needs to place 10 counters on a ten frame. She puts 6 dark gray counters on the ten fame. How many more counters does she need to make 10? **11.** There are 6 penguins. Four pengins dive into the water. How many are left? **12.** Sam has a nine-cube train. He takes it apart to make 2 trains. One train has 7 cubes. How many cubes are in the other train?

© Houghton Mifflin Harcourt Publishing Company

Name ____________________

○ 2 + 1

○ 2 + 2

○ 2   ○ 4

○ 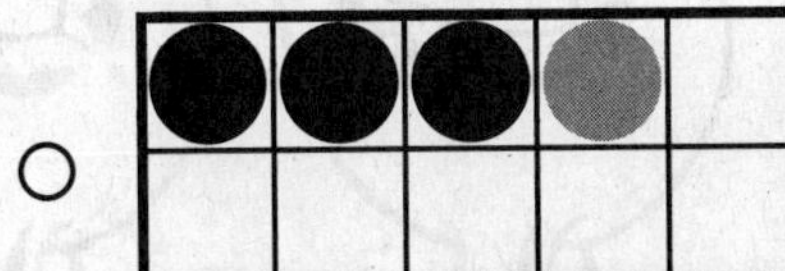

○ 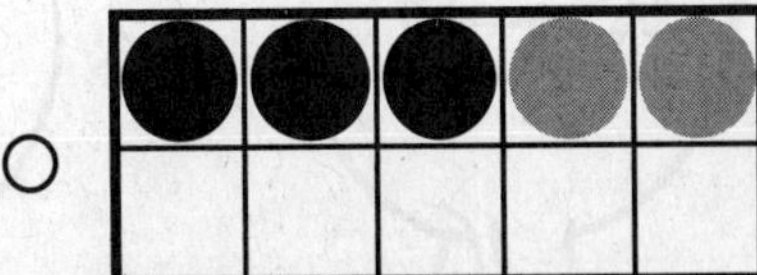

DIRECTIONS Fill in the bubble for the correct answer. **1.** There are 2 girls standing. One girl runs to them. Which numbers show the girl being added? **2.** There are 2 children hiking. Two children join them. How many children are hiking now? **3.** There are 3 striped fish in a fish tank. Jill adds 2 blue fish to the fish tank. Which shows how Jill should act out this story with counters?

GO ON

© Houghton Mifflin Harcourt Publishing Company

4 + 1

○ 5 ○ 4

○ 5 ○ 4

6

1 + 3

○ 3 ○ 4

DIRECTIONS **4.** There are 4 puppies playing. A kitten comes to play with the puppies. How many animals are playing now? **5.** There are 2 turtles. Three more turtles come. How many turtles are there now? **6.** There is 1 seal. Three more seals come to play. How many seals are there now?

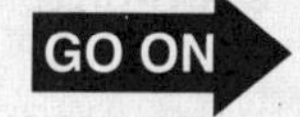

© Houghton Mifflin Harcourt Publishing Company

7

○ 3 + 1 = 4 ○ 1 + 2 = 3

8

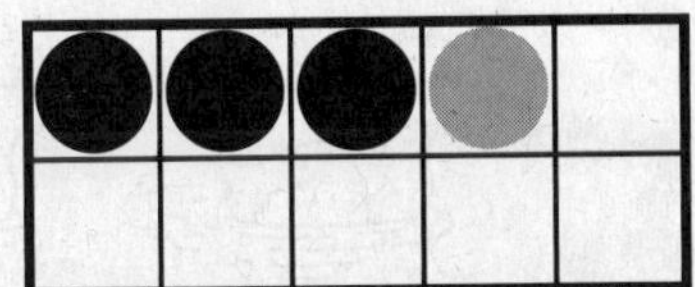
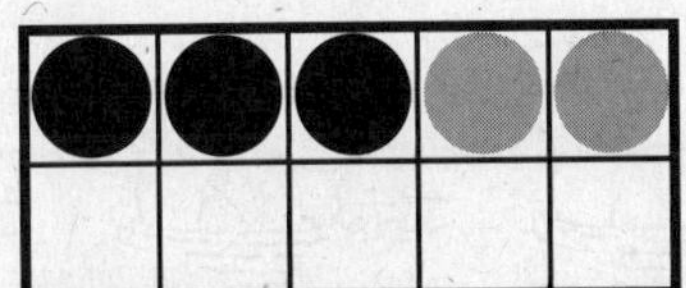

○ 3 + 1 = 4 ○ 3 + 2 = 5

9

○ 2 + 3 = 5 ○ 2 + 2 = 4

DIRECTIONS **7.** There is 1 squirrel gathering nuts. Two more squirrels come to gather nuts. How many squirrels are gathering nuts now? Which number sentence matches the story? **8.** Oliver has 3 dimes. His dad gives him 1 more dime. Which model and number sentence match this story? **9.** Two horses are in the field. Three more horses come. What does this picture show?

GO ON

© Houghton Mifflin Harcourt Publishing Company

Name ______________________________

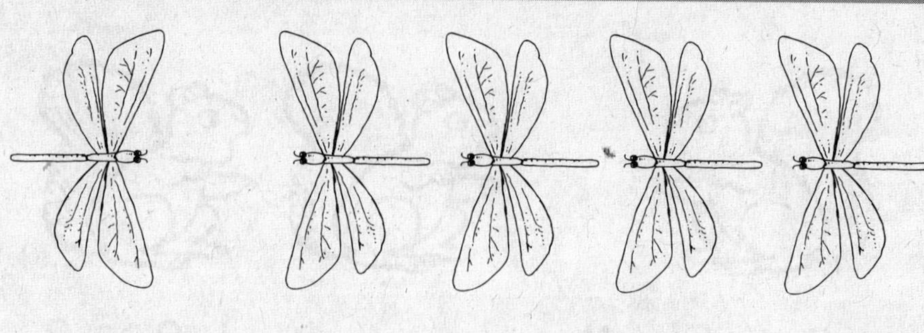

○ 1 + 4 ○ 1 + 3

○ 4 ○ 5

2 + 2

○ 3 ○ 4

DIRECTIONS **10.** There is 1 dragonfly flying. Four dragonflies come. Which shows how to find how many there are now? **11.** There are 3 ducks in the water. 2 ducks join them. How many ducks are there now? **12.** There are 2 rabbits in the garden. Two more rabbits come into the garden. How many rabbits are there now?

© Houghton Mifflin Harcourt Publishing Company

3 − 1

○ 2 ○ 1

○ 3 − 2 = 1 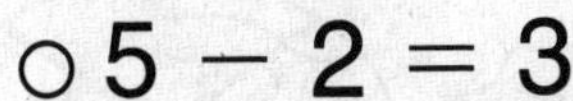
○ 5 − 2 = 3

4 − 2

○ 2 ○ 3

DIRECTIONS Fill in the bubble for the correct answer. **1.** There are 3 dogs playing. 1 dog leaves. How many dogs are left? **2.** There were 5 hamsters. 2 run away. Which number sentence matches the story? **3.** There are 4 kangaroos playing. Two of them hop away. How many kangaroos are left?

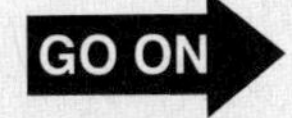

© Houghton Mifflin Harcourt Publishing Company

○ 1 − 1 = 0 ○ 2 − 1 = 1

5

○ ○

6

○ 3 ○ 2

DIRECTIONS **4.** Two butterflies are on a flower. One flies away. Which number sentence matches the story? **5.** There are 4 cars. One drives away. Which picture shows this story? **6.** There are 5 owls. Three owls leave. How many owls are left?

© Houghton Mifflin Harcourt Publishing Company

7

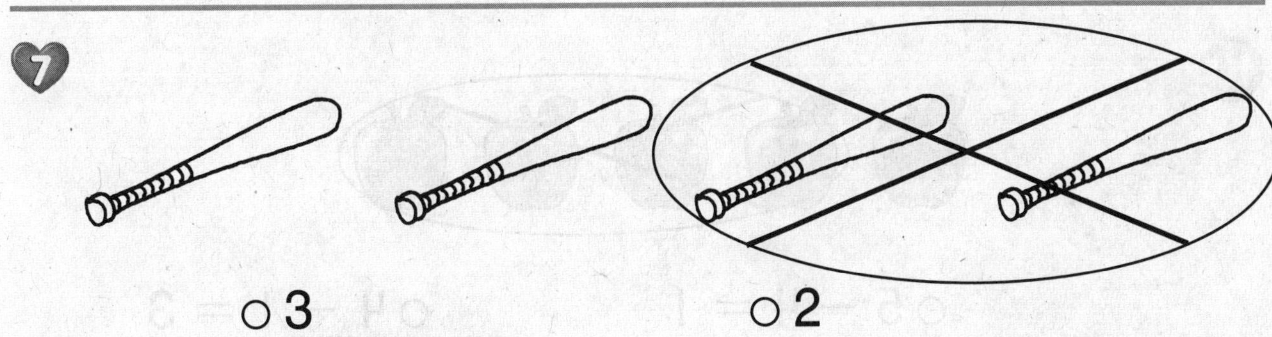

○ 3 ○ 2

8

○ 1 ○ 4

9

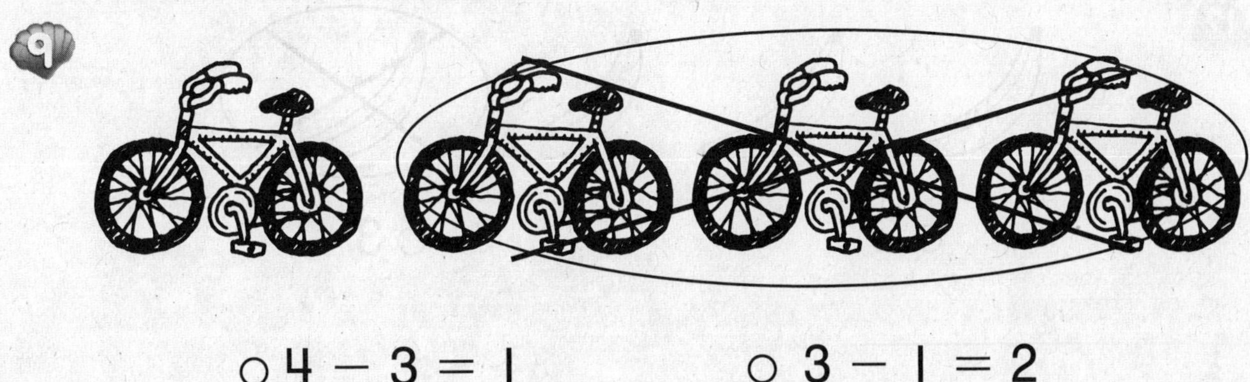

○ $4 - 3 = 1$ ○ $3 - 1 = 2$

DIRECTIONS **7.** Chris has 4 bats. He gives 2 bats to his sister. How many bats does he have now? **8.** Selene has 5 dolls. She gives one to her brother. How many dolls does she have now? **9.** There are 4 bikes at school. Children ride 3 of them away. What number sentence can you use to find how many bikes are left?

© Houghton Mifflin Harcourt Publishing Company

○ 5 − 4 = 1 ○ 4 − 1 = 3

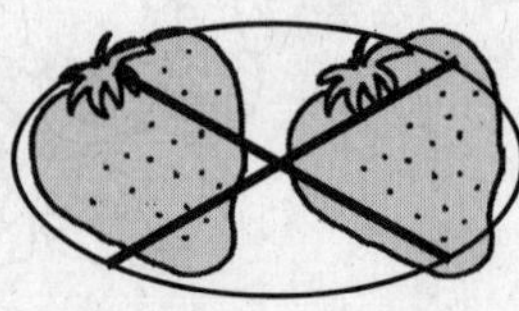

○ ○

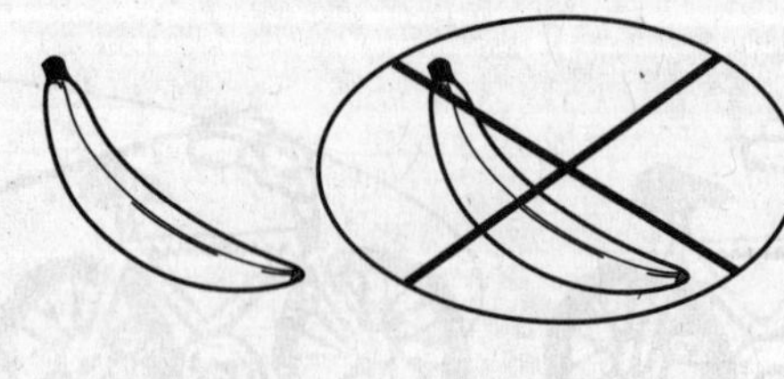

○ 2 ○ 3

DIRECTIONS **10.** Mom buys 5 apples. She uses 4 to make a pie. Which shows how to find how many apples are left? **11.** There are 3 strawberries. Amy eats 2. Which picture shows this story? **12.** Dad buys 4 bananas. He eats 1. How many are left?

STOP

© Houghton Mifflin Harcourt Publishing Company

Name ______________________________

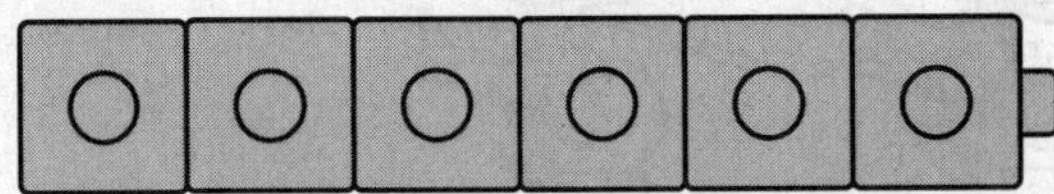

○ I more

○ I less

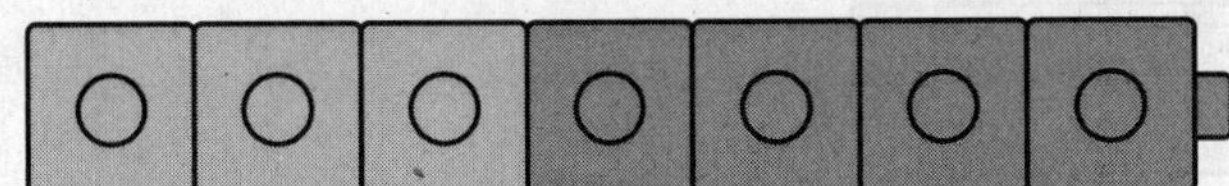

○ 7

○ 6

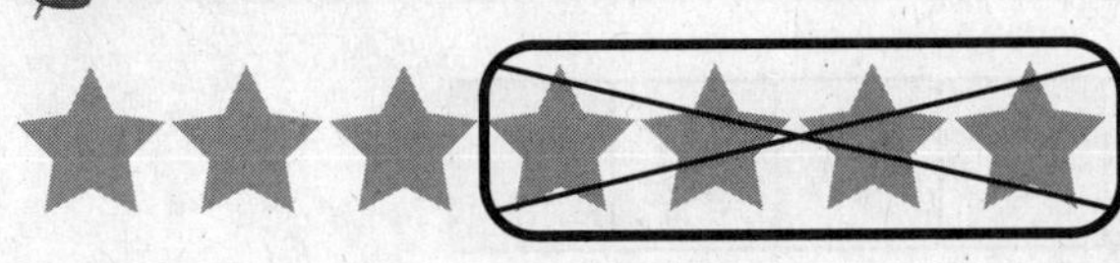

○ ○

DIRECTIONS Fill in the bubble for the correct answer. **1.** Bill has 6 cubes. Ally has 1 more cube than Bill. What should the picture show to model the story? **2.** There are 3 elephants in the circus ring. Four more join them. How many elephants are in the ring now? **3.** Harry draws 3 stars. Then he draws 5 more. Which picture shows how many he draws in all?

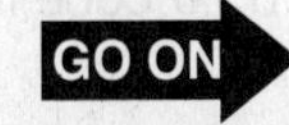

© Houghton Mifflin Harcourt Publishing Company

Name ______________________________

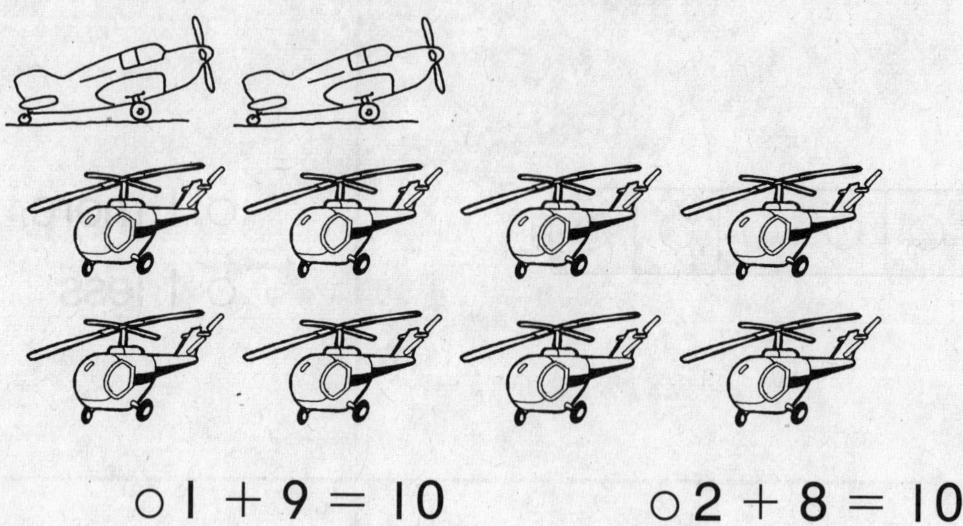

○ 1 + 9 = 10 ○ 2 + 8 = 10

5

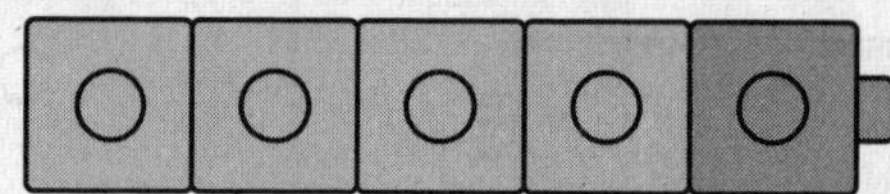

5 − 1 =

○ 6 ○ 4

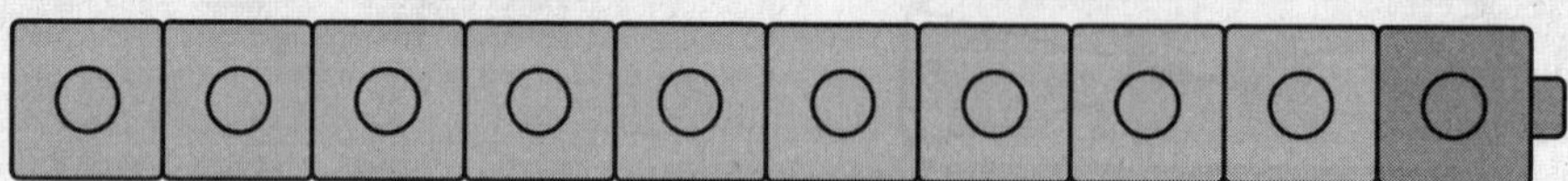

10 − 1 =

○ 9 ○ 8

DIRECTIONS **4.** There are 2 planes and 8 helicopters at the airport. What does this picture show? **5.** Hoda has 5 cubes. Rick has a number of cubes that is 1 less than Hoda has. How many cubes does Rick have? **6.** Ming has a 10-cube train. She takes away 1 cube. How many cubes are left on her train?

GO ON

© Houghton Mifflin Harcourt Publishing Company

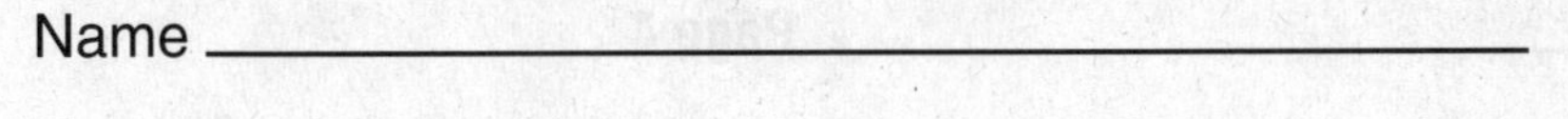

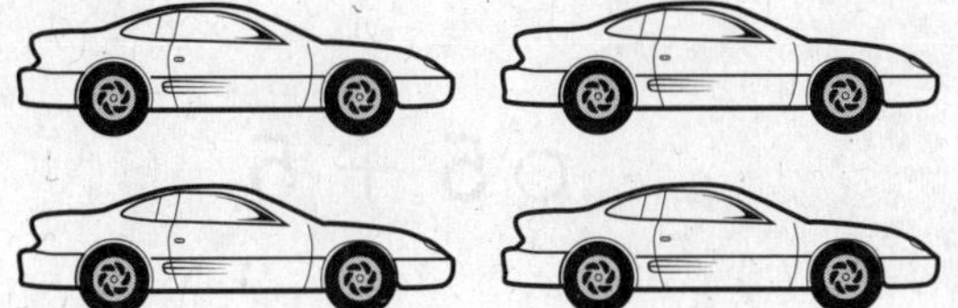

○ add ○ subtract

○ 5 + 5 = 10 ○ 6 + 3 = 9

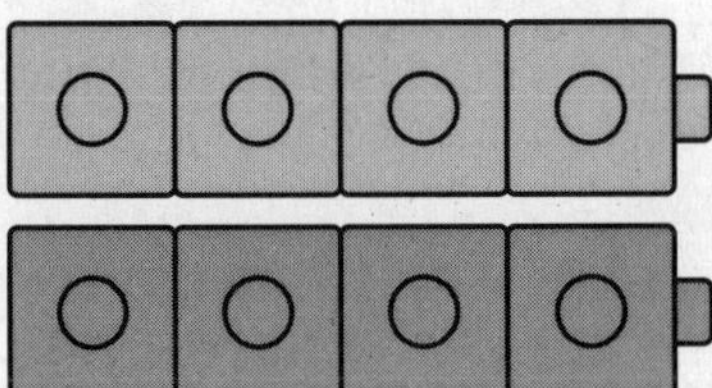

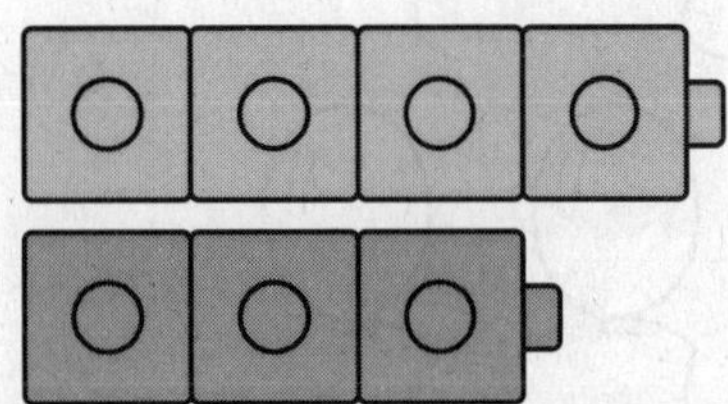

○ ○

DIRECTIONS 7. Sue Ann has 4 cars in her toy garage. She put 5 more cars inside. How can you find how many cars are in the garage now? 8. John collects 6 bugs. Then he finds 3 more. What number sentence does the picture show? 9. Which cubes show doubles?

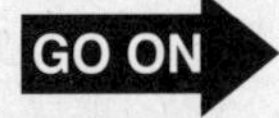

© Houghton Mifflin Harcourt Publishing Company

○ 2 + 4 ○ 5 + 5

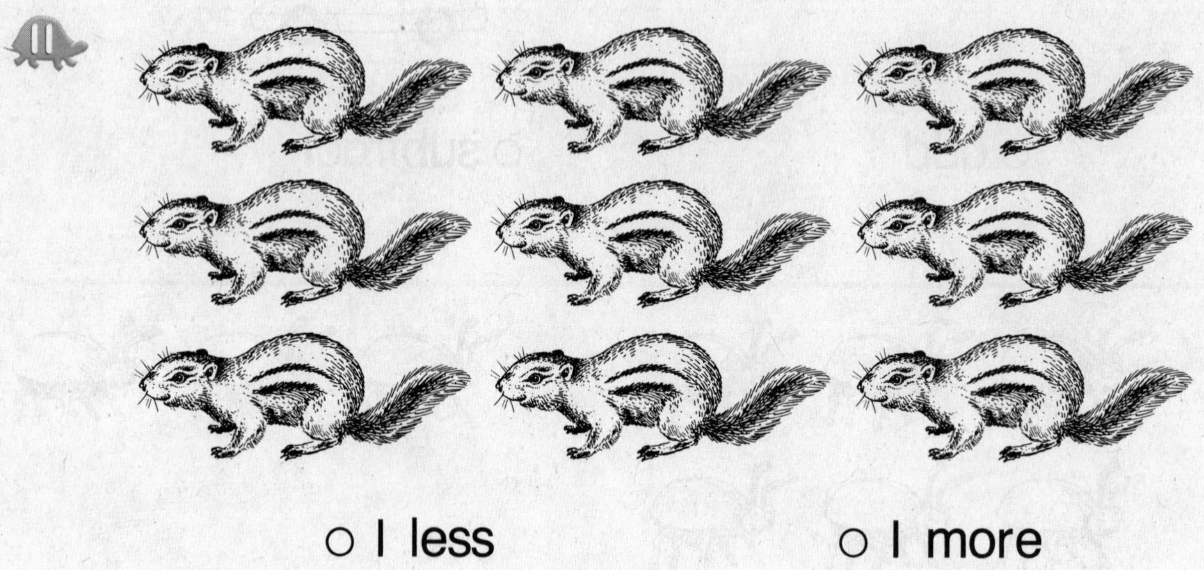

○ I less ○ I more

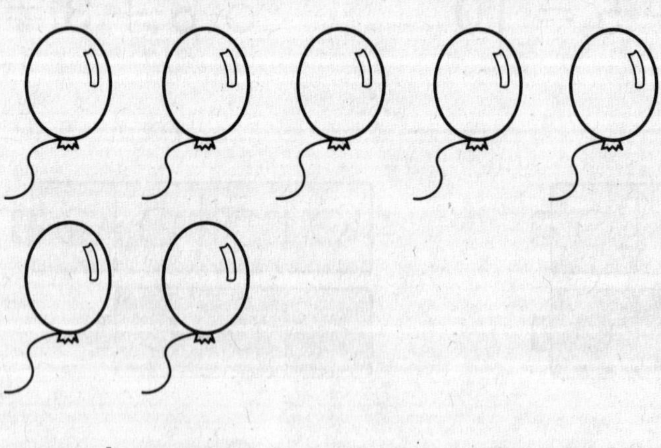

○ I more ○ I less

DIRECTIONS **10.** Which shows doubles? **11.** There are 9 chipmunks. One runs away. What should the picture show to model the story? **12.** Linda sees 7 balloons. One balloon pops. What should the picture show to model the story?

© Houghton Mifflin Harcourt Publishing Company

Name ____________________

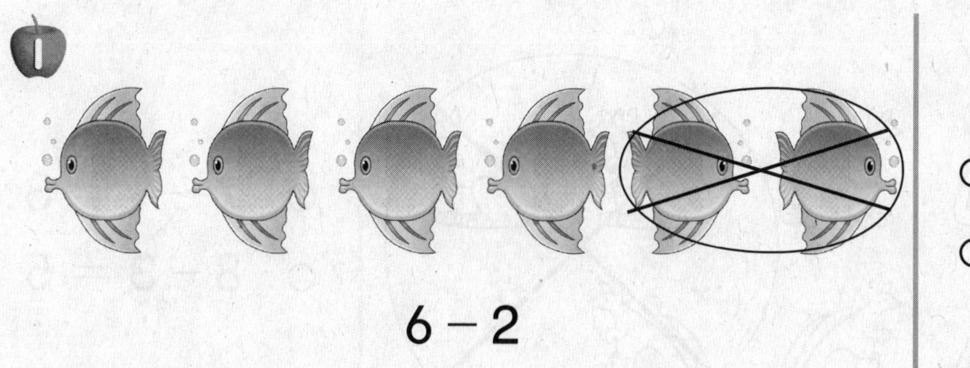

6 − 2

○ 3
○ 4

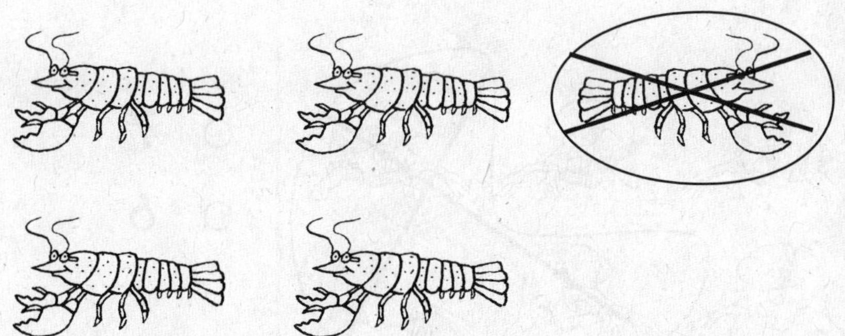

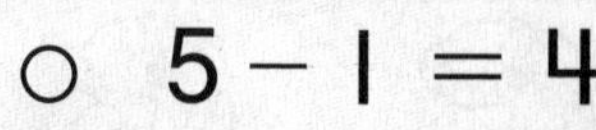

○ 5 − 1 = 4
○ 4 − 1 = 3

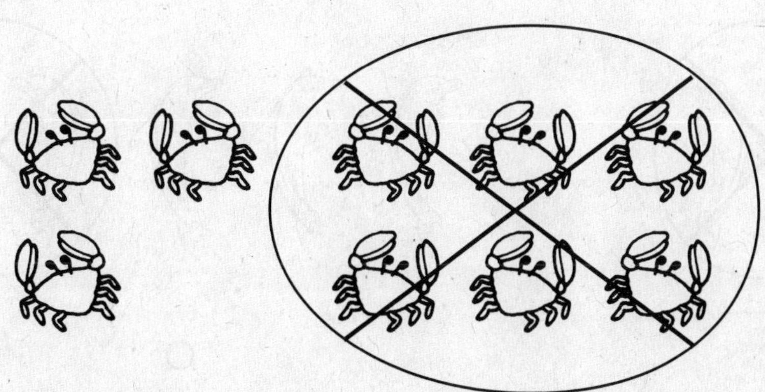

○ 6
○ 3

DIRECTIONS Fill in the bubble for the correct answer. **1.** Six fish are swimming together. Two fish swim away. How many fish are left? **2.** There are 5 lobsters. One leaves. Which number sentence shows this story? **3.** There are 9 crabs on the beach. Six go into the water. How many crabs are on the beach now?

© Houghton Mifflin Harcourt Publishing Company

4

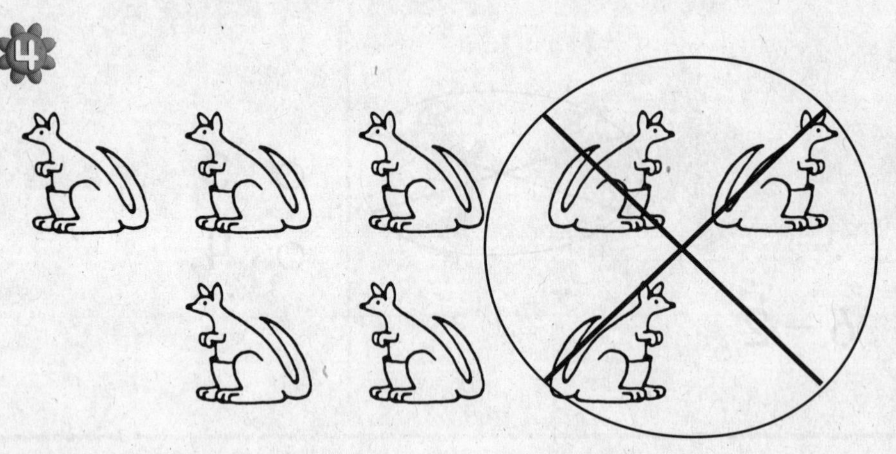

○ 7 − 4 = 3

○ 8 − 3 = 5

5

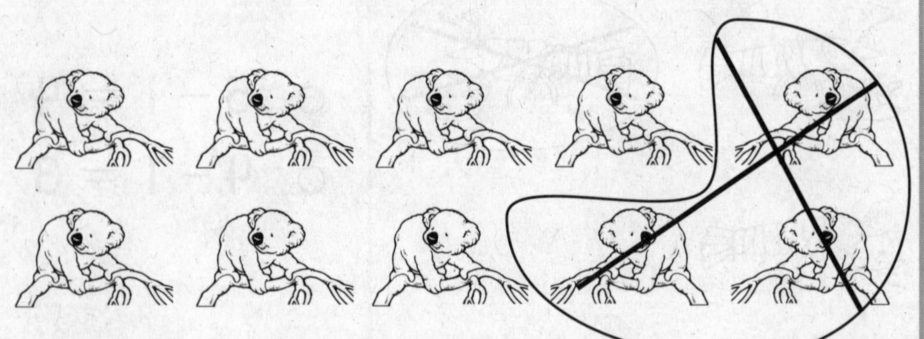

○ 7

○ 6

6

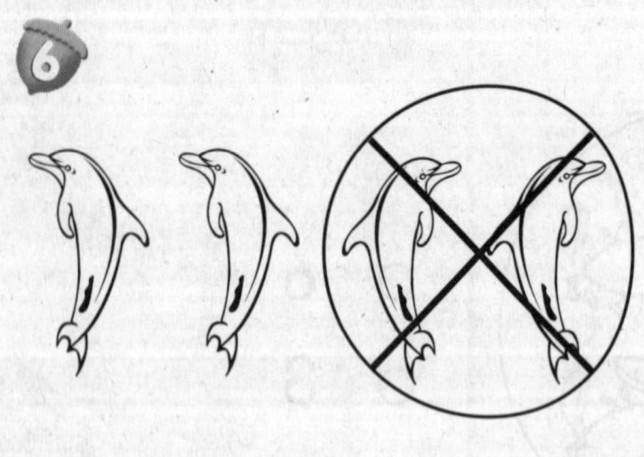

○

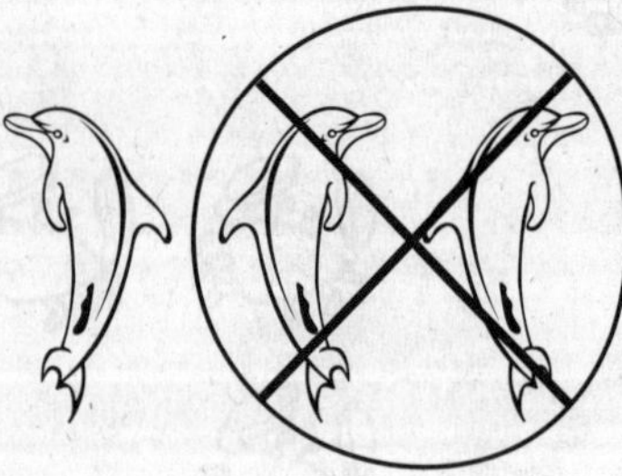

○

DIRECTIONS 4. There are 8 kangaroos. Three hop away. Which number sentence shows how many are left? **5.** Ten koalas are in the tree. Three climb down. How many are are in the tree now? **6.** There are 5 dolphins playing. Two swim away. Which picture matches the story?

GO ON

© Houghton Mifflin Harcourt Publishing Company

Name ____

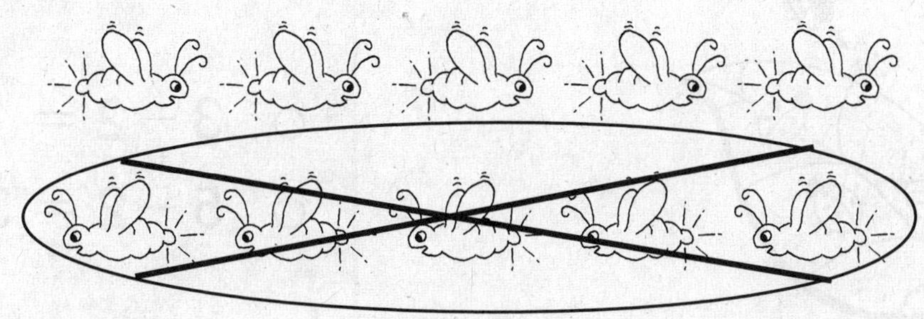

○ $10 - 5 = 5$

○ $9 - 5 = 4$

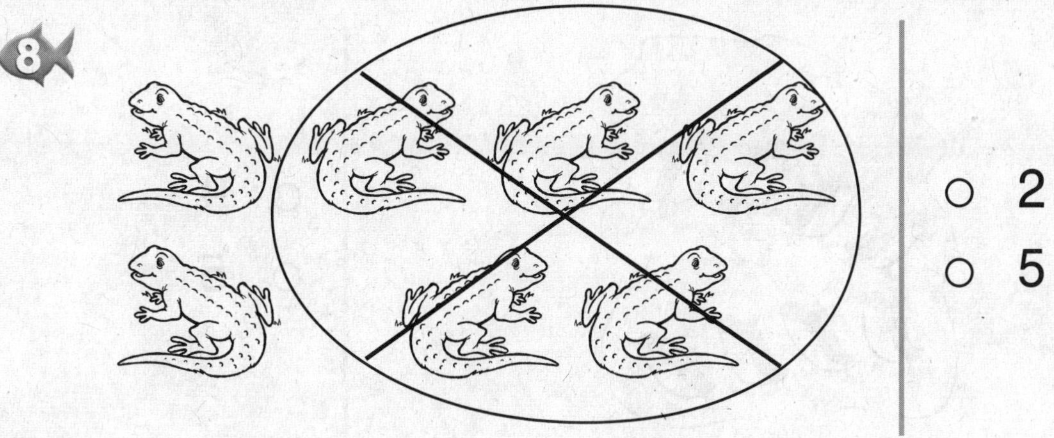

○ 2

○ 5

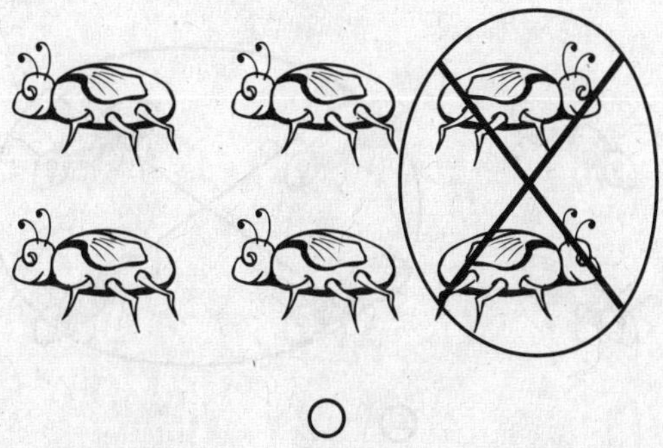

○

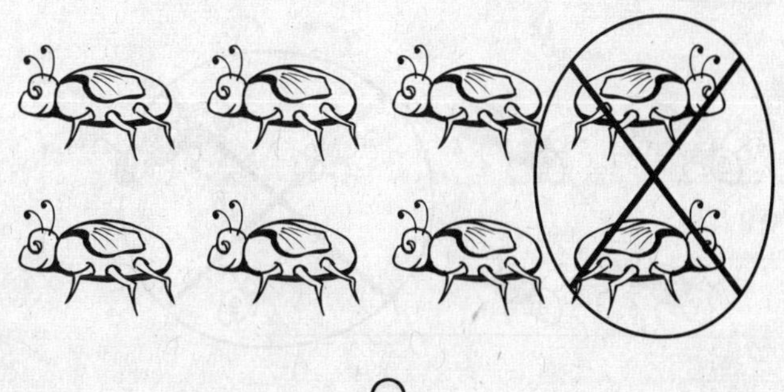

○

DIRECTIONS **7.** Ten lightning bugs are flying together. Five fly away. Which number sentence shows how to find how many are left? **8.** Seven lizards are on the beach. Five run away. How many are left? **9.** Eight bugs are on the ground. Two fly away. Which picture shows how to find how many bugs are left?

© Houghton Mifflin Harcourt Publishing Company

Name ______________________________

○ $3 - 2 = 1$

○ $5 - 2 = 3$

○ 4

○ 5

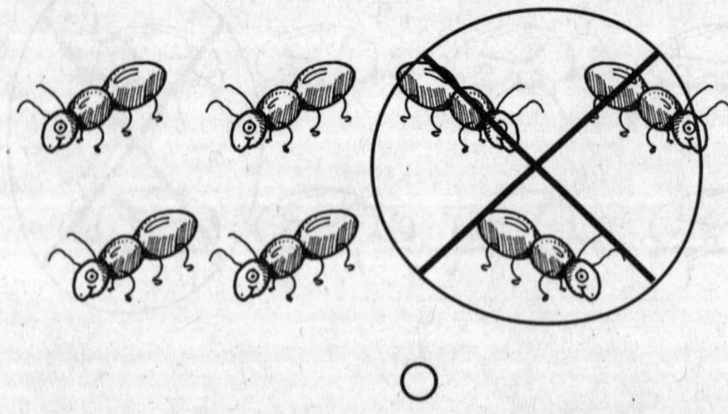

○

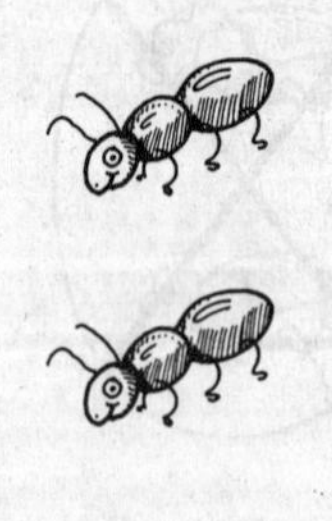

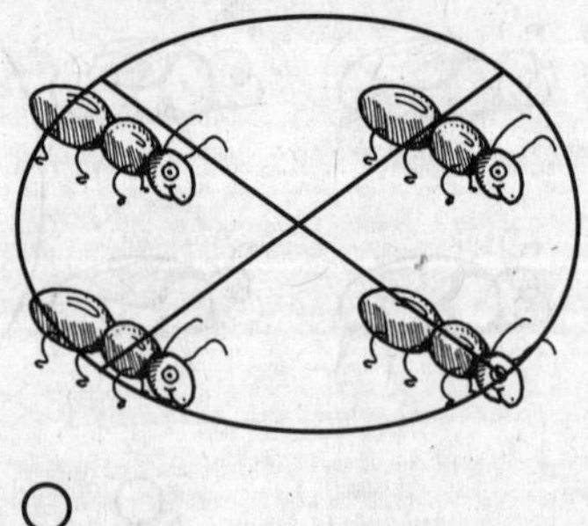

○

DIRECTIONS **10.** There are 5 ladybugs on a leaf. Two fly away. What does the picture show? **11.** There are 8 penguins. Four penguins leave. How many are left? **12.** Mr Diaz sees 7 ants. Three crawl away. Which picture shows how to find how many are left?

© Houghton Mifflin Harcourt Publishing Company

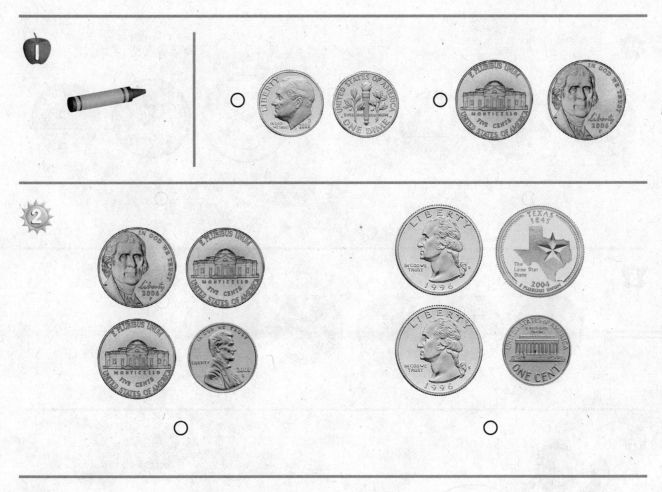

Name ______________________________

1

○ ○

2

○ ○

3

○ 2

○ 3

DIRECTIONS Fill in the bubble for the correct answer. **1.** Calvin uses 2 nickels to buy a crayon. Which set shows the coins he used? **2.** Anthony needs 3 nickels and a penny to buy a pencil. Which set shows the coins he needs? **3.** Payal wants to put quarters in the toy machine. How many quarters does she have?

© Houghton Mifflin Harcourt Publishing Company

Name ____________________

○

○

5

○ 5

○ 4

6

○

DIRECTIONS **4.** Tara needs a dime and 2 pennies to buy a sticker. Which set shows the coins she needs? **5.** Count the pennies. What number shows how many? **6.** Which set of pennies shows the number you need to buy the ring?

© Houghton Mifflin Harcourt Publishing Company

7

○ 4

○ 7

8

○ 5

○ 3

9

○ 3

○ 6

DIRECTIONS 7. Julia has the coins shown. How many nickels does she have? 8. Allen has these coins in his bank. How many nickels are in his bank? 9. Carlos found these coins in the car. How many dimes did he find?

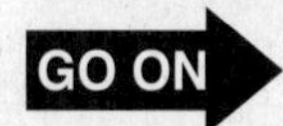

© Houghton Mifflin Harcourt Publishing Company

10

11

○ 4

○ 3

12

○ 8

○ 6

DIRECTIONS **10.** Pedro has 2 dimes and 1 nickel. Which coins belong to Pedro? **11.** How many quarters are in this group? **12.** Ana has these coins in her bank. How many quarters are in her bank?

© Houghton Mifflin Harcourt Publishing Company

Name ______________________________

○ 4
○ 5

○ 4
○ 6

DIRECTIONS Fill in the bubble for the correct answer. **1.** Count the pennies. What number shows how many? **2.** Mia finds these coins in the couch. How many nickels did she find? **3.** Bapi pays for his pencil with 3 dimes and a penny. Which coins does he use?

© Houghton Mifflin Harcourt Publishing Company

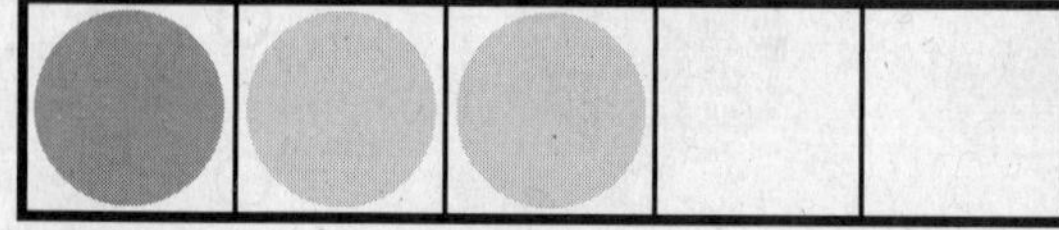

○ ○

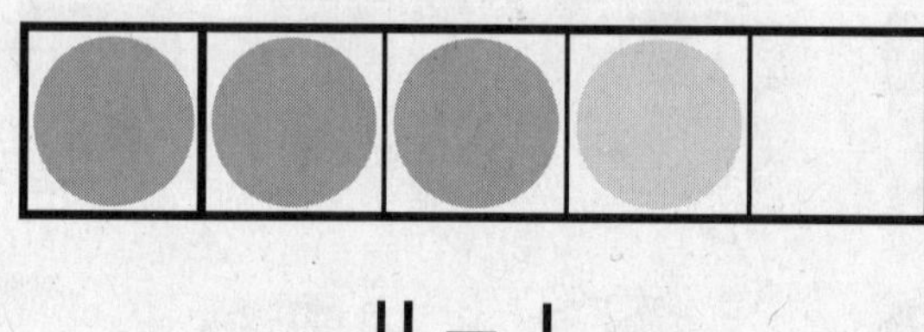

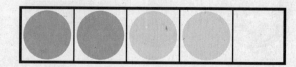

4 − 1

○ 1 ○ 3

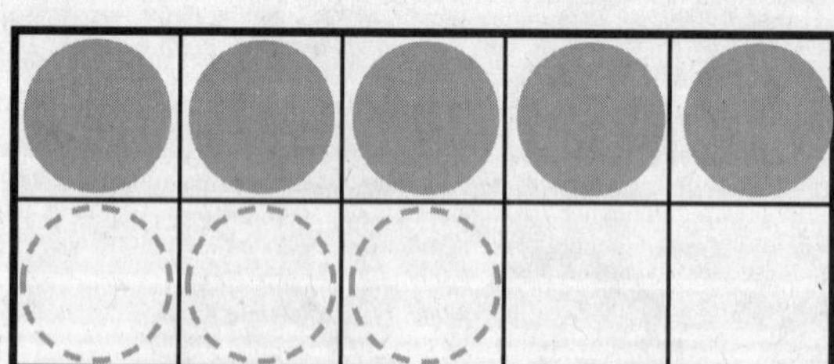

○ 3
○ 4

DIRECTIONS **4.** Which model shows 3 as 1 and 2? **5.** There are 4 counters in the five frame. One is light gray. How many are dark gray? **6.** Jordan needs to place 8 counters in the ten fame. He puts 5 dark gray counters in the ten fame. How many more counters does he need to make 8?

GO ON

© Houghton Mifflin Harcourt Publishing Company

Name ______________________

9 − 4

○ 5 ○ 3

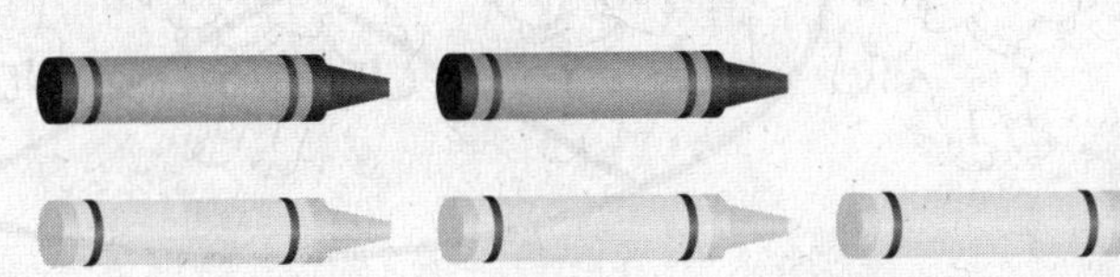

○ 2 + 3
○ 5 + 2

3 − 1

○ 1
○ 2

DIRECTIONS **7.** Lisa has a nine-cube train. She breaks it apart into 2 trains. One train has 4 cubes. How many cubes are in the other train? **8.** Sam has 2 crayons. He finds 3 more crayons. Which numbers show how many crayons Sam has now? **9.** There are 3 kittens playing. 1 kitten leaves. How many kittens are left?

GO ON

© Houghton Mifflin Harcourt Publishing Company

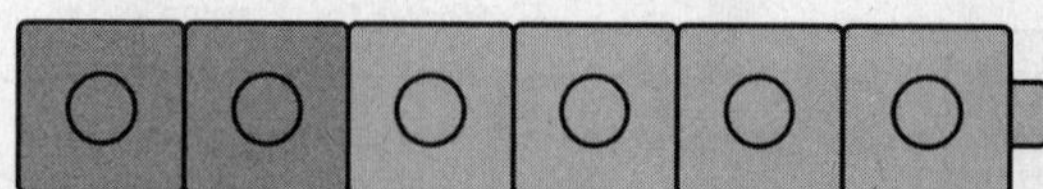

○ 6

○ 7

○ $6 - 3 = 3$ ○ $5 - 3 = 2$

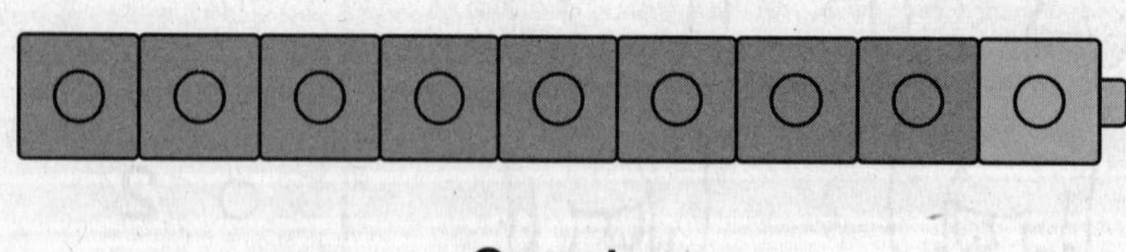

$9 - 1$

○ 10

○ 8

DIRECTIONS **10.** There are 2 children on the swings. Four more join them. How many children are on the swings now? **11.** There are 6 dogs. Three run away. Which number sentence shows this story? **12.** Ari has 9 cubes. Jennifer has a number of cubes that is 1 less than Ari has. How many cubes does Jennifer have?

© Houghton Mifflin Harcourt Publishing Company

Name ________________________________

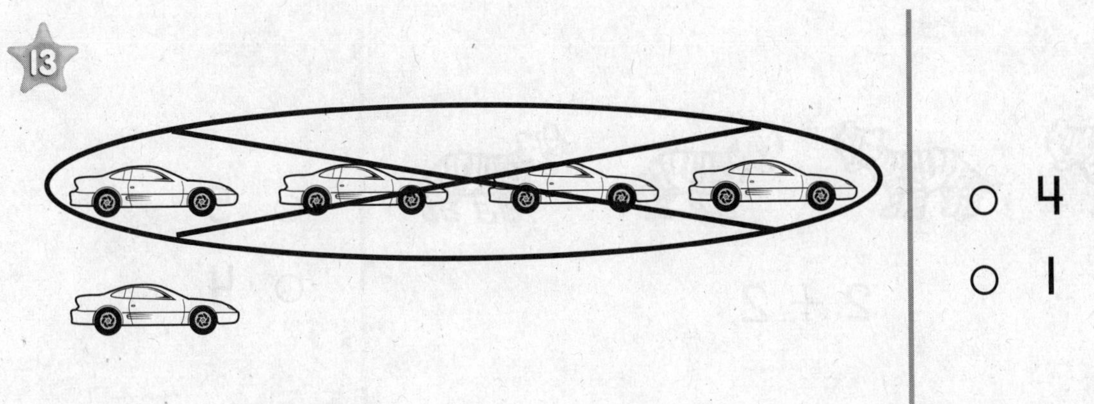

○ 4

○ 1

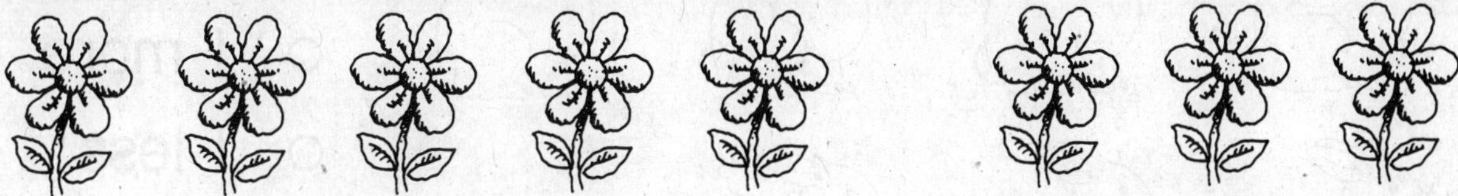

○ add ○ subtract

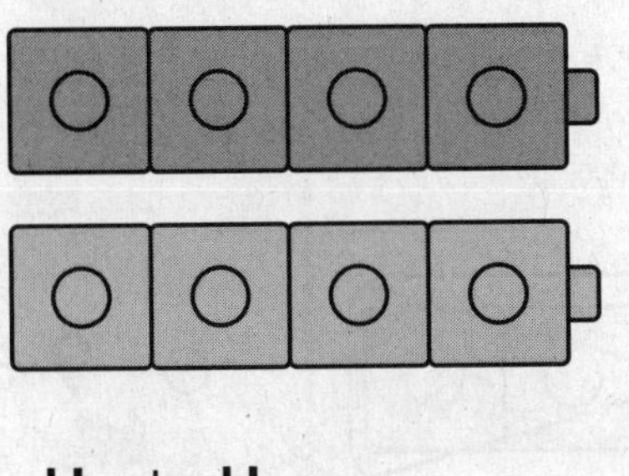

4 + 4 = ______

○ count on

○ use doubles

DIRECTIONS **13.** Dan has 5 cars. He gives 4 cars to his friend. How many cars does he have now? **14.** Amita puts 5 flowers in a vase. She put 3 more flowers in the vase. How can you find how many flowers are in the vase now? **15.** Which is the best way to solve 4 + 4?

GO ON

© Houghton Mifflin Harcourt Publishing Company

Name ______________________________

2 + 2

○ 5

○ 4

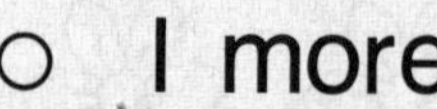

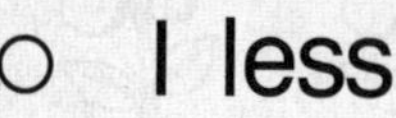

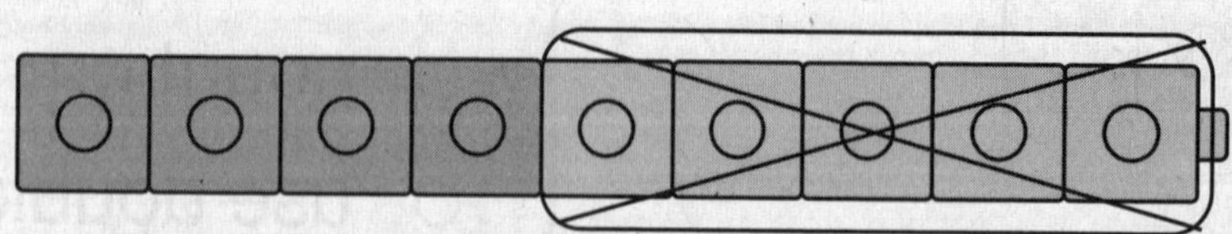

○ 9 − 5 = 4

○ 5 − 4 = 1

DIRECTIONS **16.** There are 2 tigers. Two more tiger come. How many tigers are there now? **17.** Davis sees 7 bunnies. One hops away. How will you find how many there are now? **18.** Tiffany is playing with 9 dolls. She puts away 5 dolls. What does this model show?

© Houghton Mifflin Harcourt Publishing Company

21	22	23	24	25	26	27	28	29	30
31	32	33	34	35	36	37	38	39	40

○ 33
○ 35

11	12	13	14	15	16	17	18	19	20
21	22	23	24	25	26	27	28	29	30

○ 18
○ 20

31	32	33	34	35	36	37	38	39	40
41	42	43	44	45		47	48	49	50

○ 56
○ 46

DIRECTIONS Fill in the bubble for the correct answer. **1.** What number is one more than 34? **2.** What number is one less than 19? **3.** Point to each number as you count. What is the missing number?

© Houghton Mifflin Harcourt Publishing Company

11	12	13	14	15	16	17	18	19	20
21	22	23	24	25	26	27	28	29	30

○ 21

○ 30

5

71	72	73	74	75	76	77	78	79	80
81	82	83	84	85	86	87	88	89	90

○ 89

○ 87

6

81	82	83	84	85	86	87	88	89	90
91	92	93	94	95	96	97	98	99	

○ 10

○ 100

DIRECTIONS **4.** What number comes right after 20? **5.** Look at the numbers that are "neighbors" to the number 88. Which one is greater? **6.** Point to each number as you count. What is the missing number?

© Houghton Mifflin Harcourt Publishing Company

51	52	53	54	55	56	57	58	59	60
61	62	63	64	65	66	67	68	69	70

○ 56, 57, 58

○ 59, 60, 61

61	62	63	64	65	66	67	68	69	70
71		73	74	75	76	77	78	79	80

○ 72

○ 70

71	72	73	74	75	76	77	78	79	80
81	82	83	84	85	86	87	88	89	90

○ 81, 82, 83

○ 80, 81, 82

DIRECTIONS **4.** Point to each number as you count. Which three numbers come after 58? **8.** Point to each number as you count. What is the missing number? **9.** Point to each number as you count. Which three numbers come after 79?

© Houghton Mifflin Harcourt Publishing Company

Name ______________________

1	2	3	4	5	6	7	8	9	10
11	12	13	14	15	16	17	18	19	20
21	22	23	24	25	26	27	28	29	30
31	32	33	34	35	36	37	38	39	40
41	42	43	44	45	46	47	48	49	50

○ 28

○ 26

○ 49

○ 51

○ 35

○ 33

DIRECTIONS Use this chart for the questions on this page. **10.** I am between 21 and 30. I am one less than 27. What number am I? **11.** I am greater than 48. I am less than 50. What number am I? **12.** I am between 31 and 40. I am one more than 34. What number am I?

© Houghton Mifflin Harcourt Publishing Company

1	2	3	4	5	6	7	8	9	10
11	12	13	14	15	16	17	18	19	20
21	22	23	24	25	26	27	28	29	30
31	32	33	34	35	36	37	38	39	40
41	42	43	44	45	46	47	48	49	50
51	52	53	54	55	56	57	58	59	60
61	62	63	64	65	66	67	68	69	70
71	72	73	74	75	76	77	78	79	80
81	82	83	84	85	86	87	88	89	90
91	92	93	94	95	96	97	98	99	100

○ 59 ○ 61

○ 73 ○ 71

○ 40 ○ 20

DIRECTIONS Use this chart for the questions on this page. **13.** I am greater than 60. I am less than 62. **14.** I am between 71 and 80. I am one more than 72. What number am I? **15.** You say this number when you count by tens. I am greater than 10 and less than 30. What number am I?

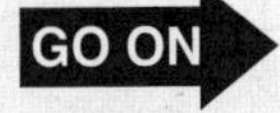

© Houghton Mifflin Harcourt Publishing Company

Name ______________________

51	52	53	54	55	56	57	58	59	60
61	62	63	64	65	66	67	68	69	70
71	72	73	74	75	76	77	78	79	
81	82	83	84	85	86	87	88	89	90
91	92	93	94	95	96	97	98	99	100

○ 71 ○ 80

10	20	30		50	60	70

○ 40 ○ 31

50	60	70	80	90	

○ 100 ○ 91

DIRECTIONS **16.** Count by tens. What is the missing number? **17.** Count by tens. What is the missing number? **18.** Count by tens. What is the missing number?

© Houghton Mifflin Harcourt Publishing Company

Name ______________________________

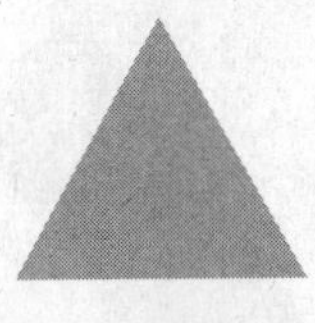

○

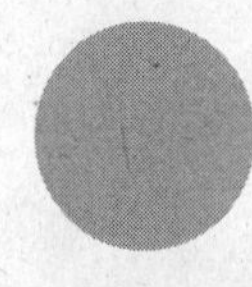

○

○

○

○

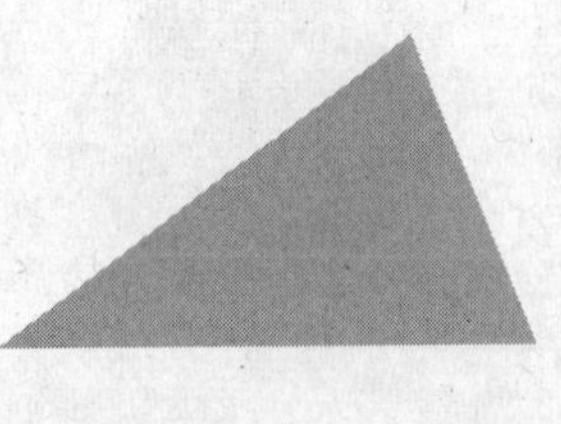

○

DIRECTIONS Fill in the bubble for the correct answer. **1.** Which shape is a circle? **2.** Which shape is a triangle? **3.** Amanda drew a shape with 3 sides and 3 vertices. Which shape did she draw?

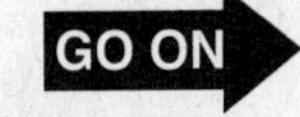

© Houghton Mifflin Harcourt Publishing Company

5

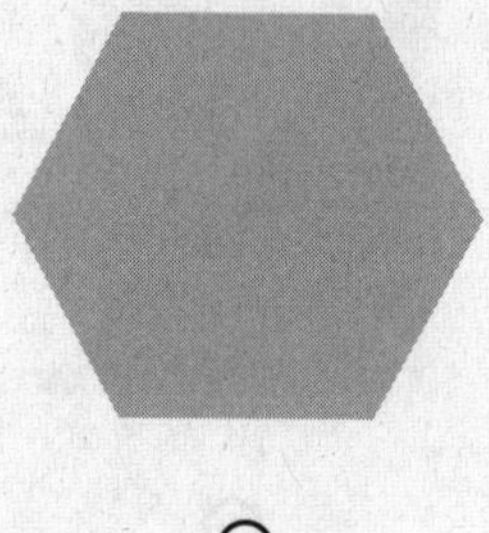

6

DIRECTIONS **4.** Which shape is a rectangle? **5.** Brian drew a shape with 4 sides and 4 vertices. Which shape did he draw? **6.** Which shape is a square?

GO ON

© Houghton Mifflin Harcourt Publishing Company

Name ____________________

7

○ ○

8

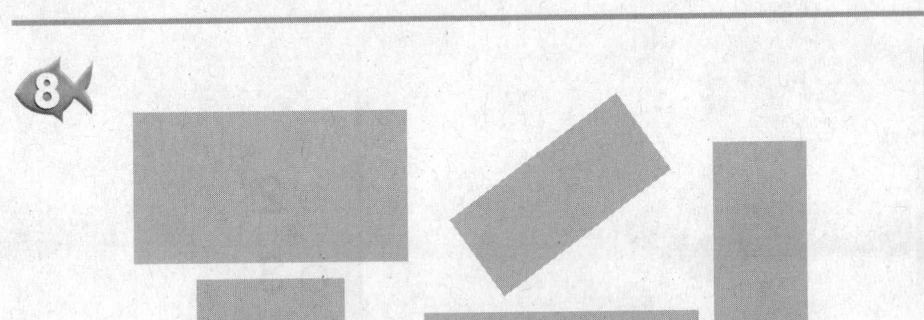

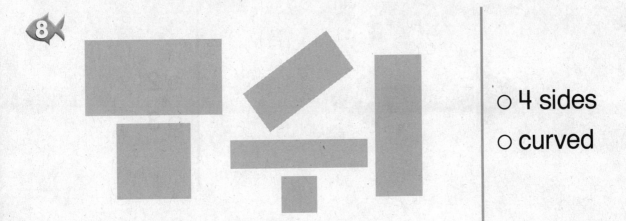

○ 4 sides

○ curved

9

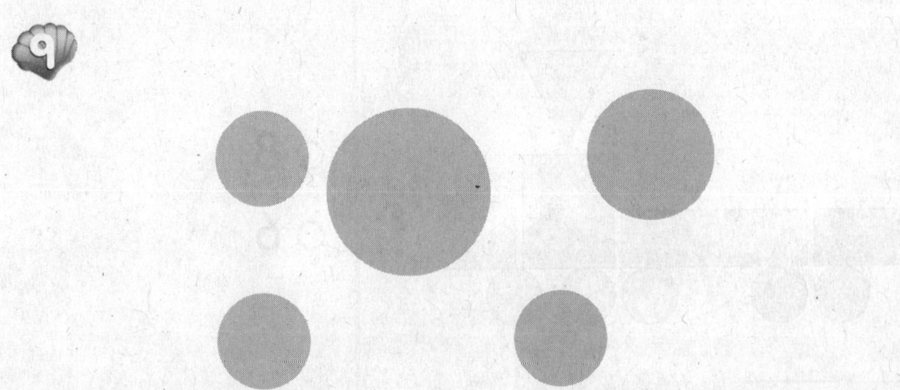

○ not circles

○ circles

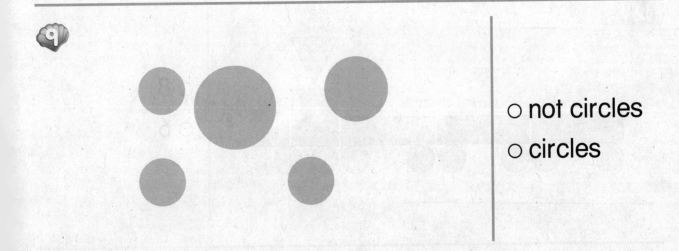

DIRECTIONS **7.** Which rectangle is a square? **8.** Look at the shapes. Which describes all the shapes? **9.** Jill sorted her shapes. What is the name of this group of shapes?

GO ON

© Houghton Mifflin Harcourt Publishing Company

Name ______________________________

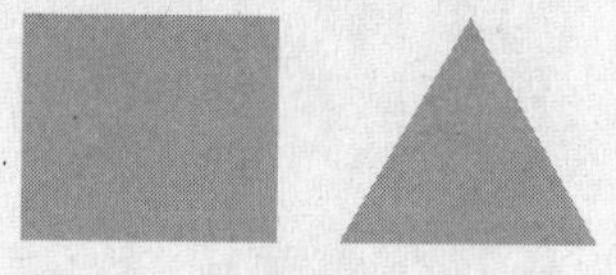

○ 2

○ 3

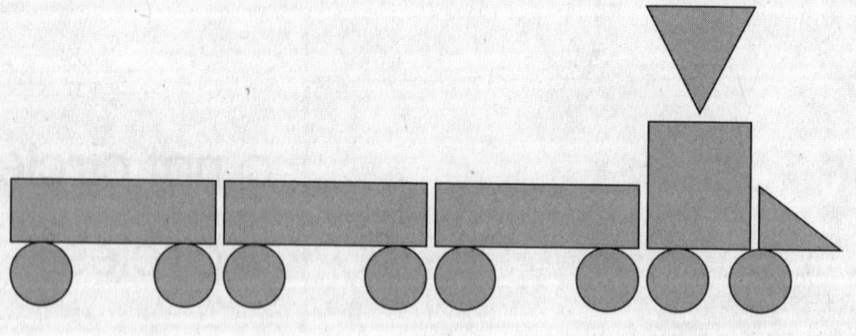

○ 8

○ 6

DIRECTIONS **10.** Shakira used 2 shapes to make a house. Which two shapes did she use? **11.** Jim made this drawing using shapes. How many triangles did he draw? **12.** Rachel drew shapes to make a train. How many circles did she draw?

STOP

© Houghton Mifflin Harcourt Publishing Company

Name ____________________

○ ○

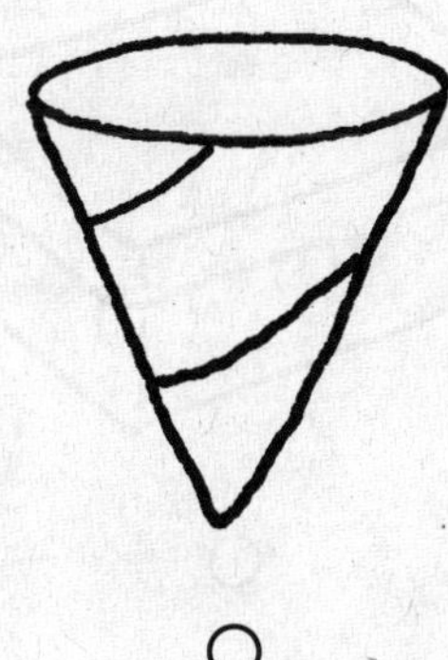

○ ○

○ ○

DIRECTIONS Fill in the bubble for the correct answer. **1.** Which object is shaped like a cylinder? **2.** Which object is shaped like a cone? **3.** Which object has 1 flat surface and a curved surface?

GO ON

© Houghton Mifflin Harcourt Publishing Company

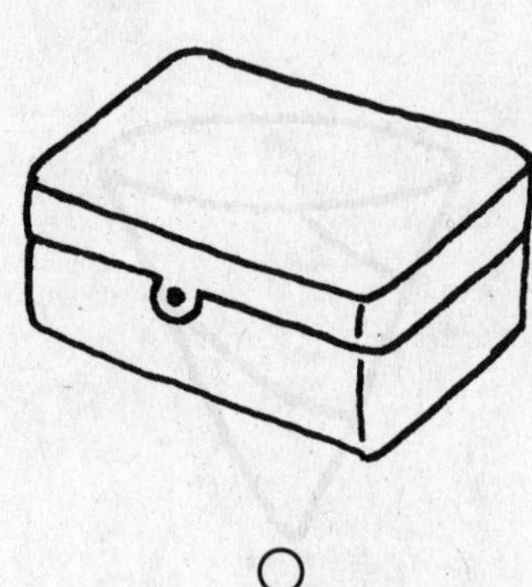

DIRECTIONS **4.** Which object is shaped like a sphere? **5.** Which object has a curved surface? **6.** Which object is shaped like a cube?

GO ON

© Houghton Mifflin Harcourt Publishing Company

○ ○

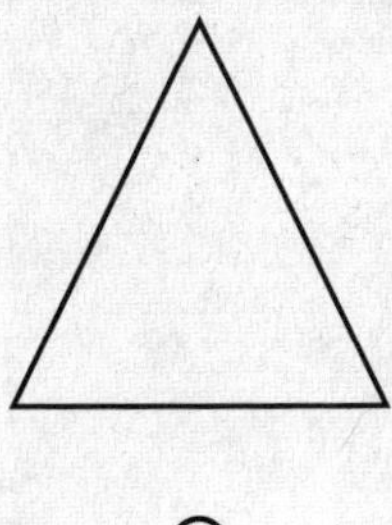

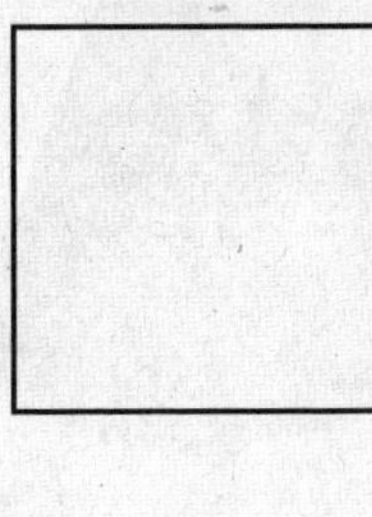

○ ○

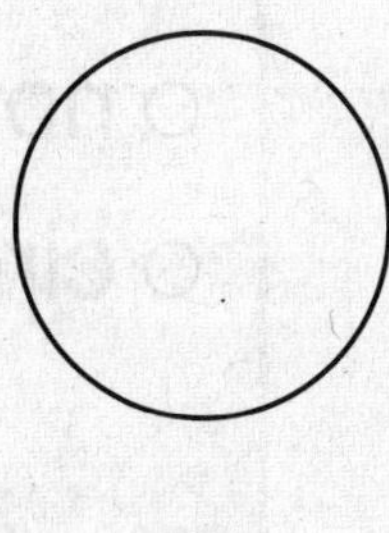

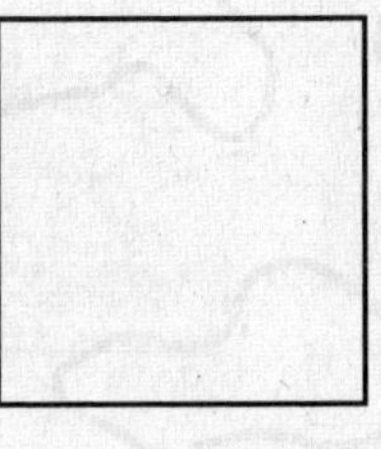

○ ○

DIRECTIONS **7.** Which shape is a flat surface on a cone? **8.** Which shape is a flat surface on a cube? **9.** Which shape is a flat surface on a cylinder?

GO ON

© Houghton Mifflin Harcourt Publishing Company

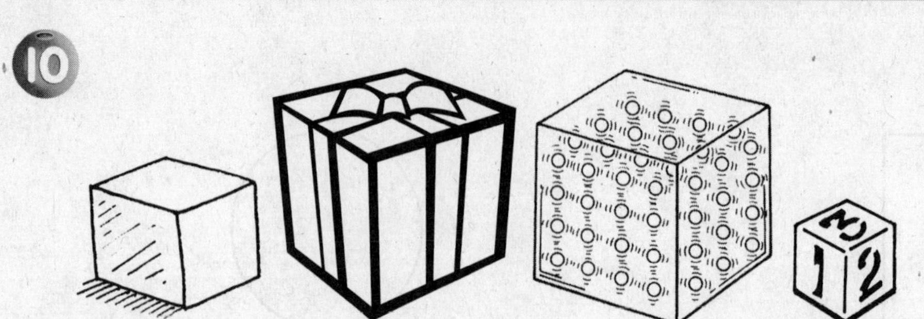

○ not cubes
○ cubes

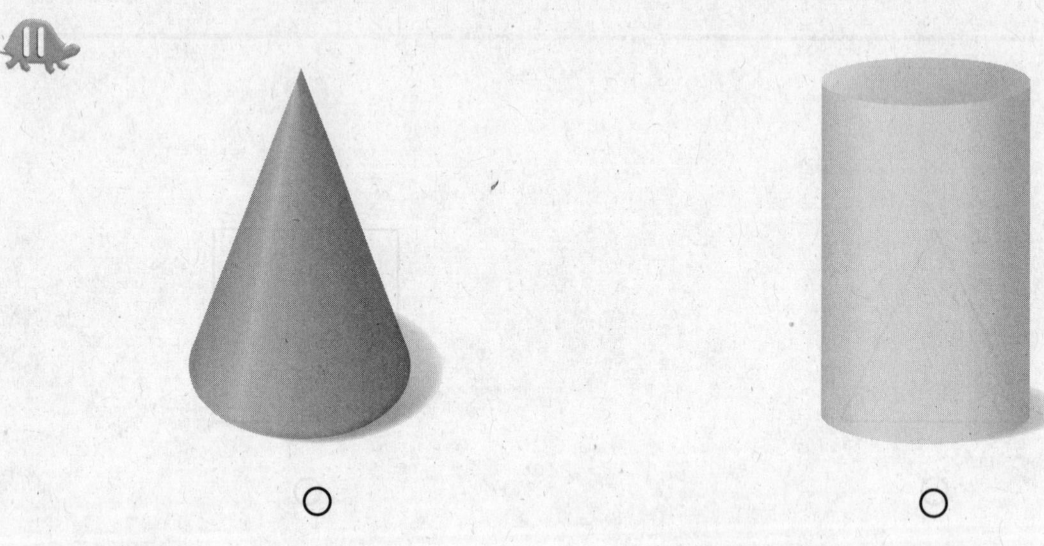

○ ○

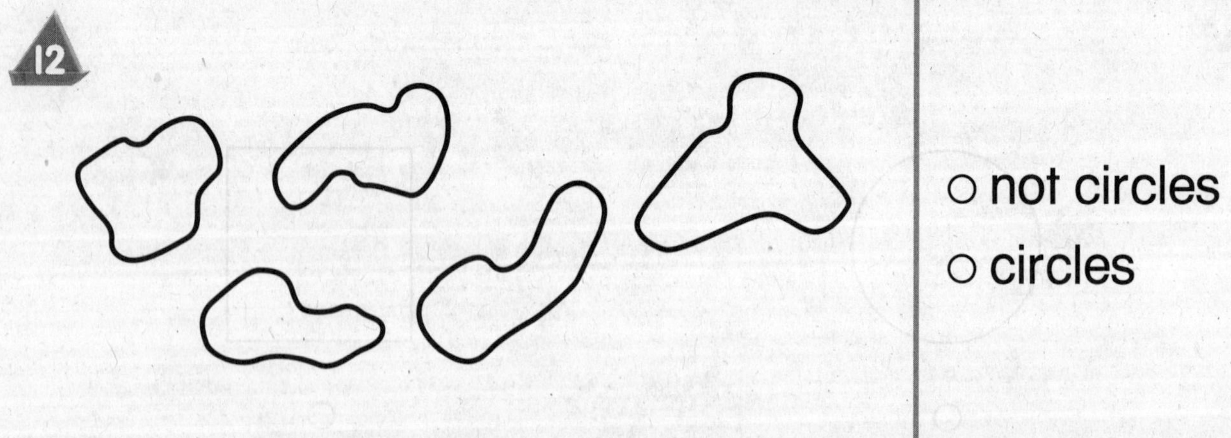

○ not circles
○ circles

DIRECTIONS **10.** Han sorted his shapes and made this set. What could he name this set? **11.** Which shape is a cone? **12.** Milena sorted her shapes and made this set. What could she name this set?

© Houghton Mifflin Harcourt Publishing Company

Name ______________________________

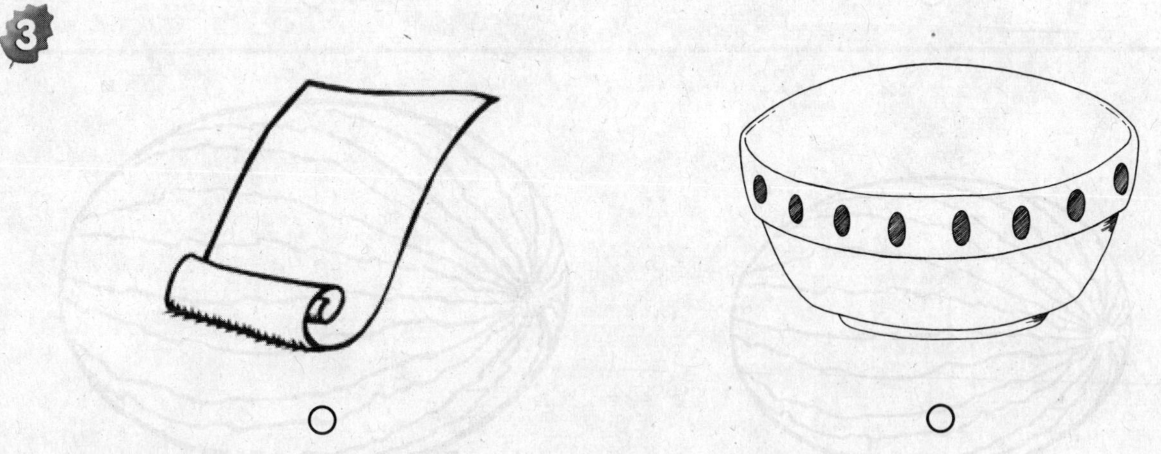

DIRECTIONS Fill in the bubble for the correct answer. **1.** Which object would you most likely measure to find out how long it is? **2.** Which object would you most likely measure to find out how much it weighs? **3.** Which object would you most likely measure to find out how much it holds?

© Houghton Mifflin Harcourt Publishing Company

4

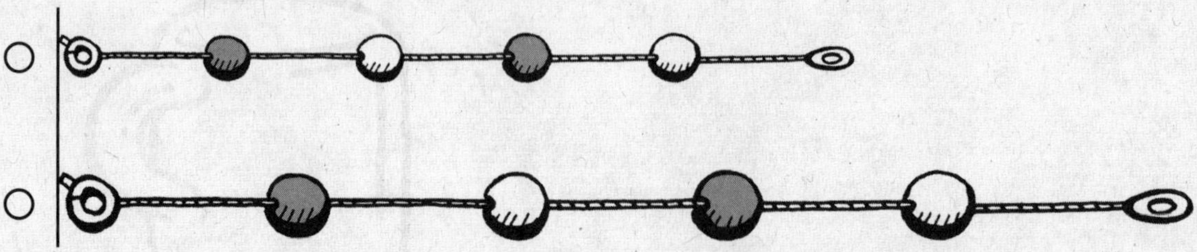

○

○

5

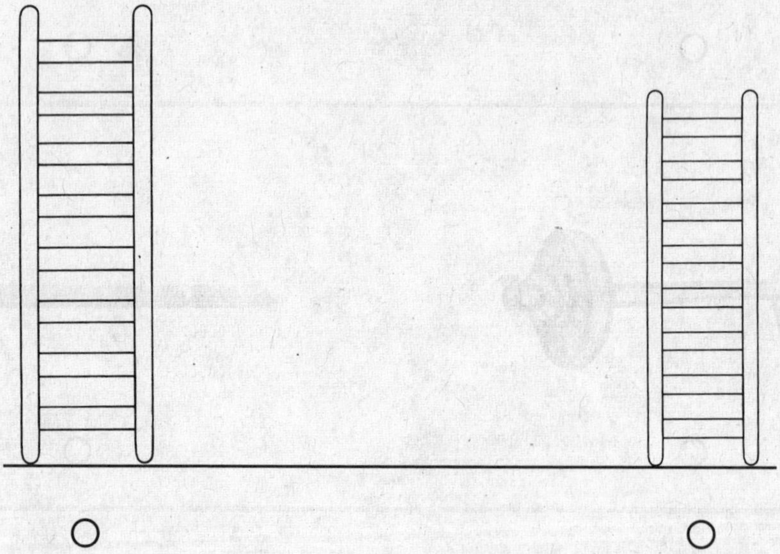

○ ○

6

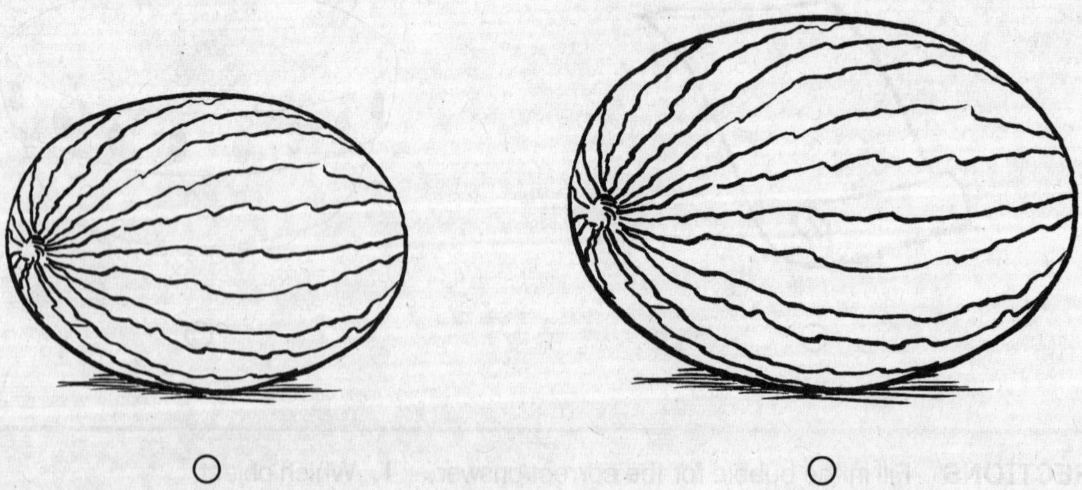

○ ○

DIRECTIONS **4.** Which bracelet is shorter? **5.** Which ladder is taller? **6.** Which watermelon is heavier?

© Houghton Mifflin Harcourt Publishing Company

7

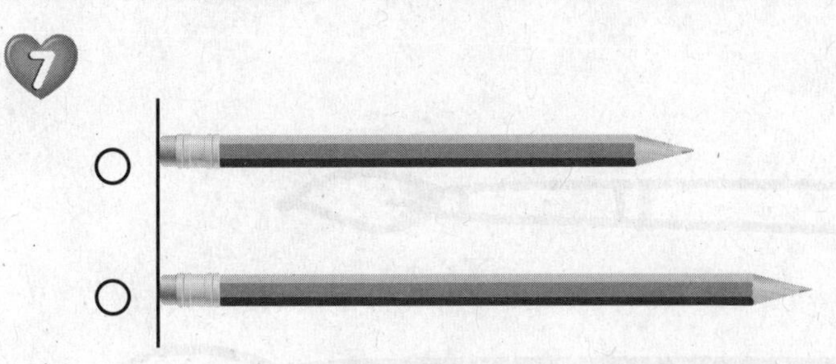

8

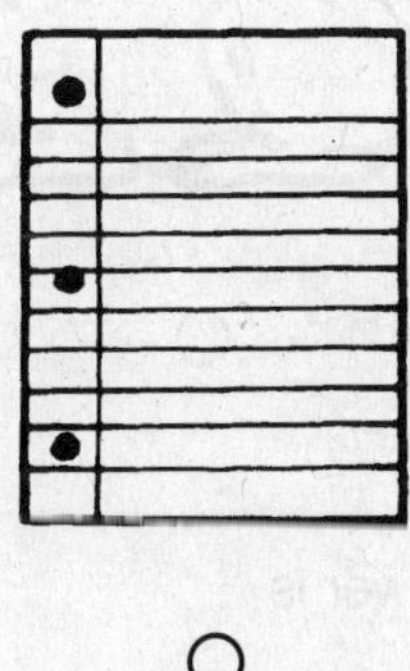

DIRECTIONS **7.** Which pencil is longer? **8.** Which tree is taller? **9.** Which object is heavier?

© Houghton Mifflin Harcourt Publishing Company

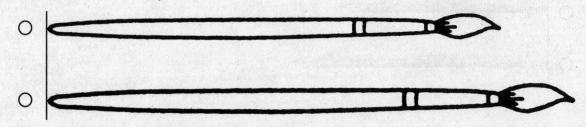

DIRECTIONS **10.** Which paintbrush is shorter? **11.** Which flower is shorter? **12.** Which is lighter?

© Houghton Mifflin Harcourt Publishing Company

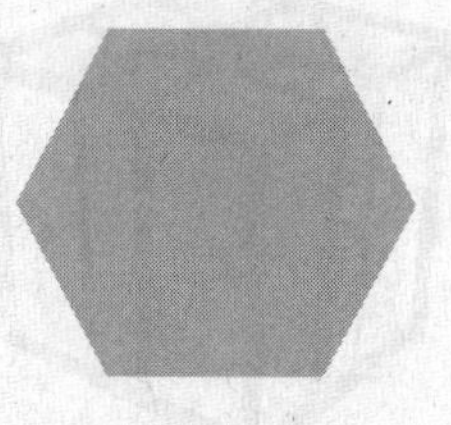

DIRECTIONS Fill in the bubble for the correct answer. **1.** Which shape is a triangle? **2.** Which shape is a rectangle? **3.** Which shape is a square?

GO ON

© Houghton Mifflin Harcourt Publishing Company

Name ______________________________

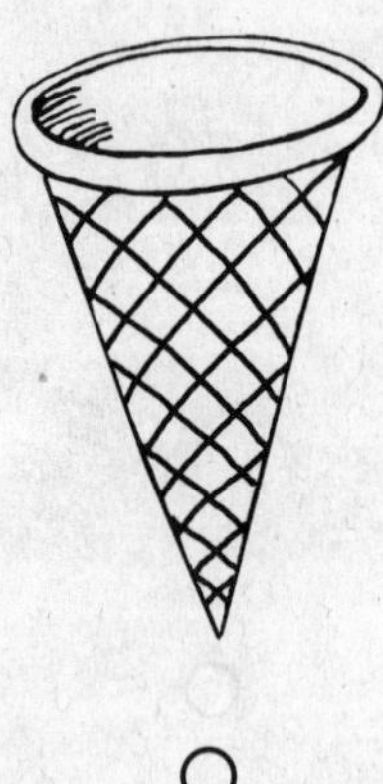

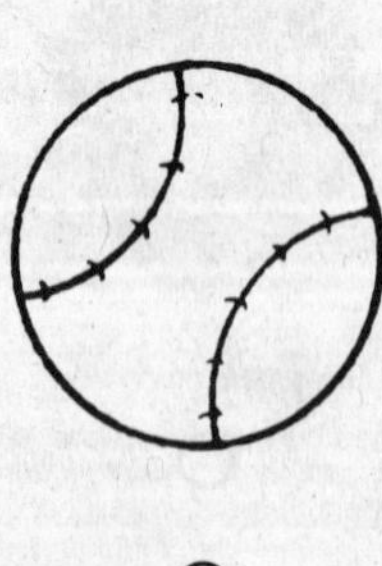

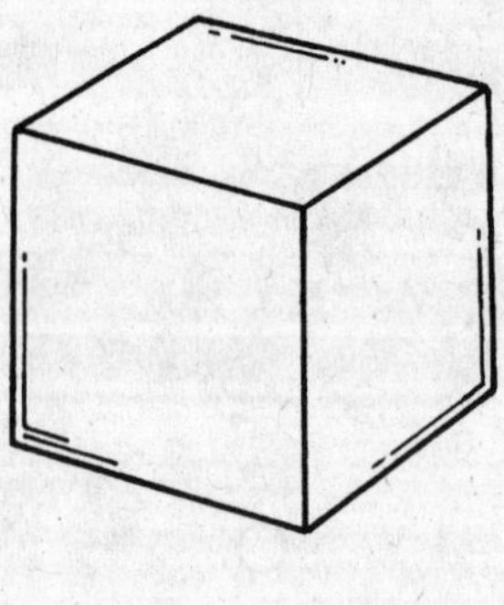

DIRECTIONS **4.** Which object is shaped like a cylinder? **5.** Which object is shaped like a cone? **6.** Which object is shaped like a sphere?

© Houghton Mifflin Harcourt Publishing Company

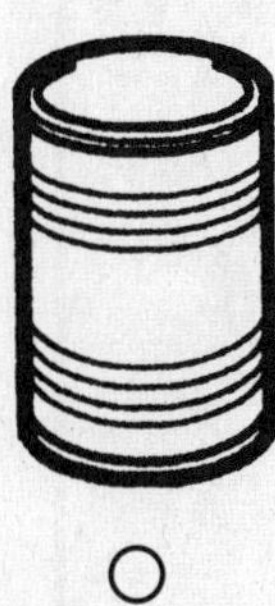
○

○

○ not circles
○ circles

○ 3 sides
○ 4 vertices

DIRECTIONS **7.** Which object is shaped like a cube? **8.** Tyrone sorted his shapes and made this set. What could he name this set? **9.** Rosa sorted her shapes and made this set. What could she name this set?

© Houghton Mifflin Harcourt Publishing Company

Name ______________________________

10

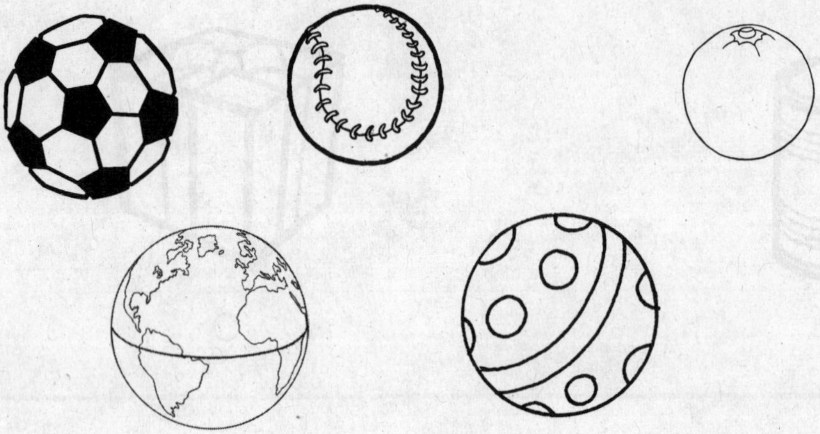

11

12

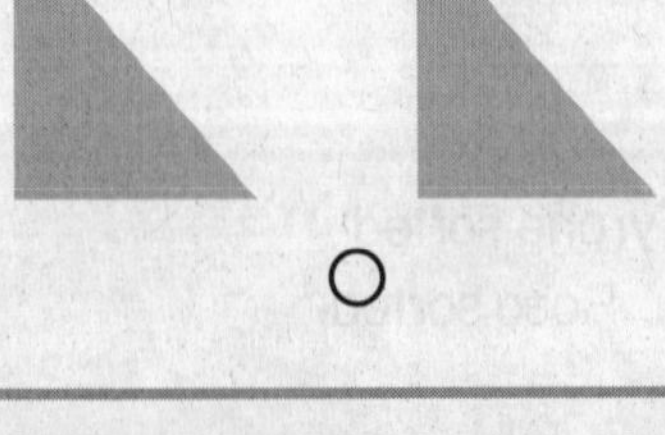

DIRECTIONS **10.** Which object belongs in this set? **11.** Which object belongs in this set? **12.** Micah uses 2 shapes to make a square. Which two shapes does he use?

© Houghton Mifflin Harcourt Publishing Company

Name ______________________________

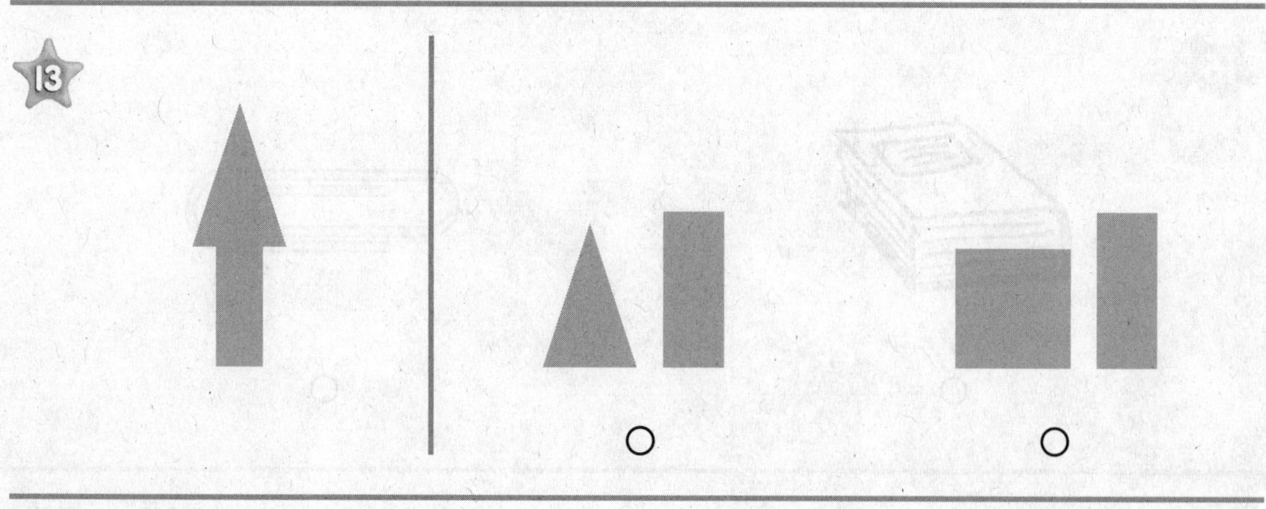

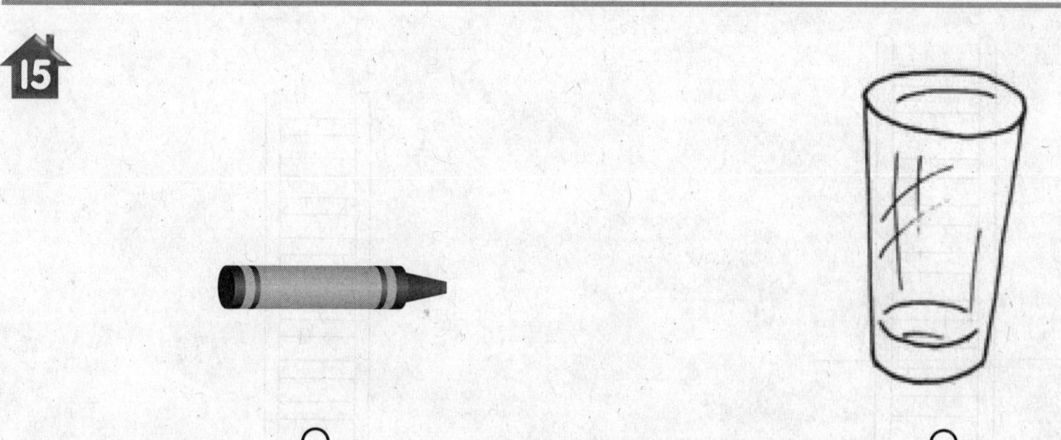

DIRECTIONS **13.** Which two shapes were used to make the first shape? **14.** Which object would you most likely measure to show how long it is? **15.** Which object would you most likely measure to show how much it holds?

© Houghton Mifflin Harcourt Publishing Company

Name ______________________________

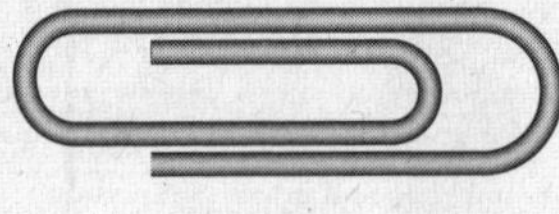

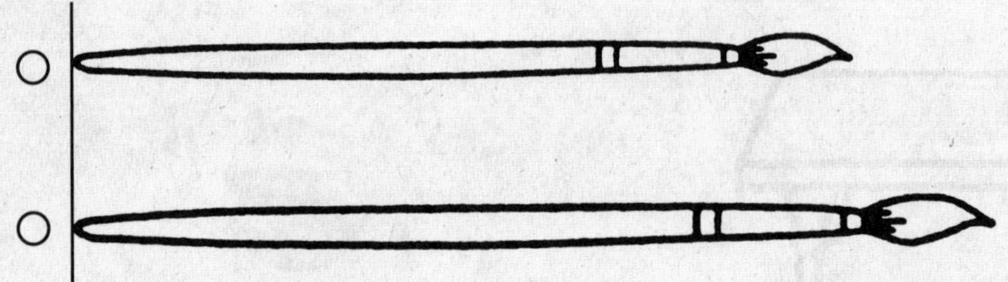

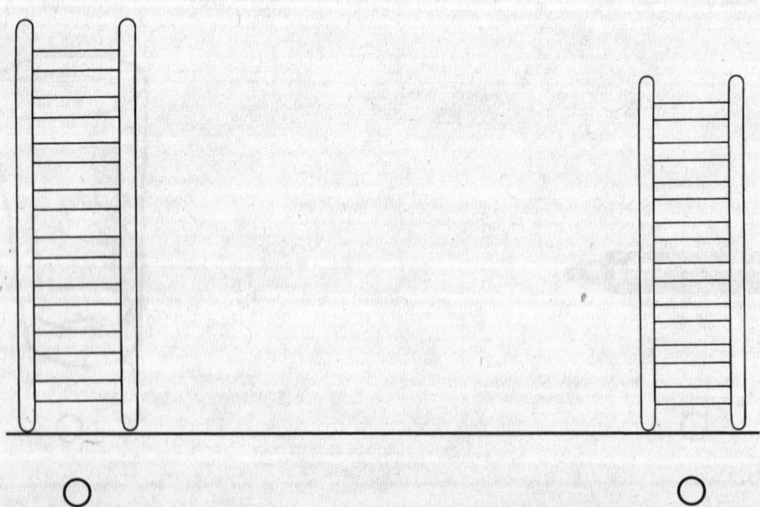

DIRECTIONS **16.** Which object would you most likely measure to show how much it weighs? **17.** Which paintbrush is longer? **18.** Which ladder is shorter?

© Houghton Mifflin Harcourt Publishing Company

Name ______________________________

1

○ ○

2

○ ○

3

○ ○

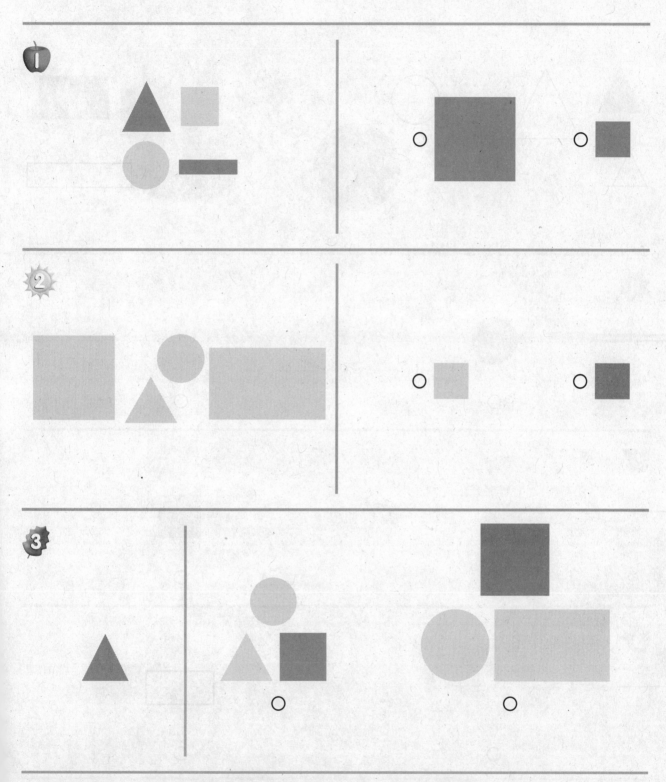

DIRECTIONS Fill in the bubble for the correct answer. **1.** Kayla sorted these shapes. Which shape belongs in this set? **2.** Adam sorted these shapes. Which shape belongs in this set? **3.** Steven sorted his shapes. Which set does the triangle belong in?

© Houghton Mifflin Harcourt Publishing Company

4

5

6

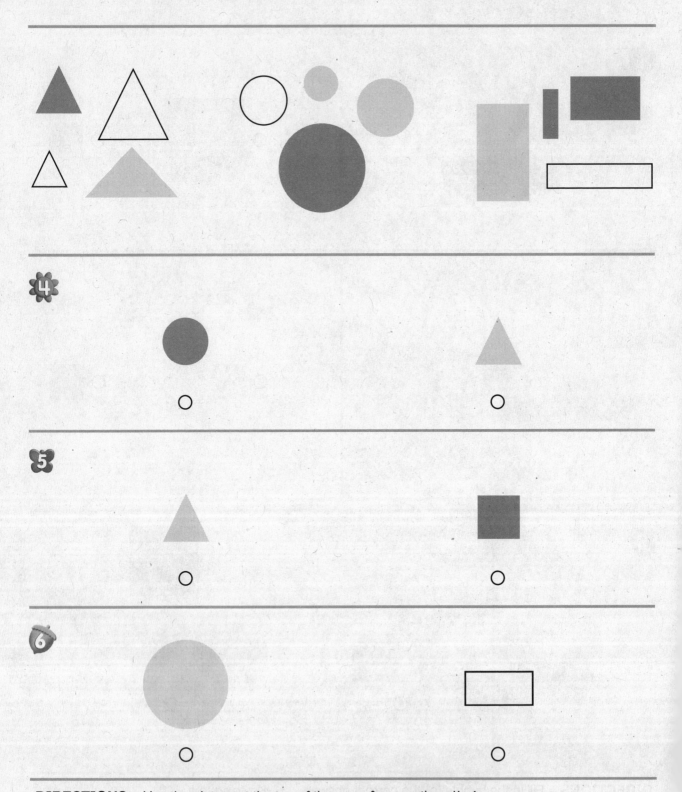

DIRECTIONS Use the picture at the top of the page for questions 4–6. **4.** Look at how the shapes are sorted. Which shape belongs in the middle category? **5.** Look at how the shapes are sorted. Which shape belongs in the first category? **6.** Look at how the shapes are sorted. Which shape belongs in the last category?

© Houghton Mifflin Harcourt Publishing Company

7

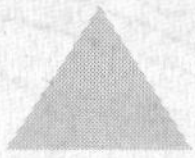

8

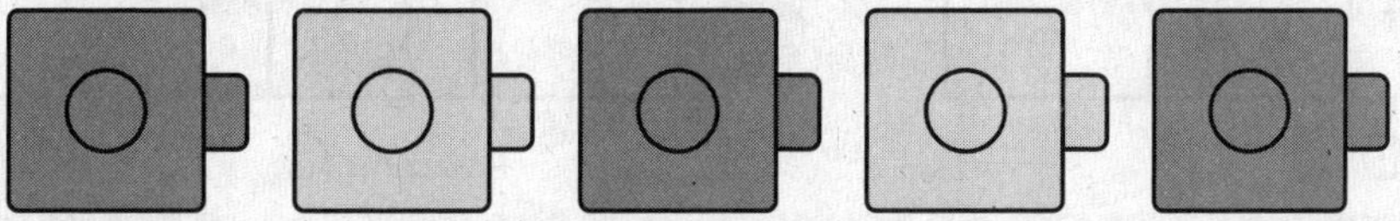

○ 3

○ 5

9

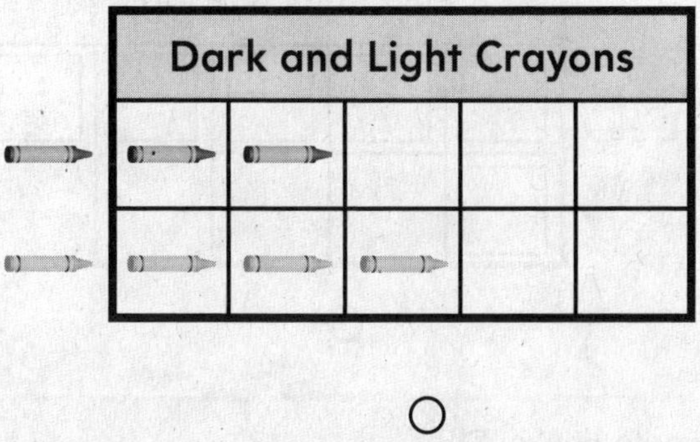

Dark and Light Crayons					

○

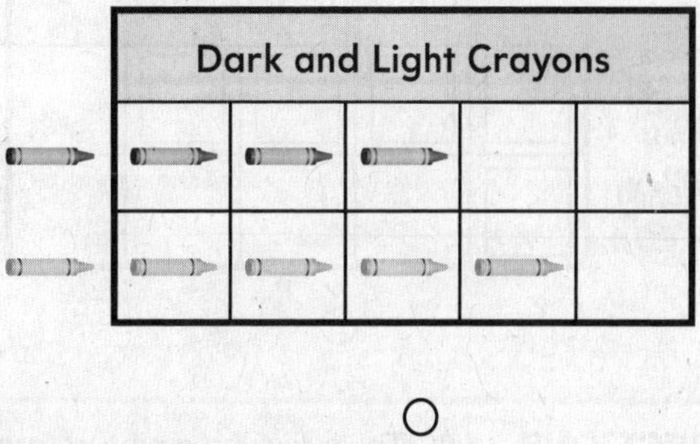

Dark and Light Crayons					

○

DIRECTIONS **7.** Look at how the shapes are sorted. Which shape belongs in the middle category? **8.** Sahil made a graph of his cubes. How many dark gray cubes should Sahil place on his graph? **9.** Look at the crayons. Which graph matches these crayons?

© Houghton Mifflin Harcourt Publishing Company

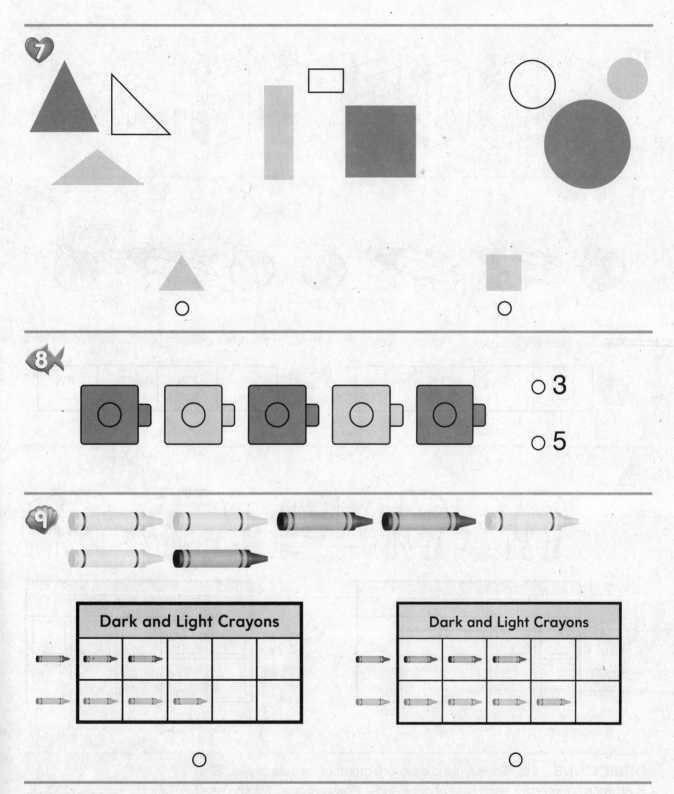

10

Apple Apple Apple Apple

○ 3
○ 4

11

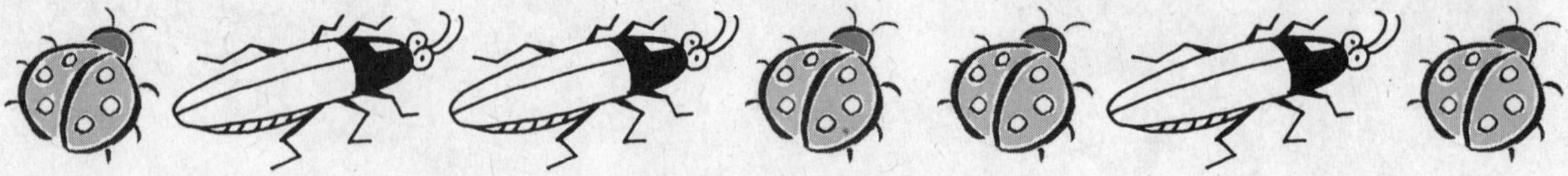

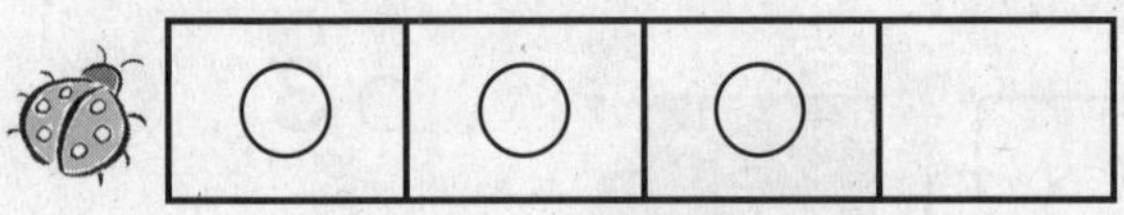

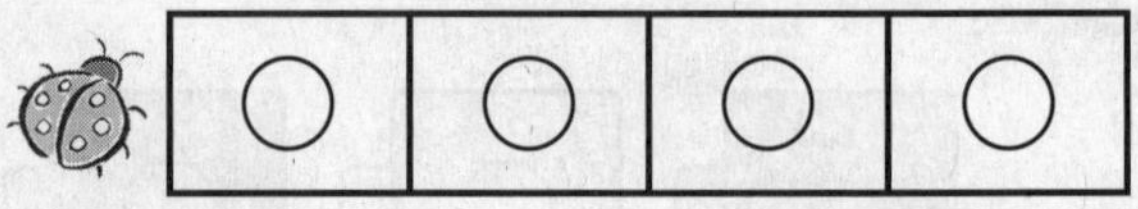

12

Elephants and Tigers

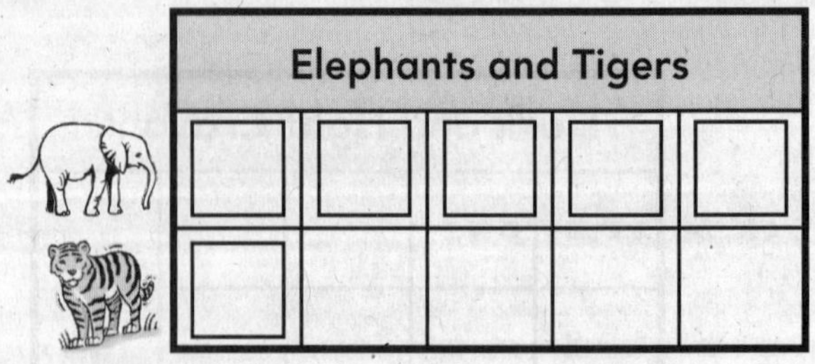

Elephants and Tigers

DIRECTIONS **10.** Thi is making a picture graph of favorite drinks. She is drawing squares for each type of drink. How many squares will she need to draw for juice boxes? **11.** Victor made a picture graph using circles for each type of bug. How should the row for ladybugs look? **12.** Ryan is using squares for each animal on his picture graph. Which graph matches the animals shown?

© Houghton Mifflin Harcourt Publishing Company

13

Light and Dark Crayons

○
○

14

Dark and Light Cubes

○ 4
○ 5

15

Light and Dark Counters

○
○

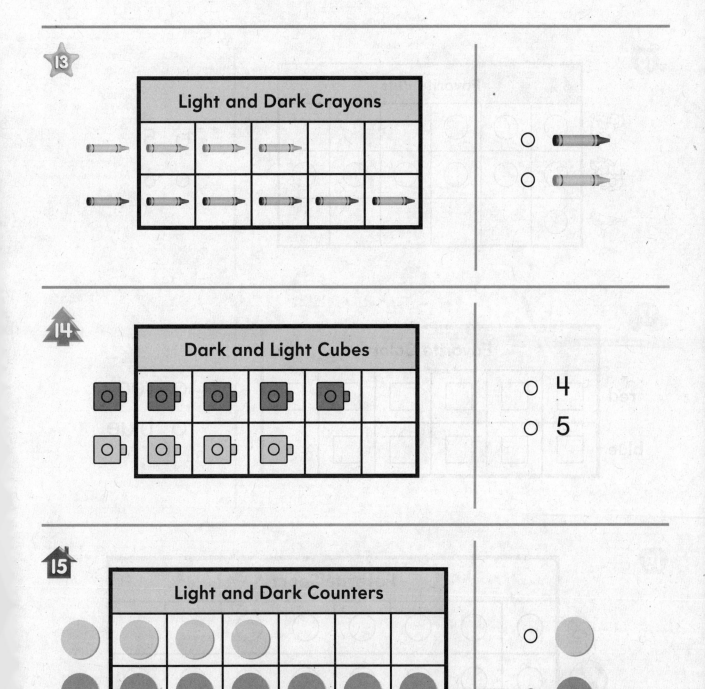

DIRECTIONS **13.** Read the graph. Are there fewer light or dark crayons? **14.** Read the graph. How many dark gray cubes are there? **15.** Read the graph. Are there more light or dark counters?

© Houghton Mifflin Harcourt Publishing Company

Name ______________________________

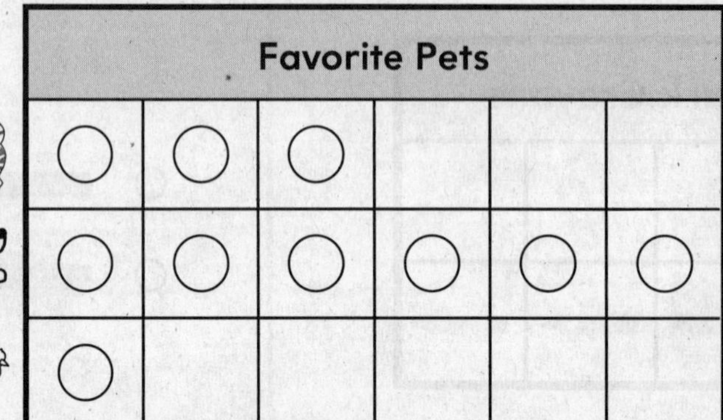

○ 5

○ 6

17

Favorite Color						
red	□	□	□	□	□	□
blue	□	□	□	□	□	

○ red

○ blue

18

Favorite Sport								
baseball	○	○	○	○	○	○		
soccer	○	○	○	○	○	○	○	○

○ 8 ○ 7

DIRECTIONS **16.** Read the graph. How many children chose dogs? **17.** Read the graph. Which color do fewer children like? **18.** Read the graph. How many children chose soccer?

© Houghton Mifflin Harcourt Publishing Company

Name ______________________________

○ ○

○ ○

○ ○

DIRECTIONS Fill in the bubble for the correct answer. **1.** Which picture shows a way to earn money? **2.** Which shows a picture of someone at work? **3.** Which shows a picture of someone working to earn income?

© Houghton Mifflin Harcourt Publishing Company

Name ______________________________

5

DIRECTIONS **4.** Which picture shows a way to earn money? **5.** Which shows a picture of someone at work? **6.** Which shows a picture of someone working to earn income?

GO ON

© Houghton Mifflin Harcourt Publishing Company

Name ____________________

○ ○

○ ○

○ ○

DIRECTIONS 7. Which picture shows a way to earn money? **8.** Which shows a picture of someone at work? **9.** Which person needs to know how to swim?

© Houghton Mifflin Harcourt Publishing Company

Name ______________________________________

○ ○

○ ○

○ ○

DIRECTIONS **10.** Which person needs to know about animals? **11.** Which person uses a hammer to do his or her job? **12.** Which man would need a hose to do his job?

© Houghton Mifflin Harcourt Publishing Company

Name ______________________________

DIRECTIONS **13.** Which shows children earning money? **14.** Which shows a child receiving money as a gift? **15.** Mr. Black used the money from his paycheck to buy something he needs. Which picture shows what he bought?

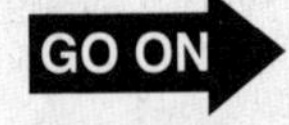

© Houghton Mifflin Harcourt Publishing Company

Name ______________________________

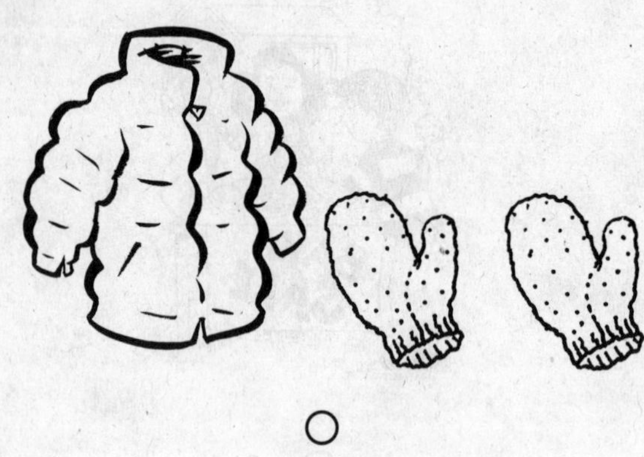

DIRECTIONS **16.** Bob eats what he wants not what he needs. Which shows what he eats? **17.** Malik wears what he wants not what he needs. What does he wear? **18.** Which picture shows a need?

© Houghton Mifflin Harcourt Publishing Company

Child's Name ____________________ Date ____________

Prerequisite Skills Inventory

Item	Common Error	Intervene with RtI*
1	May miscount the items	4
2	May miscount the items	12
3	May not understand the concept of zero	8
4	May not recognize the number 0	8
5	May forget to count an item	21
6	May count an item twice	19
7	May not understand the concept of same	22
8	May not understand the concept of more	23
9	May not understand the concept of fewer	24
10	May not understand the ways to make a number	26
11	May not understand how to make 10	27
12	May miscount the items	28
13	May not be able to match a picture to a story	30
14	May not be able to count forward starting from a number other than 1	41
15	May not be able to decide what shape belongs in a set	42

***RtI**—Response to Intervention Tier 2 Skills and Tier 3 Examples

© Houghton Mifflin Harcourt Publishing Company

Child's Name ______________________ Date ____________

Item	Common Error	Intervene with RtI*
16	May not understand the meaning of alike/different	43
17	May not understand the meaning of alike/different	44
18	May not be able to distinguish between sizes	45
19	May not understand the meaning of the word shorter	46
20	May not understand the meaning of the word heavier	23

***RtI**—Response to Intervention Tier 2 Skills and Tier 3 Examples

© Houghton Mifflin Harcourt Publishing Company

Child's Name ______________________ Date ____________

Beginning of Year Test

Item	Lesson	Standard	Common Error	Rti T1	Soar to Success
1	2.4	K.2.A	May not understand how to count backward	1	1.03
2	2.4	K.2.A	May not know the numbers in counting order	1	1.03
3	1.1	K.2.B	May not know how to represent the number 2	2	1.01
4	3.4	K.2.E	May not understand the concept of greater	32	7.06
5	3.4	K.2.E	May not understand the concept of less	32	7.06
6	3.4	K.2.E	May not understand the concept of the same	32	7.06
7	6.4	K.2.F	May not understand the concept of one more	34	7.11, 7.12
8	6.4	K.2.F	May not understand the concept of one less	34	7.11, 7.12
9	3.2	K.2.G	May not understand the concept of the same	37	7.06
10	3.3	K.2.G	May not understand the concept of one more	38	7.06
11	6.6	K.2.H	May not understand the concepts of less than and greater than	41	7.09
12	8.8	K.2.H	May not understand the concepts of less than and greater than	42	70.01
13	9.1	K.2.I	May not understand how to represent 3 as 1 and 2	43	1.03
14	10.5	K.2.I	May count all the cubes	51	11.03

*TEKS-Texas Essential Knowledge and Skills

© Houghton Mifflin Harcourt Publishing Company

Child's Name ______________________ Date ____________

Beginning of Year Test (continued)

Item	Lesson	Standard	Common Error	Rti T1	Soar to Success
15	13.1	K.3.B	May not understand the concept of one more	57	10.02, 11.01
16	11.2	K.3.B	May count only one group	58	10.03
17	14.4	K.3.C	May start with one group instead of the total	72	11.04
18	15.2	K.4	Does not distinguish between nickels and pennies	74	27.05
19	15.1	K.4	May miscount the pennies	73	27.05
20	16.1	K.5	May only look at the ones digit	78	28.1
21	16.2	K.5	May not count forward from the correct number	79	28.11, 28.12
22	17.1	K.6.A	Does not recognize a circle	82	38.02, 38.07
23	17.2	K.6.A	Does not recognize a triangle	83	38.02, 38.07
24	18.1	K.6.B	Does not recognize an object shaped like a cylinder	86	39.13, 39.26
25	18.2	K.6.B	Does not recognize a cone	87	39.13, 39.26
26	18.5	K.6.C	May not recognize a flat surface of a cube	90	39.13, 39.26
27	17.2	K.6.D	Cannot distinguish between curves and 3 sides	83	38.02, 38.07
28	17.4	K.6.E	Cannot label a sorted group of squares	85	38.02, 38.07
29	18.2	K.6.E	May not be able to classify cones	87	39.13, 39.26

*TEKS-Texas Essential Knowledge and Skills

© Houghton Mifflin Harcourt Publishing Company

Child's Name ________________________ Date ____________

Beginning of Year Test (continued)

Item	Lesson	Standard	Common Error	Rti T1	Soar to Success
30	19.1	K.7.A	May not understand the attribute of length	92	41.01
31	19.1	K.7.A	May not understand the attribute of capacity	92	41.01
32	19.2	K.7.B	May not understand the meaning of longer	93	41.02
33	20.1	K.8.A	May not recognize that the categories are sorted by size	96	38.04, 38.06
34	20.2	K.8.A	May not recognize that the categories are sorted by shape	97	38.04, 38.06, 38.05
35	20.3	K.8.C	May include the label icon in the count	98	53.02
36	20.4	K.8.C	May not understand how to read a picture graph	99	53.06
37	21.1	K.9.A	May not understand the concept of earning money	97	38.04, 38.06, 38.05
38	21.2	K.9.B	May not be able to distinguish between earning money and getting money as a gift	97	38.04, 38.06, 38.05
39	21.4	K.9.C	May not recognize the skills needed to do a job	39	7.06
40	21.3	K.9.D	May not be able to distinguish between wants and needs	97	38.04, 38.06, 38.05

*TEKS-Texas Essential Knowledge and Skills

© Houghton Mifflin Harcourt Publishing Company

Child's Name ______________________ Date ____________

Middle of Year Test

Item #	Lesson	Standard	Common Error	Rti T1	Soar to Success
1	2.4	K.2.A	May not know the numbers in counting order	1	1.03
2	2.4	K.2.A	May not understand how to count backward	1	1.03
3	6.1	K.2.B	May not know the numbers in counting order	18	28.08
4	3.4	K.2.E	May not understand the concept of less	32	7.06
5	3.4	K.2.E	May not understand the concept of same	32	7.06
6	4.6	K.2.E	May not understand the concept of greater	33	1.03
7	6.4	K.2.F	May not understand the concept of one more	34	7.11, 7.12
8	6.4	K.2.F	May not understand the concept of one less	34	7.11, 7.12
9	3.4	K.2.G	May not understand the concept of greater	32	7.06
10	3.4	K.2.G	May not understand the concept of less	32	7.06
11	6.6	K.2.H	May not understand the concepts of less than and greater than	41	7.09
12	8.8	K.2.H	May not understand the concepts of less than and greater than	42	70.01
13	9.3	K.2.I	May add instead of subtract	45	11.03
14	10.6	K.2.I	May not understand the concept of making 9	52	11.03

*TEKS-Texas Essential Knowledge and Skills

© Houghton Mifflin Harcourt Publishing Company

Child's Name ______________________ Date ____________

Middle of Year Test (continued)

Item #	Lesson	Standard	Common Error	Rti T1	Soar to Success
15	13.4	K.3.B	May not understand how to interpret a picture	64	10.09
16	13.1	K.3.B	May miscount the items	57	10.02, 11.01
17	14.4	K.3.C	May look at only the number being subtracted	72	11.04
18	15.2	K.4	May not be able to distinguish between a penny and a nickel	74	27.05
19	15.3	K.4	May not be able to distinguish between a dime and a nickel	75	27.05
20	16.4	K.5	May only look at the ones digit	81	28.11, 28.12
21	16.3	K.5	May not be able to count by tens	80	28.11, 28.12
22	17.2	K.6.A	Does not recognize a triangle	83	38.02, 38.07
23	17.3	K.6.A	Does not recognize a rectangle	84	38.02, 38.07
24	18.2	K.6.B	Does not recognize a cone	87	39.13, 39.26
25	18.3	K.6.B	Does not recognize a sphere	88	39.13, 39.26
26	18.5	K.6.C	May not recognize a flat surface of a cylinder	90	38.02, 39.13, 39.26
27	17.3	K.6.D	Cannot label a sorted group of rectangles	84	38.02, 38.07
28	17.2	K.6.E	Cannot label a sorted group of irregular shapes	85	38.02, 38.07
29	18.3	K.6.E	May not be able to classify spheres	88	39.13, 39.26

*TEKS-Texas Essential Knowledge and Skills

© Houghton Mifflin Harcourt Publishing Company

Child's Name ______________________ Date ____________

Middle of Year Test (continued)

Item #	Lesson	Standard	Common Error	Rti T1	Soar to Success
30	19.1	K.7.A	May not understand the attribute of capacity	92	41.01
31	19.1	K.7.A	May not understand the attribute of weight	92	41.01
32	19.2	K.7.B	May not understand the meaning of shorter	94	41.03
33	20.1	K.8.A	May not recognize that the categories are sorted by color	96	38.04, 38.06
34	20.2	K.8.A	May not recognize that the categories are sorted by shape	97	38.04, 38.06, 38.05
35	20.3	K.8.C	May include the label icon in the count	98	53.02
36	20.4	K.8.C	May not understand how to read a picture graph	99	53.06
37	21.1	K.9.A	May not understand the concept of earning money	97	38.04, 38.06, 38.05
38	21.2	K.9.B	May not be able to distinguish between earning money and getting money as a gift	97	38.04, 38.06, 38.05
39	21.4	K.9.C	May not recognize the skills needed to do a job	39	7.06
40	21.3	K.9.D	May not be able to distinguish between wants and needs	97	38.04, 38.06, 38.05

*TEKS-Texas Essential Knowledge and Skills

© Houghton Mifflin Harcourt Publishing Company

Child's Name ________________________ Date ____________

End of Year Test

Item #	Lesson	Standard	Common Error	Rti T1	Soar to Success
1	2.4	K.2.A	May not understand how to count backward	1	1.03
2	2.4	K.2.A	May not understand how to count backward	1	1.03
3	6.1	K.2.B	May not know the numbers in counting order	18	28.08
4	4.6	K.2.E	May not understand the concept of more	33	1.03
5	4.6	K.2.E	May not understand the concept of less	33	1.03
6	4.6	K.2.E	May not understand the concept of the same	33	1.03
7	6.4	K.2.F	May not understand the concept of one more	34	7.11, 7.12
8	6.4	K.2.F	May not understand the concept of one less	34	7.11, 7.12
9	6.2	K.2.G	May not know the meaning of greater	39	7.06
10	6.3	K.2.G	May not understand the concept of the same	40	7.09
11	6.6	K.2.H	May not understand the concepts of less than and greater than	41	7.09
12	8.8	K.2.H	May not understand the concepts of less than and greater than	42	70.01
13	9.2	K.2.I	May miscount items	44	10.03
14	10.7	K.2.I	May miscount items	53	11.03

*TEKS-Texas Essential Knowledge and Skills

© Houghton Mifflin Harcourt Publishing Company

Child's Name ______________________ Date ______________

End of Year Test (continued)

Item #	Lesson	Standard	Common Error	Rti T1	Soar to Success
15	13.1	K.3.B	May add instead of subtract	57	10.02, 11.01
16	12.2	K.3.B	May not understand to start with the total	60	11.03
17	12.4	K.3.C	May not understand to start with the total	70	11.08
18	15.3	K.4	May not be able to distinguish between a dime and a nickel	75	27.05
19	15.4	K.4	May not be able to distinguish between a quarter and a nickel	76	27.05
20	16.4	K.5	May only look at the ones digit	81	28.11, 28.12
21	16.3	K.5	May not be able to count by tens	80	28.11, 28.12
22	17.3	K.6.A	Does not recognize a rectangle	84	38.02, 38.07
23	17.4	K.6.A	Does not recognize a square	85	38.02, 38.07
24	18.3	K.6.B	Does not recognize a sphere	88	39.13, 39.26
25	18.4	K.6.B	Does not recognize a cube	89	39.13, 39.26
26	18.5	K.6.C	May not recognize a flat surface of a cube	90	39.13, 39.26
27	17.4	K.6.D	Cannot label a sorted group of squares	85	38.02, 38.07
28	18.3	K.6.E	May not be able to classify spheres	88	39.13, 39.26
29	18.4	K.6.E	May not be able to sort shapes	89	39.13, 39.26

*TEKS-Texas Essential Knowledge and Skills

© Houghton Mifflin Harcourt Publishing Company

Child's Name ____________________ Date ____________

End of Year Test (continued)

Item #	Lesson	Standard	Common Error	Rti T1	Soar to Success
30	19.1	K.7.A	May not understand the attribute of capacity	92	41.01
31	19.1	K.7.A	May not understand the attribute of weight	92	41.01
32	19.2	K.7.B	May not understand the meaning of shorter	95	42.02
33	20.2	K.8.A	May not recognize that the categories are sorted by shape	97	38.04, 38.06, 38.05
34	20.1	K.8.A	May not recognize that the categories are sorted by color	96	38.04, 38.06
35	20.3	K.8.C	May include the label icon in the count	98	53.02
36	20.4	K.8.C	May not understand how to read a picture graph	99	53.06
37	21.1	K.9.A	May not understand the concept of earning money	97	38.04, 38.06, 38.05
38	21.2	K.9.B	May not be able to distinguish between earning money and getting money as a gift	97	38.04, 38.06, 38.05
39	21.4	K.9.C	May not recognize the skills needed to do a job	39	7.06
40	21.3	K.9.D	May not be able to distinguish between wants and needs	97	38.04, 38.06, 38.05

*TEKS-Texas Essential Knowledge and Skills

© Houghton Mifflin Harcourt Publishing Company

Child's Name ______________________ Date ____________

Module 1 Test

Item	Lesson	TEKS*	Common error	Intervene with RtI* Tier 1 Lessons	Soar to Success
1	1.3	K.2.B	May miscount the items	4	1.02
2	1.4	K.2.B	May not understand to add 1	5	2.01, 1.02
3	1.2	K.2.B	May not understand the value of 2	3	2.01
4	1.3	K.2.B	May count boxes instead or counters	4	1.02
5	1.3	K.2.B	May count an item twice	4	1.02
6	1.4	K.2.B	May not recognize the number 4	5	2.01, 1.02
7	1.4	K.2.B	May not represent all the objects	5	2.01, 1.02
8	1.1	K.2.B	May not understand the value of 1	2	1.01
9	1.2	K.2.B	May not be able to read the number	3	2.01
10	1.2	K.2.B	May not recognize the number 1	3	2.01
11	1.4	K.2.B	May not understand the concept of same	5	2.01, 1.02
12	1.1	K.2.B	May not count with one to one correspondence	2	1.01

***TEKS**—Texas Essential Knowledge and Skills; **RtI**—Response to Intervention

© Houghton Mifflin Harcourt Publishing Company

Child's Name ______________________ Date ____________

Module 2 Test

Item	Lesson	TEKS*	Common error	Intervene with RtI* Tier 1 Lessons	Soar to Success
1	2.3	K.2.D	May miscount the items	31	1.03
2	2.5	K.2.B	May misread the number words	8	2.04
3	2.4	K.2.A	May not understand concept of counting backward	1	1.03
4	2.1	K.2.B	May not represent all the objects	6	1.03
5	2.4	K.2.A	May not understand how to represent counting forward	1	1.03
6	2.5	K.2.B	May not understand the value of zero	8	2.04
7	2.2	K.2.B	May miscount the items	7	2.03
8	2.5	K.2.B	May not understand the value of zero	8	2.04
9	2.4	K.2.A	May not know the numbers in counting order	1	1.03
10	2.1	K.2.B	May not count all the objects	6	1.03
11	2.5	K.2.B	May count an item twice	8	2.04
12	2.4	K.2.A	May not understand how to count backward	1	1.03

***TEKS**—Texas Essential Knowledge and Skills; **RtI**—Response to Intervention

© Houghton Mifflin Harcourt Publishing Company

Child's Name ______________________ Date ______________

Module 3 Test

Item	Lesson	TEKS*	Common error	Intervene with RtI* Tier 1 Lessons	Soar to Success
1	3.3	K.2.G	May not understand the meaning of greater	38	7.06
2	3.3	K.2.G	May not understand the meaning of less	38	7.06
3	3.2	K.2.E	May not understand the meaning of same	37	7.06
4	3.1	K.2.C	May count only the top row	29	1.04
5	3.1	K.2.C	May not understand the meaning of counting order	29	1.04
6	3.2	K.2.E	May not understand the meaning of same	37	7.06
7	3.4	K.2.E	May not understand the meaning of greater	32	7.06
8	3.4	K.2.E	May miscount the items	32	7.06
9	3.1	K.2.C	May not understand counting order	29	1.04
10	3.4	K.2.E	May not understand the meaning of greater	32	7.06
11	3.1	K.2.C	May miscount the items	29	1.04
12	3.4	K.2.C	May not understand the meaning of less	32	7.06

***TEKS**—Texas Essential Knowledge and Skills; **RtI**—Response to Intervention

© Houghton Mifflin Harcourt Publishing Company

Child's Name ______________________ Date __________

Module 4 Test

Item	Lesson	TEKS*	Common error	Intervene with RtI* Tier 1 Lessons	Soar to Success
1	4.6	K.2.E	May not add 2 more	33	1.03
2	4.1	K.2.B	May miscount the items	9	1.03
3	4.5	K.2.B	May misread the numbers	13	1.03, 2.03
4	4.4	K.2.B	May count an item twice	12	1.03, 2.03
5	4.1	K.2.B	May miscount the items	9	1.03
6	4.6	K.2.E	May not add one more	33	1.03
7	4.2	K.2.B	May misread the numbers	10	2.03
8	4.3	K.2.B	May count an item twice	11	1.03
9	4.5	K.2.B	May try to fill the ten frame	13	1.03, 2.03
10	4.2	K.2.B	May count only 1 row	10	2.03
11	4.6	K.2.E	May find only 1 less	33	1.03
12	4.6	K.2.E	May add only 1 more	33	1.03

***TEKS**—Texas Essential Knowledge and Skills; **RtI**—Response to Intervention

© Houghton Mifflin Harcourt Publishing Company

Child's Name ______________________ Date ______________

Module 5 Test

Item	Lesson	TEKS*	Common error	Intervene with RtI* Tier 1 Lessons	Soar to Success
1	5.1	K.2.B	May count the counters in only the top row	14	1.03, 2.03
2	5.3	K.2.B	May count shaded cubes	16	1.06, 2.09
3	5.4	K.2.B	May count only top row	17	1.11
4	5.3	K.2.B	May misread the number	16	10.6, 2.09
5	5.1	K.2.B	May miscount the items	14	1.03, 2.03
6	5.2	K.2.B	May miscount the items	15	1.03, 2.03
7	5.2	K.2.B	May misread the number	15	1.03, 2.03
8	5.3	K.2.B	May not understand the concept of 10	16	10.6, 2.09
9	5.4	K.2.B	May not understand the concept of 10	17	1.11
10	5.2	K.2.B	May not understand the concept of 9	15	1.03, 2.03
11	5.4	K.2.B	May not understand the concept of representing a number	17	1.11
12	5.1	K.2.B	May miscount the items	14	1.03, 2.03

*TEKS—Texas Essential Knowledge and Skills; RtI—Response to Intervention

© Houghton Mifflin Harcourt Publishing Company

Child's Name ______________________ Date ____________

Module 6 Test

Item	Lesson	TEKS*	Common error	Intervene with RtI* Tier 1 Lessons	Soar to Success
1	6.6	K.2.H	May not understand the concepts of less and/or greater	41	7.09
2	6.1	K.2.C	May miscount the items	18	28.08
3	6.5	K.2.E	May not understand the concept of less	35	7.06
4	6.4	K.2.F	May not understand the concept of 1 less	34	7.11, 7.12
5	6.4	K.2.B	May not understand the concept of 1 less and 1 more when ordering numbers	34	7.11, 7.12
6	6.2	K.2.G	May not understand the concept of less	39	7.06
7	6.4	K.2.F	May not understand the concept of 1 more	34	7.11, 7.12
8	6.5	K.2.E	May not understand the concept of the same	35	7.06
9	6.5	K.2.E	May not understand the concept of more	35	7.06
10	6.3	K.2.B	May miscount the items	40	7.09
11	6.5	K.2.E	May not understand the concept of less	35	7.06
12	6.5	K.2.E	May not understand the concept of more	35	7.06

***TEKS**—Texas Essential Knowledge and Skills; **RtI**—Response to Intervention

© Houghton Mifflin Harcourt Publishing Company

Child's Name ______________________ Date ______________

Module 7 Test

Item	Lesson	TEKS*	Common error	Intervene with RtI* Tier 1 Lessons	Soar to Success
1	7.4	K.2.B	May miscount the items	22	2.10
2	7.3	K.2.B	May not understand the concept of 13	21	1.07
3	7.2	K.2.B	May not recognize the number 12	20	2.10
4	7.6	K.2.F	May not understand the concept of one more	36	7.11, 7.12
5	7.2	K.2.B	May miscount the items	20	2.10
6	7.6	K.2.F	May not understand the concept of one less	36	7.11, 7.12
7	7.2	K.2.B	May not recognize the number 11	20	2.10
8	7.6	K.2.F	May not understand the concept of one more	36	7.11, 7.12
9	7.4	K.2.B	May miscount the items	22	2.10
10	7.5	K.2.B	May not understand the concept of 15	23	1.08, 2.11
11	7.3	K.2.B	May not recognize the number 14	21	1.07
12	7.1	K.2.B	May miscount the items	19	1.07

*TEKS—Texas Essential Knowledge and Skills; RtI—Response to Intervention

© Houghton Mifflin Harcourt Publishing Company

Child's Name ________________________ Date ______________

Module 8 Test

Item	Lesson	TEKS*	Common error	Intervene with RtI* Tier 1 Lessons	Soar to Success
1	8.2	K.2.F	May not understand the concept of 1 more	25	2.11
2	8.1	K.2.B	May not recognize 16	24	1.08
3	8.8	K.2.H	May not understand the concepts of less and greater	42	70.01
4	8.7	K.2.F	May not understand the concept of 1 more	34	7.11, 7.12
5	8.5	K.2.B	May miscount the items	28	1.09, 2.12
6	8.3	K.2.B	May not understand the concept of 18	26	1.08
7	8.6	K.2.C	May miscount the items	30	7.14
8	8.4	K.2.B	May misread the number words	27	2.11
9	8.2	K.2.B	May miscount the stars	25	2.11
10	8.3	K.2.B	May miscount the counters	26	1.08
11	8.2	K.2.B	May choose the sum instead of an addend	25	2.11
12	8.7	K.2.B	May not understand the concept of 16	34	7.11, 7.12

*TEKS—Texas Essential Knowledge and Skills; RtI—Response to Intervention

© Houghton Mifflin Harcourt Publishing Company

Child's Name ____________________ Date ____________

Unit 1 Test

Item	Lesson	TEKS*	Common error	Intervene with RtI* Tier 1 Lessons	Soar to Success
1	3.4	2.E	May not understand the concept of less	32	7.06
2	5.3	2.B	May miscount the items	16	1.06, 2.09
3	3.3	2.G	May not understand the concept of 1 less	38	7.06
4	8.8	2.H	May not undertand concept of less/greater	42	70.01
5	7.6	2.F	May not understand the concept of 1 more	36	7.11, 7.12
6	1.4	2.B	May not read number words correctly	5	2.01, 1.02
7	2.3	2.D	May not recognize a set of 2	31	1.03
8	8.6	2.C	May miscount the items	30	7.14
9	4.6	2.E	May not understand the concept of representing a number	33	1.03
10	6.5	2.E	May not understand the concept of more	35	7.06
11	6.1	2.A	May not understand the concept of count forward	18	28.08
12	4.4	2.B	May miscount the items	12	1.03, 2.03
13	3.4	2.E	May not understand the concept of same	32	7.06
14	2.4	2.A	May not understand the concept of counting backward	1	1.03
15	6.1	2.C	May miscount the items	18	28.08
16	6.4	2.F	May not understand the concept of 1 less	34	7.11, 7.12
17	6.4	2.E	Not not understand how to show a representation of a set that is less	34	7.11, 7.12
18	2.4	2.A	May not understand how to order numbers	1	1.03

***TEKS**—Texas Essential Knowledge and Skills; **RtI**—Response to Intervention

© Houghton Mifflin Harcourt Publishing Company

Child's Name ______________________ Date ____________

Module 9 Test

Item	Lesson	TEKS*	Common error	Intervene with RtI* Tier 1 Lessons	Soar to Success
1	9.3	K.2.I	May count all the counters as first number	45	11.03
2	9.1	K.2.I	May count only the large item	43	1.03
3	9.4	K.2.I	May count the gray counters	46	10.03, 11.03
4	9.3	K.2.I	May miscount the counters	45	11.03
5	9.2	K.2.I	May only count one row	44	10.03
6	9.1	K.2.I	May not understand how to represent the concept of 2 and 1	43	1.03
7	9.4	K.2.I	May miscount the counters	46	10.03, 11.03
8	9.3	K.2.I	May not count all the items	45	11.03
9	9.3	K.2.I	May miscount the counters	45	11.03
10	9.3	K.2.I	May not understand the concept of in all	45	11.03
11	9.2	K.2.I	May miscount the groups	44	10.03
12	9.1	K.2.I	May not understand the concept of 0	43	1.03

***TEKS**—Texas Essential Knowledge and Skills; **RtI**—Response to Intervention

© Houghton Mifflin Harcourt Publishing Company

Child's Name ______________________ Date ______________

Module 10 Test

Item	Lesson	TEKS*	Common error	Intervene with RtI* Tier 1 Lessons	Soar to Success
1	10.1	K.2.I	May miscount the items	47	10.03, 10.09
2	10.2	K.2.I	May not understand the concept of making 8	48	10.03, 10.09
3	10.3	K.2.I	May not understand the concept of making 9	49	10.03, 10.09
4	10.5	K.2.I	May count all the cubes	51	11.03
5	10.6	K.2.I	May count the wrong group	52	11.03
6	10.7	K.2.I	May count the dark gray cubes	53	11.03
7	10.8	K.2.I	May count all the cubes	54	11.03
8	10.8	K.2.I	May count the wrong group	54	11.03
9	10.3	K.2.I	May not understand the concept of making 9	49	10.03, 10.09
10	10.4	K.2.I	May not understand the concept of making 10	50	1.11
11	10.5	K.2.I	May miscount the items	51	11.03
12	10.6	K.2.I	May not understand the concept of taking apart a number	52	11.03

***TEKS**—Texas Essential Knowledge and Skills; **RtI**—Response to Intervention

© Houghton Mifflin Harcourt Publishing Company

Child's Name ______________________ Date ______________

Module 11 Test

Item	Lesson	TEKS*	Common error	Intervene with RtI* Tier 1 Lessons	Soar to Success
1	11.1	K.3.A	May miscount one set	55	10.03, 10.04, 10.09
2	11.1	K.3.A	May count only one set	55	10.03, 10.04, 10.09
3	11.1	K.3.A	May not know how to model a problem	55	10.03, 10.04, 10.09
4	11.1	K.3.A	May not have added	55	10.03, 10.04, 10.09
5	11.2	K.3.B	May miscount the items	58	10.03
6	11.2	K.3.B	May not add both sets	58	10.03
7	11.3	K.3.B	May not understand what the addends are	59	10.09
8	11.3	K.3.B	May not understand how to model a problem	59	10.09
9	11.4	K.3.C	May not understand how to match a number sentence to a picture	69	10.03, 10.04, 10.09
10	11.4	K.3.C	May miscount one set	69	10.03, 10.04, 10.09
11	11.4	K.3.C	May miscount the items	69	10.03, 10.04, 10.09
12	11.4	K.3.C	May not add correctly	69	10.03, 10.04, 10.09

***TEKS**—Texas Essential Knowledge and Skills; **RtI**—Response to Intervention

© Houghton Mifflin Harcourt Publishing Company

Child's Name ______________________ Date ____________

Module 12 Test

Item	Lesson	TEKS*	Common error	Intervene with RtI* Tier 1 Lessons	Soar to Success
1	12.1	K.3.A	May mistake the number leaving for how many are left	56	11.03
2	12.1	K.3.A	May use numbers in the two sets instead of starting with number in all	56	11.03
3	12.1	K.3.A	May miscount the items	56	11.03
4	12.1	K.3.A	May not start with the number in all	56	11.03
5	12.2	K.3.B	May not know how to model a problem	60	11.03
6	12.2	K.3.B	May count the set leaving	60	11.03
7	12.3	K.3.B	May miscount the items	61	11.08
8	12.3	K.3.B	May count the set being taken away	61	11.08
9	12.4	K.3.C	May use incorrect numbers to represent problem	70	11.08
10	12.4	K.3.C	May begin with the number being subtracted	70	11.08
11	12.4	K.3.C	May not be able to represent a subtraction problem	70	11.08
12	12.4	K.3.C	May miscount the items	70	11.08

***TEKS**—Texas Essential Knowledge and Skills; **RtI**—Response to Intervention

© Houghton Mifflin Harcourt Publishing Company

Child's Name ________________________ Date ____________

Module 13 Test

Item	Lesson	TEKS*	Common error	Intervene with RtI* Tier 1 Lessons	Soar to Success
1	13.1	K.3.C	May not understand the concept of 1 more	57	10.02, 11.01
2	13.2	K.3.B	May miscount the items	62	10.09
3	13.3	K.3.B	May not understand how to represent a problem	63	10.09
4	13.4	K.3.B	May not understand how to interpret a picture	64	10.09
5	13.1	K.3.B	May not understand the concept of 1 less	57	10.02, 11.01
6	13.1	K.3.B	May miscount the items	57	10.02, 11.01
7	13.6	K.3.C	May not understand the concept of more	65	10.05
8	13.6	K.3.C	May not understand how to represent a problem	65	10.05
9	13.5	K.3.C	May not understand the concept of doubles	71	10.03
10	13.5	K.3.C	May not understand the concept of doubles	71	10.03
11	13.1	K.3.C	May not understand the concept of 1 less	57	10.02, 11.01
12	13.1	K.3.C	May not understand the concept of 1 less	57	10.02, 11.01

***TEKS**—Texas Essential Knowledge and Skills; **RtI**—Response to Intervention

© Houghton Mifflin Harcourt Publishing Company

Child's Name ______________________ Date ____________

Module 14 Test

Item	Lesson	TEKS*	Common error	Intervene with RtI* Tier 1 Lessons	Soar to Success
1	14.1	K.3.B	May miscount the items	66	11.03
2	14.1	K.3.B	May not start with the number in all	66	11.03
3	14.2	K.3.B	May count items crossed off	67	11.03
4	14.2	K.3.B	May miscount the items	67	11.03
5	14.3	K.3.B	May miscount the items	68	11.04
6	14.3	K.3.B	Man not understand how to use a drawing to match story	68	11.04
7	14.4	K.3.C	May miscount the starting number	72	11.04
8	14.4	K.3.C	May count the items crossed off	72	11.04
9	14.4	K.3.C	May look at only the number being subtracted	72	11.04
10	14.4	K.3.C	May not understand which is the starting number	72	11.04
11	14.4	K.3.C	May miscount the items	72	11.04
12	14.4	K.3.C	May confuse the number subtracted and the number left	72	11.04

*TEKS—Texas Essential Knowledge and Skills; RtI—Response to Intervention

© Houghton Mifflin Harcourt Publishing Company

Child's Name ______________________ Date ____________

Module 15 Test

Item	Lesson	TEKS*	Common error	Intervene with RtI* Tier 1 Lessons	Soar to Success
1	15.5	K.4	Does not distinguish between nickels and dimes	77	3.08
2	15.5	K.4	Does not recognize a nickel	77	3.08
3	15.5	K.4	Does not recognize a quarter	77	3.08
4	15.5	K.4	Does not distinguish between different coins	77	3.08
5	15.1	K.4	May miscount the pennies	73	27.05
6	15.1	K.4	May miscount the pennies	73	27.05
7	15.2	K.4	May count only nickels that are shown on heads	74	27.05
8	15.2	K.4	May not distinguish between nickels and pennies	74	27.05
9	15.3	K.4	May count only dimes that are shown on heads	75	27.05
10	15.3	K.4	May not distinguish between nickels and dimes	75	27.05
11	15.4	K.4	May not recognize a quarter	76	27.05
12	15.4	K.4	May not distinguish between nickels and quarters	76	27.05

*TEKS—Texas Essential Knowledge and Skills; RtI—Response to Intervention

© Houghton Mifflin Harcourt Publishing Company

Child's Name ______________________ Date ______________

Unit 2 Test

Item	Lesson	TEKS*	Common error	Intervene with RtI* Tier 1 Lessons	Soar to Success
1	15.2	K.4	May miscount the pennies	74	27.05
2	15.3	K.4	May count only the nickels that are shown on heads	75	27.05
3	15.4	K.4	May not distinguish between nickels and dimes	76	27.05
4	9.1	K.2.I	May not understand the concept of making 3	43	1.03
5	9.3	K.2.I	May count the wrong group	45	11.03
6	10.2	K.2.I	May not understand the concept of making 8	48	10.03, 10.09
7	10.6	K.2.I	May not understand the concept of taking apart a number	52	11.03
8	11.1	K.3.A	May start with the number in all	55	10.03, 10.04, 10.09
9	12.1	K.3.A	May mistake the number leaving for how many are left	56	11.03
10	13.2	K.3.B	May miscount the items	62	10.09
11	14.1	K.3.B	May not start with the number in all	66	11.03
12	13.1	K.3.B	May not understand the concept of 1 less	57	10.02, 11.01

***TEKS**—Texas Essential Knowledge and Skills; **RtI**—Response to Intervention

© Houghton Mifflin Harcourt Publishing Company

Child's Name ________________________ Date ______________

Unit 2 Test (continued)

Item	Lesson	TEKS*	Common error	Intervene with RtI* Tier 1 Lessons	Soar to Success
13	12.3	K.3.B	May count the set being taken away	61	11.08
14	13.6	K.3.C	May not understand what operation to use	65	10.05
15	13.5	K.3.C	May not understand the concept of doubles	71	10.03
16	11.4	K.3.C	May not add correctly	69	10.03, 10.04, 10.09
17	13.1	K.3.C	May not understand the concept of 1 less	57	10.02, 11.01
18	14.4	K.3.C	May not understand which is the starting number	72	11.04

***TEKS**—Texas Essential Knowledge and Skills; **RtI**—Response to Intervention

© Houghton Mifflin Harcourt Publishing Company

Child's Name ______________________ Date ______________

Unit 3 Test

Item	Lesson	TEKS*	Common error	Intervene with RtI* Tier 1 Lessons	Soar to Success
1	16.1	K.5	May not understand the concept of 1 more	78	28.10
2	16.1	K.5	May not understand the concept of 1 less	78	28.10
3	16.1	K.5	May look only at the ones digit	78	28.10
4	16.1	K.5	May not understand how to read the chart	78	28.10
5	16.2	K.5	May not understand the concept of greater	79	28.11, 28,12
6	16.2	K.5	May not know how to represent 100	79	28.11, 28,12
7	16.2	K.5	May not count forward from correct number	79	28.11, 28,12
8	16.2	K.5	May not count forward	79	28.11, 28,12
9	16.2	K.5	May skip to the next row	79	28.11, 28,12
10	16.4	K.5	May not understand the concept of 1 less	81	28.11, 28,12
11	16.4	K.5	May not understand the concepts of greater than and less than	81	28.11, 28,12
12	16.4	K.5	May not understand the concept of 1 more	81	28.11, 28,12

***TEKS**—Texas Essential Knowledge and Skills; **RtI**—Response to Intervention

© Houghton Mifflin Harcourt Publishing Company

Child's Name ______________________ Date ______________

Unit 3 Test (continued)

Item	Lesson	TEKS*	Common error	Intervene with RtI* Tier 1 Lessons	Soar to Success
13	16.4	K.5	May not understand the concepts of greater than and less than	81	28.11, 28,12
14	16.4	K.5	May not understand the concept of 1 more	81	28.11, 28,12
15	16.3	K.5	May not understand the concepts of greater than and less than	80	28.11, 28,12
16	16.3	K.5	May not be able to count by tens	80	28.11, 28,12
17	16.3	K.5	May not be able to count by tens	80	28.11, 28,12
18	16.3	K.5	May not be able to count by tens when starting at a number other than 10	80	28.11, 28,12

***TEKS**—Texas Essential Knowledge and Skills; **RtI**—Response to Intervention

© Houghton Mifflin Harcourt Publishing Company

Child's Name ______________________________ Date ______________

Module 17 Test

Item	Lesson	TEKS*	Common error	Intervene with RtI* Tier 1 Lessons	Soar to Success
1	17.1	K.6.A	Does not recognize a circle	82	38.02, 38.07
2	17.2	K.6.A	Does not recognize a triangle	83	38.02, 38.07
3	17.2	K.6.A	Does not recognize the attributes of a triangle	83	38.02, 38.07
4	17.3	K.6.A	Does not recognize a rectangle	84	38.02, 38.07
5	17.3	K.6.A	Does not recognize a shape with 4 sides and 4 vertices	84	38.02, 38.07
6	17.4	K.6.A	Does not recognize a square	85	38.02, 38.07
7	17.4	K.6.A	Does not know attributes of a square	85	38.02, 38.07
8	17.3	K.6.D	Cannot distinguish between curved sides and 4 sides	84	38.02, 38.07
9	17.1	K.6.E	Cannot label a sorted group of circles	82	38.02, 38.07
10	17.5	K.6.F	Cannot visualize composite shapes	91	38.02, 38.07
11	17.5	K.6.F	Counts all the shapes	91	38.02, 38.07
12	17.5	K.6.F	Does not count all the circles	91	38.02, 38.07

***TEKS**—Texas Essential Knowledge and Skills; **RtI**—Response to Intervention

© Houghton Mifflin Harcourt Publishing Company

Child's Name ______________________ Date ______________

Module 18 Test

Item	Lesson	TEKS*	Common Error	Intervene with RtI* Tier 1 Lessons	Soar to Success Math
1	18.1	K.6.B	May not recognize the shape of a cylinder	86	39.13, 39.26
2	18.2	K.6.B	May not recognize the shape of a cone	87	39.13, 39.26
3	18.2	K.6.B	May not know the attributes of a cone	87	39.13, 39.26
4	18.3	K.6.B	May not recognize the shape of a sphere	88	39.13, 39.26
5	18.3	K.6.B	May not know the attributes of a sphere	88	39.13, 39.26
6	18.4	K.6.B	May not recognize the shape of a cube	89	39.13, 39.26
7	18.5	K.6.C	May not know a circle is a flat surface on a cone	90	39.13, 39.26
8	18.5	K.6.C	May not know a square is a flat surface on a cube	90	39.13, 39.26
9	18.5	K.6.C	May not know a circle is a flat surface on a cylinder	90	39.13, 39.26
10	18.4	K.6.E	May not be able to recognize the sorting rule	89	39.13, 39.26
11	18.3	K.6.B	May not recognize a cone	88	39.13, 39.26
12	18.2	K.6.E	May not be able to recognize the sorting rule	87	39.13, 39.26

***TEKS**—Texas Essential Knowledge and Skills; **RtI**—Response to Intervention

© Houghton Mifflin Harcourt Publishing Company

Child's Name ______________________ Date ____________

Module 19 Test

Item	Lesson	TEKS*	Common Error	Intervene with RtI* Tier 1 Lessons	Soar to Success
1	19.1	K.7.A	May not understand the attribute of length	92	41.01
2	19.1	K.7.A	May not understand the attribute of weight	92	41.01
3	19.1	K.7.A	May not understand the attribute of capacity	92	41.01
4	19.2	K.7.B	May not understand the meaning of shorter	93	41.02
5	19.3	K.7.B	May not understand the meaning of taller	94	41.03
6	19.4	K.7.B	May not understand the meaning of heavier	95	42.02
7	19.2	K.7.B	May not understand the meaning of longer	93	41.02
8	19.3	K.7.B	May not understand the meaning of taller	94	41.03
9	19.4	K.7.B	May not understand the meaning of heavier	95	42.02
10	19.2	K.7.B	May not understand the meaning of shorter	93	41.02
11	19.3	K.7.B	May not understand the meaning of shorter	94	41.03
12	19.4	K.7.B	May not understand the meaning of lighter	95	42.02

*TEKS—Texas Essential Knowledge and Skills; RtI—Response to Intervention

© Houghton Mifflin Harcourt Publishing Company

Child's Name ______________________ Date ______________

Unit 4 Test

Item	Lesson	TEKS*	Common Error	Intervene with RtI* Tier 1 Lessons	Soar to Success Math
1	17.2	K.6.A	May not recognize a triangle	83	38.02, 38.07
2	17.3	K.6.A	May not recognize a rectangle	84	38.02, 38.07
3	17.4	K.6.A	May not recognize a square shown in a different orientation	85	38.02, 38.07
4	18.1	K.6.B	May not recognize the shape of a cylinder	86	39.13, 39.26
5	18.2	K.6.B	May not recognize the shape of a cone	87	39.13, 39.26
6	18.3	K.6.B	May not recognize the shape of a sphere	88	39.13, 39.26
7	18.4	K.6.B	May not recognize the shape of a cube	89	39.13, 39.26
8	17.1	K.6.E	May not recognize circles	82	38.02, 38.07
9	17.2	K.6.E	May not be able to recognize the sorting rule	82	38.02, 38.07
10	18.3	K.6.E	May not be able to recognize the sorting rule	88	39.13, 39.26
11	18.2	K.6.E	May not be able to recognize the sorting rule	87	39.13, 39.26
12	17.5	K.6.F	May not be able to visualize composite shapes	91	38.02, 38.07
13	17.5	K.6.F	May not be able to visualize composite shapes	91	38.02, 38.07
14	19.1	K.7.A	May not understand the attribute of length	92	41.01
15	19.1	K.7.A	May not understand the attribute of capacity	92	41.01

***TEKS**—Texas Essential Knowledge and Skills; **RtI**—Response to Intervention

© Houghton Mifflin Harcourt Publishing Company

Child's Name ______________________________ Date ____________

Unit 4 Test (continued)

Item	Lesson	TEKS*	Common Error	Intervene with RtI* Tier 1 Lessons	Soar to Success Math
16	19.1	K.7.A	May not understand the attribute of weight	92	41.01
17	19.2	K.7.B	May not understand the meaning of longer	93	41.02
18	19.3	K.7.B	May not understand the meaning of shorter	94	41.03

***TEKS**—Texas Essential Knowledge and Skills; **RtI**—Response to Intervention

© Houghton Mifflin Harcourt Publishing Company

Child's Name ____________________ Date ____________

Unit 5 Test

Item	Lesson	TEKS*	Common Error	Intervene with RtI* Tier 1 Lessons	Soar to Success
1	20.1	K.8.A	May not recognize that the set is sorted by size	96	38.04, 38.06
2	20.1	K.8.A	May not recognize that the set is sorted by color	96	38.04, 38.06
3	20.1	K.8.A	May not recognize that the categories are sorted by size	96	38.04, 38.06
4	20.2	K.8.A	May not recognize that the categories are sorted by shape	96	38.04, 38.06
5	20.2	K.8.A	May not recognize that the categories are sorted by shape	97	38.04, 38.06, 38.05
6	20.2	K.8.A	May not recognize that the categories are sorted by shape	97	38.04, 38.06, 38.05
7	20.2	K.8.A	May not recognize that the categories are sorted by number of sides	97	38.04, 38.06, 38.05
8	20.3	K.8.B	May count all the objects	98	53.02
9	20.3	K.8.B	May include the label picture in the count	98	53.02
10	20.4	K.8.B	May miscount the items	99	53.06
11	20.4	K.8.B	May count the wrong objects	99	53.06
12	20.4	K.8.B	May miscount the items	99	53.06

***TEKS**—Texas Essential Knowledge and Skills; **RtI**—Response to Intervention

© Houghton Mifflin Harcourt Publishing Company

Child's Name ______________________ Date ____________

Unit 5 Test (continued)

Item	Lesson	TEKS*	Common Error	Intervene with RtI* Tier 1 Lessons	Soar to Success
13	20.3	K.8.C	May not understand the concept of fewer	98	53.02
14	20.3	K.8.C	May include the label icon in the count	98	53.02
15	20.5	K.8.C	May not understand the concept of more	100	53.06
16	20.4	K.8.C	May miscount the circles	99	53.06
17	20.5	K.8.C	May not understand how to read the graph	100	53.06
18	20.5	K.8.C	May miscount the circles	100	53.06

***TEKS**—Texas Essential Knowledge and Skills; **RtI**—Response to Intervention

© Houghton Mifflin Harcourt Publishing Company

Child's Name ______________________ Date ____________

Unit 6 Test

Item #	Lesson	Standard	Common Error	Rti T1	Soar to Success
1	21.1	K.9.A	May not understand the concept of earning money	97	38.04, 38.06, 38.05
2	21.1	K.9.A	May not recognize someone at work	97	38.04, 38.06, 38.05
3	21.1	K.9.A	May not understand the concept of earning an income	97	38.04, 38.06, 38.05
4	21.1	K.9.A	May not understand the concept of earning money	97	38.04, 38.06, 38.05
5	21.1	K.9.A	May not recognize someone at work	97	38.04, 38.06, 38.05
6	21.1	K.9.A	May not understand the concept of earning an income	97	38.04, 38.06, 38.05
7	21.1	K.9.A	May not understand the concept of earning money	97	38.04, 38.06, 38.05
8	21.1	K.9.A	May not recognize someone at work	97	38.04, 38.06, 38.05
9	21.4	K.9.C	May not understand the skills needed to do a job	39	7.06

*TEKS-Texas Essential Knowledge and Skills

© Houghton Mifflin Harcourt Publishing Company

Child's Name ______________________ Date __________

Unit 6 Test (continued)

Item #	Lesson	Standard	Common Error	Rti T1	Soar to Success
10	21.4	K.9.C	May not understand the skills needed to do a job	39	7.06
11	21.4	K.9.C	May not understand the tool needed to do a job	39	7.06
12	21.4	K.9.C	May not understand the tool needed to do a job	39	7.06
13	21.2	K.9.B	May not be able to distinguish between earning money and getting money as a gift	97	38.04, 38.06, 38.05
14	21.2	K.9.B	May not be able to distinguish between earning money and getting money as a gift	97	38.04, 38.06, 38.05
15	21.3	K.9.D	May not be able to distinguish between wants and needs	97	38.04, 38.06, 38.05
16	21.3	K.9.D	May not be able to distinguish between wants and needs	97	38.04, 38.06, 38.05
17	21.3	K.9.D	May not be able to distinguish between wants and needs	97	38.04, 38.06, 38.05
18	21.3	K.9.D	May not be able to distinguish between wants and needs	97	38.04, 38.06, 38.05

*TEKS-Texas Essential Knowledge and Skills

© Houghton Mifflin Harcourt Publishing Company

Correlations

	Knowledge and Skills	Test: Item Number
K.2	**Number and operations.** The student applies mathematical process standards to understand how to represent and compare whole numbers, the relative position and magnitude of whole numbers, and relationships within the numeration system. The student is expected to:	
K.2.A	count forward and backward to at least 20 with and without objects;	Module 2 Test: 3, 5, 9, 12 Unit 1 Test: 11, 14, 18 Beginning-/Middle-/End-of-Year Tests: 1–2
K.2.B	read, write, and represent whole numbers from 0 to at least 20 with and without objects or pictures;	Module 1 Test: 1–12 Module 2 Test: 1–2, 4, 6–8, 10–11 Module 4 Test: 2–5, 7–10 Module 5 Test: 1–12 Module 6 Test: 5, 10 Module 7 Test: 1–3, 5, 7, 9–12 Module 8 Test: 2, 5–6, 8–12 Unit 1 Test: 2, 6, 12 Beginning-/Middle-/End-of-Year Tests: 3
K.2.C	count a set of objects up to at least 20 and demonstrate that the last number said tells the number of objects in the set regardless of their arrangement or order;	Module 3 Test: 4–5, 9, 11–12 Module 6 Test: 2 Module 8 Test: 7 Unit 1 Test: 8, 15
K.2.D	recognize instantly the quantity of a small group of objects in organized and random arrangements;	Unit 1 Test: 7
K.2.E	generate a set using concrete and pictorial models that represents a number that is more than, less than, and equal to a given number up to 20;	Module 3 Test: 3, 6–8, 10 Module 4 Test: 1, 6, 11–12 Module 6 Test: 3, 8–9, 11–12 Unit 1 Test: 1, 9–10, 13, 17 Beginning-/Middle-/End-of-Year Tests: 4–6
K.2.F	generate a number that is one more than or one less than another number up to at least 20;	Module 6 Test: 4, 7 Module 7 Test: 4, 6, 8 Module 8 Test: 1, 4 Unit 1 Test: 5, 16 Beginning-/Middle-/End-of-Year Tests: 7–8
K.2.G	compare sets of objects up to at least 20 in each set using comparative language;	Module 3 Test: 1–2 Module 6 Test: 6 Unit 1 Test: 3 Beginning-/Middle-/End-of-Year Tests: 9–10
K.2.H	use comparative language to describe two numbers up to 20 presented as written numerals; and	Module 6 Test: 1 Module 8 Test: 3 Unit 1 Test: 4 Beginning-/Middle-/End-of-Year Tests: 11–12
K.2.I	compose and decompose numbers up to 10 with objects and pictures.	Module 9 Test: 1–12 Module 10 Test: 1–12 Unit 2 Test: 4–7 Beginning-/Middle-/End-of-Year Tests: 13–14

© Houghton Mifflin Harcourt Publishing Company

Correlations

Knowledge and Skills		Test: Item Number
K.3	**Number and operations.** The student applies mathematical process standards to develop an understanding of addition and subtraction situations in order to solve problems. The student is expected to:	
K.3.A	model the action of joining to represent addition and the action of separating to represent subtraction;	Module 11 Test: 1–4 Module 12 Test: 1–4 Unit 2 Test: 8–9
K.3.B	solve word problems using objects and drawings to find sums up to 10 and differences within 10; and	Module 11 Test: 5–8 Module 12 Test: 5–8 Module 13 Test: 2–6 Module 14 Test: 1–6 Unit 2 Test: 10–13 Beginning-/Middle-/End-of-Year Tests: 15–16
K.3.C	explain the strategies used to solve problems involving adding and subtracting within 10 using spoken words, concrete and pictorial models, and number sentences.	Module 11 Test: 9–12 Module 12 Test: 9–12 Module 13 Test: 1, 7–12 Module 14 Test: 7–12 Unit 2 Test: 14–18 Beginning-/Middle-/End-of-Year Tests: 17
K.4	**Number and operations.** The student applies mathematical process standards to identify coins in order to recognize the need for monetary transactions. The student is expected to identify U.S. coins by name, including pennies, nickels, dimes, and quarters.	Module 15 Test: 1–12 Unit 2 Test: 1–3 Beginning/Middle/End of Year Tests: 18–19
K.5	**Algebraic reasoning.** The student applies mathematical process standards to identify the pattern in the number word list. The student is expected to recite numbers up to at least 100 by ones and tens beginning with any given number.	Unit 3 Test: 1–18 Beginning-/Middle-/End-of-Year Tests: 20–21
K.6	**Geometry and measurement.** The student applies mathematical process standards to analyze attributes of two-dimensional shapes and three-dimensional solids to develop generalizations about their properties. The student is expected to:	
K.6.A	identify two-dimensional shapes, including circles, triangles, rectangles, and squares as special rectangles;	Module 17 Test: 1–7 Unit 4 Test: 1–3 Beginning-/Middle-/End-of-Year Tests: 22–23
K.6.B	identify three-dimensional solids, including cylinders, cones, spheres, and cubes, in the real world;	Module 18 Test: 1–6, 11 Unit 4 Test: 4–7 Beginning-/Middle-/End-of-Year Tests: 24–25
K.6.C	identify two-dimensional components of three-dimensional objects;	Module 18 Test: 7–9 Beginning-/Middle-/End-of-Year Tests: 26
K.6.D	identify attributes of two-dimensional shapes using informal and formal geometric language interchangeably;	Module 17 Test: 8 Beginning-/Middle-/End-of-Year Tests: 27

© Houghton Mifflin Harcourt Publishing Company

Correlations

	Knowledge and Skills	Test: Item Number
K.6.E	classify and sort a variety of regular and irregular two- and three-dimensional figures regardless of orientation or size; and	Module 17 Test: 9 Module 18 Test: 10, 12 Unit 4 Test: 8–11 Beginning-/Middle-/End-of-Year Tests: 28–29
K.6.F	create two-dimensional shapes using a variety of materials and drawings.	Module 17 Test: 10–12 Unit 4 Test: 12–13
K.7	**Geometry and measurement.** The student applies mathematical process standards to directly compare measurable attributes. The student is expected to:	
K.7.A	give an example of a measurable attribute of a given object, including length, capacity, and weight; and	Module 19 Test: 1–3 Unit 4 Test: 14–16 Beginning-/Middle-/End-of-Year Tests: 30–31
K.7.B	compare two objects with a common measurable attribute to see which object has more of/less of the attribute and describe the difference.	Module 19 Test: 4–12 Unit 4 Test: 17–18 Beginning-/Middle-/End-of-Year Tests: 32
K.8	**Data analysis.** The student applies mathematical process standards to collect and organize data to make it useful for interpreting information. The student is expected to:	
K.8.A	collect, sort, and organize data into two or three categories;	Unit 5 Test: 1–7 Beginning-/Middle-/End-of-Year Tests: 33–34
K.8.B	use data to create real-object and picture graphs; and	Unit 5 Test: 8–12
K.8.C	draw conclusions from real-object and picture graphs.	Unit 5 Test: 13–18 Beginning-/Middle-/End-of-Year Tests: 35–36
K.9	**Personal financial literacy.** The student applies mathematical process standards to manage one's financial resources effectively for lifetime financial security. The student is expected to:	
K.9.A	identify ways to earn income;	Unit 6 Test: 1–8 Beginning-/Middle-/End-of-Year Tests: 37
K.9.B	differentiate between money received as income and money received as gifts;	Unit 6 Test: 13–14 Beginning-/Middle-/End-of-Year Tests: 38
K.9.C	list simple skills required for jobs; and	Unit 6 Test: 9–12 Beginning-/Middle-/End-of-Year Tests: 39
K.9.D	distinguish between wants and needs and identify income as a source to meet one's wants and needs.	Unit 6 Test: 15–18 Beginning-/Middle-/End-of-Year Tests: 40

© Houghton Mifflin Harcourt Publishing Company